THE

TIMELESS NOW

Healing from Grief and Loss
Mystical Meditation
The Sacred Law of Impermanence

JAI

THE TIMELESS NOW

Healing from Grief and Loss
Mystical Meditation
The Sacred Law of Impermanence

THE TIMELESS NOW:
Healing from Grief and Loss
Mystical Meditation
The Sacred Law of Impermanence
by JAI

Copyright © 1990-2018 by JAI (Dream Universal Media)

ISBN-13: 978-1-7324068-0-3

Edited by: Timothy Rodd
             D. Christopher Rodd
             Nicholas T.O. Rodd

All rights reserved, including the right to reproduce or scan this book or portions thereof in any form whatsoever without the prior written permission of JAI, Dream Universal Media except where permitted by law. Please do not participate in or encourage piracy of copyrighted materials in violation of the author's rights.

Disclaimer:

The materials contained in this text are provided for the purpose of general information only and do not constitute professional medical or psychological advice. The author/publisher accepts no responsibility for any loss which may arise from ill-advised reliance on, and/or practice of information contained herein. The author will arrange Q&A sessions, if any are needed after reading this manual.

The contents of this book and the recordings of the meditations herein are protected by Copyright Law under international https://www.facebook.com/messages/t/1284311126/conventions, and the reproduction or retransmission of the contents of this text and/or related recordings and/or artwork is prohibited, without the prior written consent of the author.

The content of this text and related recordings, including all music, all text, all downloads, all music samples, and all other material are owned and controlled by Dream Universal Media. ALL RIGHTS RESERVED. Unauthorized use, duplication, or distribution of this content is strictly prohibited.

Consecration

May the words of my mouth and the meditations of my heart be acceptable to the Most High, Creator of all the worlds and Timeless realms. I pray that my will and Thy Will are as One. I write from that Oneness.

I offer this book in the Name of the One Holy True and Living God, from Whom all emanate and to Whom all return. It is important to our soul's illumination that we know our Oneness with The Divine, and live from that place in our consciousness. It is a breach of reason to perpetuate the divisive labels we may seek to assign and define That Which Created all things. There must be no division in personal attention with regard to dangerously unfocused spiritual interests and associations with That Which Created us all of the Essence of Itself. There is no division in Spirit regarding That Which cannot be divided.

> *I have learned*
> *so much from God*
> *that I can no longer*
> *call myself*
> *a Christian, a Hindu, a Muslim,*
> *a Buddhist, a Jew.*
> *The truth has shared so much of itself*
> *with me*
> *that I can no longer call myself*
> *a man, a woman, an angel,*
> *or even a pure Soul.*
> *Love has*
> *befriended Hafiz so completely,*
> *it has turned to ash*
> *and freed me*
> *of every concept and image*
> *my mind has ever known.*
>
> ~ *Hafiz* ~

There is none like The Creator, and none deserves to be worshipped or served beside the Most High, the Ultimate Light. I bear witness to the truth of Divine Wisdom delivered by the prophets, apostles, messengers, saints, angels, and servants of The Divine Light. The God is sovereign and has neither partner nor patron.

My soul is thankful for The Protection, Love, and Guidance of The Comforter, The Holy Spirit. I accept that the Faces that have been shown to us as Manifestations of The Creator, known and unknown, seen and unseen, were and are among us as we prepare ourselves to be among the worthy.

All gender references to The God in this text reflect terminology that is not necessarily intended to be gender-specific. I accept that the Holy Names of The God and the Holy Attributes of The God, both known and unknown, know nothing of contradiction in opposites of polarities … only the Union of Spirit. Both the Yin and the Yang energies must exist to be our cause and continuation. The masculine and feminine energies are compelled to engage in this grand mystical dance of existence equally respected and acknowledged as being mutually responsible for the emanation of all creation in its myriad glorious forms. The God is called by many names from many traditions. My focus remains on The One … That Which defies our marginalized, limited comprehension, that which cannot be named, known, or defined.

I offer this journal from no position of authority. I am but a traveler. I am a student, a seeker, lifting my pen and voice to express praise and thanks to The Almighty, the Most High, for the blessing of this opportunity to share this journey with you.

Acknowledgments

The Timeless Now has been writing itself through me with inspired structure and intention over the course of many years. Its earliest beginning was a poem that wrote itself through me at the age of nine, named Ashes. As morbid a preoccupation as death is for a child that young, it has been a consistent theme in my writing and my life. When my beloved mother passed away, it got personal.

I thank her for teaching me that there is no such thing as death, as her life still breathes through me and all of the lives she so graciously touched. She was one of the most powerful mystics I have ever known. I am so grateful to her for all of the love she brought to my life. She was my biggest fan and often my only fan. She was a warrior … a peacemaker … a counselor … a healer … a real, live angel. I thank The God every day for ever having known her.

Many thanks to Timothy Rodd for opening your Third Eye wide enough to see a finish line I almost lost sight of, and for tirelessly helping me cross it. Thank you for sharing your energy and refusing to stop just short of the journey's victory. I may have given up had you not been inspired to see that and become an intervention in my life. Ma would have loved that. Like she was, you are my biggest fan. I know that somewhere she is smiling about your dedication to sharing some of her perspectives on life and death, and her story of having touched them both. I know she loves that you helped me share this story of healing. Thank you for graphic design, cover art, and all your editing work.

I thank The Most High for that first trip to the other side for evidence that there is no "veil" between worlds. You showed me that the realm of Maya was just the tip of the iceberg. You smiled Transcendence upon me from one dimension into the next, and back. Thank you for opening the portal to the Mystic and showing me that this is not all there is. You showed me that death is only a figment of the collective imagination. You taught me that people really can change. You've shown me a higher Love. You know who you are.

Christopher … Thank you for your help with some of the most brutal bouts with research and editing ever. Thank you for helping with the conquering of the "devil in the details." Thank you for the brilliant photography for the cover art; Jamil … Thank you for your intuitive guidance in marketing and distribution. Because of the wisdom you shared, many people who might not otherwise have been able to access this offering will be given a chance to embrace a healing, spiritual perspective; Nicholas … Thank you for lending your beautiful voice to the I Transcend My Ego Self Meditation. The vibration of your voice brought a powerful healing spirit to the meditation. Thank you for believing in me and pushing me to reach higher; Rahmon … Thank you for your help with sound engineering, your invaluable research, and thank you for your prayers. The Light you each have brought into my life will always illuminate my path and give me a sense of purpose. Unconditional love is more than a philosophy. It's what we are made of. More than anything, thank you for your love.

Thank you, Richard Allen, for pulling me out of the perfect storm. I give thanks for the braided twists and turns of fate and circumstance the Universe delivered to my doorstep that caused our paths to cross. Your spiritual strength and guidance helped me to bear the unbearable. Thank you for being the angel that tore Nicholas and me away from the grip of the reaper. The Natural Mystic is alive and well in your heart of hearts.

Thank you, Joe Stecher, for your introduction to the concept and practice of the I AM Meditation in the tradition of Gurdjieff. It was deep, insightful, and contributed greatly to directing my path toward the perspectives of Advaita consciousness, out of which the Light of this book emanated.

Daniel Hernandez, my teacher … my friend. Thank you for all you shared with me and taught me. I will never stop reeling from the shock of your passing. Now you live in every star I see in the sky. I miss you.

Arthur Hakalani Pacheco … Mahalo! I miss you! Thank you for teaching me more about death than I ever wanted to know. I will always remember your radiant smile, your melodic laughter, and looking forward to current stories of your dramatic inter-dimensional journeying … each with a wild metaphysical twist, pouring out more Light and Love than anyone could contain all at once. Thank you for sharing your ethereal world until we could see that we can see it too. You made such a graceful dance of living in the Light and singing the blues at the same time.

Akihiro (Calvin) Moriwaki … I thumbed through the final edit of this book and felt your spirit alive on every page. There is no way to measure how much of your wisdom and magick you shared with me. I was truly blessed to have even known you, not to mention to have had you as one of my 'awakening' teachers. You are appreciated, loved, and missed. I thank you for helping drag me kicking and screaming into the Timeless understanding of what is beyond the veils between the limitless dimensions of consciousness … Until there is no such thing as a veil. Goodbye feels like just another ash rising from the fire of impermanence.

Reverend Harley Robert 'Hal' Beagle of Religious Science/Science of Mind Church, Honolulu, Dr. William Hornaday of Science of Mind Church, Los Angeles … Thank you for making me understand that a rapport with the spirit world is a practical and very normal part of the physical world.

Matthias Swaby – I thank you for your prayers. Your life is a testament to the power of God over life and death. I thank God for you and for the spiritual intervention that performed a profound healing in my life. I can never repay you for your bravery, persistence, and courage, fearlessly confronting demons with the touch of an angel of God. Your humble manner and your chosen surrendered life are a soul's inspiration. I am blessed to have been welcomed into your spiritual family.

Night Shift Editing Team – Thank you all for your energy, time, and diligence. The devil is in the details. Thank you for following it through to the last breath of exorcising that beast.

I give thanks to my ancestors, who remembered me before I was the thought that is me, who delivered me to my understanding, who speak from their watery and earthly graves from the realm of the Timeless to remind me there is no such thing as death. You are the vibration of an ancient drum beating itself into Ultimate relevance, telling true stories time wrote in the Ether of their erasure. The Spirit of cultures of origin occupied, set aside, and buried under the Earth from which a new world rises, snatching Light back from thieves and raiders, grave robbers, and soul traders. Scientists, still unsure of what the magic means, can only wonder as it surfaces in dreams of clandestine things that rise like the phoenix to be known again. This magic cannot be burned down with a library. It will not be mocked. It breathes a sacred breath that cannot be choked out or gunned down with silver bullets. It is airborne and cannot be buried, disguised, or replaced with lies. It flows through the bloodline of the body of consciousness that is waking up from this dream. The mouthless whispers emerge from a mosaic of inspired visions of prophetic graffiti, inscribed upon the walls of what will not be forgotten. Voices ride the whirlwinds of the unborn realm into the eye of the cyclone, that place of stillness and silence and Light.

The Light Meditation

Written by JAI
Tim Rodd: Narration, Copy Editing, Post Production, Cover Design
Rahmon Muhammad: Sound Engineer
Sebastian Robertson: Sound Engineer
Levi Chen: Chinese Harp or Zither

I Transcend My Ego Self Meditation

Written by JAI
Narration: Nicholas Rodd, JAI
Tim Rodd: Copy Editing, Post Production, Cover Design
Rahmon Muhammad: Sound Engineer
Sebastian Robertson: Sound Engineer
Levi Chen: Chinese Harp or Zither

Many thanks to prolific composer, producer, visionary musician, and performing artist … the heart and soul of Yin Yang Records and Liquid Gardens, Levi Chen. Dream Universal extends immense appreciation, love, and light for your participation in our healing Mystical Meditation journeys. The East meets West meets the Cosmos, ethereal soundscapes of Meditation of my Soul, featuring the interplay of ambient electric guitar textures and the traditional Gu Zheng, Chinese harp, formed a sound that perfectly complements our catalog of healing meditations.

THE TIMELESS NOW

Healing from Grief and Loss
Mystical Meditation
The Sacred Law of Impermanence

Table of Contents

Consecration

Acknowledgments

Prologue   01

Ashes   02
Prologue   05
Mirror Mirror   11
Frequency of the Natural Mystic   13

The Sacred Law of Impermanence   19

What is the Sacred Law of Impermanence?   20
The Three Marks of Existence   26
Understanding the Experience of Grief   29
Forms of Grief   34
We are Bodies of Light   40
What is The Light body?   43
The Body System (Diagram)   50
The Body System   51
    <u>The Light/Subtle Body</u>   51
    <u>The Mental Self</u>   52

The Emotional Self	53
The Physical Self	54
The Soul, The Ether, The True Self	55
How Grief Affects the Aura	57
Healthy Aura (Diagram)	64
Aura Affected by Grief (Diagram)	65
Polluted Aura (Diagram)	66
Aura Affected by Drugs and Alcohol (Diagram)	67
The Refuge (Diagram)	68

What is Death? 69

Nameless	70
Death: The Final Illusion	72
Meditation and Ego Death	75
Death the Archetype: Removing the Veil	80
The Shadow of Death: The Archetype	82
Our Glass	87
The Tower: The Archetype	88
Two Storms	94
Do Not Stand at My Grave and Weep	96
The Emotional Impact of Grief	98
Is It Even Possible To Kill One's Self?	101
Out	102
Foul Play	117
The Dark Night of the Soul	120
Beyond the Veil of Turiya	127
Turiya (Diagram)	129
Turiya: The Meaning of Bindi	130

What is the Meaning of Union?	131
Turiya Meditation	134
Reincarnation	142
Near Death Experience (NDE)	146
Ego-Annihilation	149

Mystical Meditation & the Law of Impermanence — 151

The Stilling of the Mind	153
The Waking Dream	185
Planes of Existence	189
Meditation: The Bridge Between Worlds of Consciousness	192
Mystical Meditation and Death	195
Concept of I Transcend My Ego Self	199
Mystical Meditation and Monotheism	205
Graven Images	209
The Meaning of the I AM	212
Yin Yang (Diagram)	216
The I AM Meditation	217
Our Attachment to Maya (Illusory Material World)	224
Our Attachment to the Physical Form	235
The War Within	239
The Dance of Duality	241
Unchanging	245

The Chakra System, & the Aura — 249

Basic Human Chakra System (Diagrams)	250
Meditation and the Chakra System	252

Basic Guidelines for Mystical Meditation	261
Meditation Posture (Diagram)	267
Chakra Meditation and Visualization Exercise	268
Meditation Exercise to Strengthen the Seven Energy Centers	299

The Light Meditation — 301

The Light Meditation	302
The Light Meditation Transcript	303

Featured Meditation: I Transcend My Ego Self — 317

I TRANSCEND MY EGO SELF	318
I TRANSCEND MY EGO SELF: The Meditation	319
Inspiration Behind the I TRANSCEND MY EGO SELF Meditation	325
I TRANSCEND MY EGO SELF Meditation Instructions	327
Journaling	330
How to Practice the I TRANSCEND MY EGO SELF Meditation	333
I TRANSCEND MY EGO SELF Meditation Transcript	337
Dreamcatcher Journal	355
The Power of Affirmation	359

The Power of Prayer, Intervention, and Faith — 369

The Power of Prayer, Intervention, and Faith	370
The Power of Repetitive Prayer	381
The Sacred OM/AUM (Diagram)	384
The SACRED OM/AUM	385
Service as Meditation and Healing	388

Epilogue	395
Dedication	402
My Mother My Friend	405
The Dreamcatchers	407
I Will Rise Again	408
About the Author	411
Works Cited	413
Meditation Download Instructions	414
Recommended Reading	415
Recommended Music	416

You are invited to join The Timeless Now: Healing from Grief and Loss, an online support group, designed with a recovery theme for times of grief and loss. It serves as a resourceful, interactive site offering healing and inspiration in times of suffering and despair connected with the experience of loss. Click on, scroll down, and reflect on the posts until you feel better. In times of overwhelm, seek professional medical and psychological help, support from family, friends, and wise spiritual counsel. It gets better.

When references are made to The Source, The God, in this text, these words appear with an initial capital letter. A reference expressing Divinity, used in a casual reference, such as light, vs. "Light," self, vs. "Self," is distinguished here with a capital letter. References to the Most High God are intended to be gender non-binary, consistent with the non-dual, true nature of The God. References are made to magic (magic tricks performed as entertainment) vs. "magick" (the Science and Art of causing Change to occur in conformity with Will … mundane and esoteric).

I share my journey with you

through the worlds within, where we become

the dreams that are born mature, the nightmares we cannot forget

We never die to the Timeless, beyond yesterday, today, and forever

We explore the dance of consciousness

from the non-physical, into the physical realm, and back again

This sacred dance is Eternal.

There is no past ... The First Moment

There is no future ... The Second Moment

All time is Now ... The Third Moment

In the subtle, spaceless space between them

Beyond Samadhi

Outside of Time

There is only

The Fourth Moment

The Timeless Now

We embrace this Oneness

with respect, gratitude, and Love.

I. WANT. MY. MOMMY!!! I have lived under the shadow of that unreasonable demand every day since the day she passed away ... the forlorn mantra of a petulant child. I realized that I could no longer talk to her. We could no longer hang out together. We could no longer travel together. We would no longer be the witness of each other's lives. I lost my best friend. I spiralled into an abyss of grief from what I thought was an evolved spiritual consciousness. Despair sought to eclipse the incredible Light her soul brought my life, that not even death could steal. Though so many years have passed, it will always feel like it just happened yesterday. The pain I was left in became the crossroad I stood in. The longing and resultant spiritual phenomenon known as ego-death nearly devastated my life. I was forced to find a way to survive it. *The Timeless Now* is the story of my mystical journey.

I am still emerging from behind the walls of sacred temples, circles, and ashrams ... from under the tutelage and mentorship of enlightened spiritual teachers, Light-working Energy healers, hierophants, priestesses, and mystics from diverse paths and traditions. I was guided to embrace a shift in perspective that escapes time and the lies it told. She donned the qualities of a Queen, a Priestess in her own right, one who had traversed the Sea of Eternity and returned with a page from the most ancient of scriptures. The message was we must not succumb to the fear of death ... because there is no such thing. She inspired my research and experience of Mystical Meditation as a practice which reveals the healing potential of surrendering and releasing fearful, egoic attachments that bind us to our suffering. Rising out of grief is not an event, it is a process. We seek our healing in the Timeless Realms.

The Timeless Now offers a powerful meditation, "I Transcend My Ego Self" which points to what is already within us, just waiting to be awakened. The spirit of a directive to awaken induces an evolved perspective of Self and the states of consciousness we are capable of experiencing. It inspires a dynamic shift in awareness ... a gentle letting go of the limiting, crippling illusions that seek to destroy the quality and meaning of life. We free ourselves of clinging to the delusion that temporary feelings and states will last forever and practice stripping away false identities. We explore and embrace the changeless, the Essential Being of the energetic body that cannot be diminished by transient states and circumstances. From the changeful world, we rise together in consciousness to affirm that only the unchanging is real. Only the Timeless Self is real. Only *The Timeless Now* is real.

Prologue

ASHES

The sad ritual had begun
Dirt and tears
fell to the ground
I looked to the Earth
and said goodbye
I screamed to the Heavens
demanding, "WHY!"
Then something called out
that I couldn't see
It wasn't a vision
It wasn't a dream

Whispers and echoes
from
mouthless faces
opened doors to
nameless
places
It was
so beautiful

Something much stronger
than life, death, and time
made my soul stand apart
from my body and mind

At that moment
something in me was sure
that beyond this world
there exists something more

I saw the pipe dreams of man
and how happy life makes him
the sorrow and grief
when death overtakes him

I watched the veil being lifted
to a soul reborn
brilliant white Light
emerged as his new form

He spoke
He smiled
and gently affirmed
that forever alive
is all that is loved
and all that is
learned

I heard
the flutter
of a night bird's wings
mocking this world
and such transient things

Deep inside the chrysalis
wherein all my stories
and drama dwell
lie the mysteries
and the secrets
of heaven
and hell

The faithful
spread wide
freedom's wings
ascending beyond
all worldly things
defying gravity
escaping time
leaving all mortal
worries behind

Taking off
on a ten-ticket ride
with nothing to fear
and nothing to hide
escaping this life
and all its confusion
with peace being
more than a
fleeting illusion

If I should leave this world
this very day
I am grateful
for having passed this way
I know that my soul
will never die
but will go with the wind
and forever fly

No hole in the
ground
No box can
contain me
The stillness
upon me
cannot restrain me

If my spirit
should ever
look back
and yearn
I may once again
gather dust
and return
to be born
of another woman
and a strong will to live
and find even more
to love
learn
and give

~ JAI ~
Smoke & Mirrors

Prologue

"Ashes" is the first poem I ever wrote. I was nine years old. My mom did not believe I wrote it until I showed her the pencil scribblings on the side of a furnace wall in our old-school family kitchen. I was supposed to be washing the dishes, but an energy seized me and did not let go until the poem was finished. She told me it was morbid, but it reminded her of the writing of Omar Khayyam, her favorite poet. She had often recited certain verses of The Rubaiyat that she had memorized. She taught me, at the age of three, her favorite lines, and we would recite them together.

> *"I sent my soul through the invisible*
> *with some letter of that afterlife to spell;*
> *and by and by my soul returned to me*
> *and said that I myself am heaven and hell;*
> *Heaven but a vision of fulfilled desire;*
> *hell, but the shadows of a soul on fire ..."*

She loved me so much. She exposed me to many philosophies that she had no context for. In her heart, she lived in some parallel Universe where there were no identifying labels, a place where freedom of spirit was the only definition of being alive. She was profound in both her abstract and concrete logic, as though she had one foot planted firmly in the tangible and one in the invisible realm, fluid rather than fixed, elegant in her dance between them. She had a fascination with Eastern philosophies, especially as expressed in poetry. She wanted to name me Omar for Omar Khayyam had I been a boy. She died giving birth to me with a copy of The Rubaiyat that had comforted her through labor. The delivery went wrong. My mother told me my cries brought her back. After she had been pronounced dead, my father was told the baby survived, but his wife didn't make it. Crushed, he called his sister with the news from the hospital lobby. They had neglected to tell him the heart specialist had miraculously revived her. The entire story was recounted to me by my mother. She did not understand how she had "seen" all of this because she was supposed to have been busy at the time being dead, rather than observing specific details of what was going on in the hospital.

My mother had never heard of a Near Death Experience (NDE). She had never read about the studies of Dr. Raymond Moody or Dr. Elisabeth Kübler-Ross, Dr. Edgar Cayce, or the many others who have shared their experiences and research. She told me of a tunnel of light, of beings clad in elegant flowing robes. She could not describe them as anything but beautiful and loving, as they reached out to her, welcoming her to the other side. She saw vibrant colors, picturesque landscapes, rivers, a lake. She heard unique tones and experienced a "knowing" beyond words, beyond language.

She recalled every beautiful sight in nature that one could imagine … sprawling meadows, an alluring body of water she pulled away from because she was conscious of the fact that she could not swim. She said it looked like what one might envision of heaven. When she was given a choice to stay or go back, she confessed that she did not want to come back here. She heard me crying. She chose me. She came back. When the heart specialist arrived, he was told it was too late to save her, and there was no point in trying, even if he could bring her back, he said she had been out too long and would most likely be brain damaged. When she regained consciousness, they asked her a series of questions, including her social security number, all of which she answered 'correctly' … except for one. She was asked, "Where are you from?" She replied, "Heaven." She believed that to be the place she had just come from.

She reported her life as having changed so dramatically after that experience that she did not feel like the same person. Her senses and perceptions were heightened and intensified. Her value system had changed. Her priorities in life had changed. She dedicated her life to feeding the hungry, caring for the ill and the homeless, helping the youth and the aged, giving hope to the hopeless. Her consciousness had changed in a way that brought a flavor of mysticism to everything about her brand-new life.

Her ideas and beliefs about death changed. She taught me never to fear death. On her death bed at eighty-two years of age, some of her last words expressed her embrace of the eternal and fearlessness in the face of rebirth into a world she had already tasted. She said, "I'm ready. I'm tired. I had a good time. I'm not afraid. I did this already … and I liked it. It was so beautiful." The spirit of pure bliss would sweep across her face as she drifted beyond suffering.

Growing up, over the years my writing continued, and the poetry flowed. The mystical and spiritual aspects of death have been a recurrent theme. The mysticism was the seasoning of my visions and dreams. My mom and dad would say, "That's not mystical. That's normal! We are from African and Creole. What do you expect? We come from the Geechee people out of Africa and the Cherokee tribe. It's normal!" I used to think their version of "normal" was something out of a science fiction movie. Now I know that all of existence is mystical. The fact that we are here at all is mystical. The fact that we appear to die is not only mystical, it is sacred.

I am not qualified to liberate anyone from the innate fears associated with death. After my mother passed away, the joy faded from my life, and since then nothing feels real according to my prior understanding of reality. She did not raise me like that. She taught me that we do not die. I am not a good example of a more "enlightened" acceptance of inevitable death. I buckled and fell completely apart. She was my soul mate … my twin flame. I did not know how to live without her.

No one escapes the tremors of death in the hour of its arrival. It does not matter how many books of Rumi's poetry one has read, the hour of separation is bitter. I write this, aware that today is December 17th ... Rumi's Wedding Night (Seb-I Arus) ... the anniversary of his physical death and spiritual reunion with The Beloved, The Divine One. Every year, thousands of people from all over the world make a pilgrimage to the Thirteenth-century mausoleum of the great mystic, Rumi. This day is celebrated by participating in the symbolic, choreographed, whirling dance of the Dervishes. A tall cap, representing the tomb of carnal existence, and a white robe, which is its shroud, are worn for this exacting and sacred ceremony.

I can imagine Rumi somewhere in the Timeless, spinning in circles of ecstasy, enveloped in the loving embrace of The Eternal One, The Beloved ... As I cry for my mother like an infant, the sweet words of Rumi comfort me. I am haunted by a line from *The Sufi Path of Love: The Spiritual Teachings of Rumi by William C. Chittick* ... Quote

"This body keeps you in torment.
The bird of your spirit is imprisoned with a bird of another kind."

I understand that she is free now. I feel the spirit of Rumi. I feel Oneness with the Light into Which he returned. One phone call had changed my life forever. She was gone ... dead, I was told. Just like that. Gone. An unfortunate illness ... gone. She didn't make it, and nothing would ever be the same again. It would have been different if I had not touted such a well-steeped potion of metaphysics and old-world wisdom. I was shattered. It was over. A plane ticket later, I was thrust into an unfamiliar Caribbean culture and mindset for many years. I found myself among people whose philosophy of both life and death speaks to the transcendent mystical journey of the soul, from the point of its origin, into the full bloom of its manifestation in the material realm, and back.

Dazed and numb, I stumbled out of a deep sleep one morning at the crack of dawn and slipped through the sliding doors of an island, beachfront cottage. I coasted along the stepping stone walkway that led to the shore of a private cove. I walked into the welcoming sea, all dressed up with nowhere to go … and just stood there. The glistening waves of a warm, gentle current lifted me up into its embrace. I began to pray. I began to cry. I allowed the sea to dissolve my sorrow into ten thousand peacock blues and greens, a watery turquoise meditation, where salt meets salt … the salt of an endless, tear-filled stream of vain longing meets the current of reality … Tears with no answers, prayers with no questions. I floated as if dead, praying, "Oh my God, I am yours. There is nothing left of me. I don't know who I am anymore. She was everything to me. You will have to show me how to live without her. I don't know how."

A tourist catamaran that I never saw approaching in the distance commanded my attention and drew me out of my prayerful meditation, into the listening of … "There's a Natural Mystic blowing in the air. If you listen carefully, you will hear. This could be the first trumpet … Might as well be the last …" The haunting incantation of Robert Nesta "Bob" Marley skipped across the waves and struck me as if to say, "The healing has begun." I stood up and walked out of the water and across the sand and went back inside. When I returned to that beach a little while later, I found the sand covered with what looked to me to be a million jellyfish left scattered there by the receding tide. They had been my companions in the sea as I prayed a prayer to be delivered from the sting of my insufferable loss … from this death … from this grief.

From that level of surrender, it was foreseeable that I would eventually have to embrace the study of the Sacred Law of Impermanence if I wanted to survive. It would be all that could heal me. I would have to understand the suffering caused by attachment to that which comes into being, and dissolves into the essence from which it arises ... fearfully, desperately clinging to the transient, the temporal. A trendy, yoga pants and yin yang tee shirt kind of transcendental meditation course of study would not be able to heal this death blow. I was blessed with the intervention of many opportunities to experience profoundly healing mystical traditions, from A Course in Miracles to the Orisha Yemaya, to the Temple of Neith, to the Hall of Ma'at; from the Kahunas of Hawaii to the Nyabinghi ceremonial chant downs in the Caribbean mountains, to Lakota Inipi sweat lodges; from the Tao and Zen to Vipassana ... from Shambala to Mokichi Okada to Nichiren Shoshu; from the Sufi's sacred breath to whirling circles of Dervishes, into being knocked flat on the floor, slain in the Spirit, under the speaking of tongues in Jesus' name ... to Advaita style, ego-stripping, Self-Realization. After dropping all of the story and drama, even after dropping the physical form, we are all right back to who we truly are already ... the Light, the Breath, the True Self, energy, and vibration. We are a body of conscious awareness, untouched by anything, not even death.

I knew that my spiritual survival depended on a journey that began with one question: Who am I, really?

MIRROR MIRROR

I am one
with mirrored
reflections
life & image
as one
appears to be real
the other illusion
how fine
the line
between the two

I do not grasp
or cling to imagery
I keep nothing
I hold nothing
I witness what is there
a flat surface portal
to inner dimensions
that reveals the me
in the mirror
but not the I

Just beneath surface
shadows of bitterness
suffering and pain
is love … learning
and healing
On the other side
of my most dreadful nightmares
are my wildest dreams
coming true

I reflect on
life's duality
I challenge darkness
embrace
Light
I accept them
both as one

Pain & pleasure
humanity & Divinity
the darkness of confusion
the brilliance of growth
are all one
a part of the other
Life's experience
is the soul's quest for knowledge
longing for truth ... for completion
before its return home

~ JAI ~
Smoke & Mirrors

Frequency of the Natural Mystic

It was as though two unknown dimensions collided somewhere between the gates of two airports, LAX and Montego Bay. It started as a not so funny joke. Through Xanax-laced declarations, I let it be known that I was, "going to the Rastafarian Bobo Hill in Jamaica and chant Nyabinghi … That. Is. All." My subconscious mind was full and spilling over with the hypnotic rhythms of the Nyabinghi drums, the conscious lyrics, delicately woven into the fabric of an awakening waiting to happen, cleverly disguised as entertainment.

I had a short list of reggae tunes by Bob Marley and his sons, that had been on auto-shuffle and repeat for weeks. "The body is just a vehicle that transports the soul. It's what's inside the vehicle, a beauty to behold. It was written in the Book of Life, a man shall endure forevermore." I was still in shock. I was stuck on repeat. I touched her face. It was cold, and it was hard, and she felt like furniture … like she wasn't even in there. All I could see was her face, for the wrapping.

I instinctively understood I had no choice but to embrace the true meaning of the old Zen saying that has since been reduced to memes in my Facebook news feed, "Pain is inevitable, suffering is a choice." How could something that sounded so cliché, possibly apply to me about the loss of my mother? She was my best friend.

Peeking out over the top of a downward spiraling depression that seemed to have no bottom or end, I whispered, "I'm going to Bobo Hill and chant Nyabinghi … That. Is. All." A Divine intervention, through a friend, had caused me to leave my mother's funeral, and a comfortable life in Mexico, for Jamaica. She told me I probably wouldn't come back and that it was okay, she wouldn't take it personally. She told me that I would have to stay there until I could remember myself and that I was there to meet a teacher.

It didn't take me long to figure out that this new postcard-pretty world had not properly introduced itself to me. Just beneath the mask of palm trees and pristine beaches, this haven of refuge for unsuspecting tourists was lit up like a Christmas tree. Eerily familiar, ancient spirits walked about and never slept. From the White Witch of Rose Hall to the travelers on a seaside road that no longer exists and no one still alive remembers, spirits revealed themselves in many forms ... some quite terrifying ... others stunningly beautiful like the magical cave spirits in Green Grotto Caves, Runaway Bay. Some seemed to be unaware of their ethereal state of existence.

I was lost and empty, but I intuitively knew that I needed a powerful form of meditation, a higher frequency would be required if I was going to survive this death blow. I was tightrope walking without a net to break the fall of my accelerating spiritual and emotional descent. I had been spinning in the whirlwind of approaching the finish line of a book I had written on divination, Western and Eastern occultism, and advanced metaphysical practice. I thought I was pretty deep. I saw little difference between one side of time and the other, of the fragile line between the spirit and physical world. I commonly had experiences that defied logical explanation and felt that I had a good relationship with the concept of "death" and the illusion of its existence. But when I touched the face of my mother and found an empty, cold, hard shell, I was delivered a most sobering message of the finality of the "transition" from physical to non-physical existence. That ineffable silence sent me to the only place I had left to go ... within.

The scent of peanut porridge, jerk chicken, and Ital stew drifted on the evening ocean breeze at Dead End Beach. It was there I first heard the voice of my teacher. In an emotionally paralyzed daze, I set out on a mission to find the Bobo Ashanti Rasta camp, at Bull's Bay, Bobo Hill in Jamaica. I wanted to go up into the hills, get lost in the drums echo, and chant the Eternal Spirit of Nyabinghi, to my last breath. I wanted to disappear into the Timeless portal in the mountains near Portland, where the culture of simplicity, freedom, and healing through spiritual practice is a lifestyle.

The meditation of a Rasta begins with chanting a verse from Psalms each day with the rising Sun. The intention is to manifest peace, freedom, justice, and equality for all of humanity. They ceremonially "chant down" all that threatens that … literally speaking it out of existence. The practice of metaphorically "chanting down" Babylon is a combination of vibration, breath, fire, and water, being grounded into the realm of manifestation, to accomplish an elemental cleansing and healing. "Babylon" refers to the dominant cultural energies of materialism and capitalism that lead to many levels of destruction and suffering … profit over people. Ceremonially becoming this powerful fusion of energy is a process, as it moves back and forth, between the conscious and subconscious minds of everyone and everything it touches.

I was fortunate enough to have encountered the one person who I couldn't coax, at any price, to take me there. In fresh culture shock himself, his first few days out of a lengthy stay at Bobo Hill, my teacher had appeared. I was told that "they didn't want me up there, in my present condition," … pointing out my Western or "Babylonian" attire and cultural mindset. After giving me the list of criteria for entrance into the circle of the Bobo Hill Rastas, I had to rethink my journey. Their myriad rules and requirements sounded too intense and extreme for me at the time. I had to agree that I wasn't ready.

I couldn't imagine not having my cell phone, laptop, iPod, internet, e-mail, manicurist, pedicurist, hairdresser, hairstyle, and I didn't own one item of what they would call appropriate clothing for the occasion. I couldn't imagine not "eating the flesh and drinking the blood of murdered animals" (they are strict vegans). I couldn't imagine not having cable TV, unconscious music blasting songs, ceaselessly channeling lyrical mindless emptiness … and NO INTERNET signal!!! … that was a deal-breaker. I really couldn't imagine having any kind of responsibility for, or interest in agricultural issues.

I never made it up to Bobo Hill, but after many years of living totally immersed in parallel Rastafarian influenced cultural circles, some aspects of the profoundly mystical energies of Bobo Hill found their way to me. Within the first heartbeat of that first Nyabinghi drum, I encountered a vortex of magickal energy and vibration so strong, that it ultimately changed many sacred aspects of my life. All of the mysticism I'd ever learned, and had yet to learn, made "natural" common sense to me. I had returned to the starting point of a very large circle. Full circle is never a loss. It is never the same person who started it, that completes it.

My path had evolved enough to send me back to the drawing board to revise my book in conformance with my new, and yet hauntingly familiar, standard of spiritual practice. I was exposed to energies so intense that my spirit was set off its axis, or rather, had begun a process of regenerating the brilliance of my true inner Light. Messages came in visions, in dreams, in synchronicities that defied rational explanation. It wasn't as though I was really "learning" anything. I was being made to remember. It was a process. Like the layers of an onion being peeled back, all the way to the heart, "Babylon" began to fall away … left behind, gasping for last breaths, on the floor of a Rastafarian tabernacle, on a hilltop in Jamaica. Spirits rising up in the smoke of the meditation fire ceremony, petitioned for the healing of a profoundly sick and suffering world … affirming the protection of, the recognition of, the shared energies of The Most High, as the Ultimate Natural Mystic.

I lost track of just how many years had passed, perhaps because the meaning of time had changed ... evolved into a vast energy field of all time as One tense ... no past, no future, only the Timeless Now. Reduced to fading memories, were the little boxes with labels on them, that we are pressured to force-fit into. Disappearing was the expectation that our inner and outer reality will either conform to, or be harshly judged, and dismissed. Both inner and outer reality is insulted to be fragmented and defined as such hollow, designer-labeled pieces of a Divinely complex puzzle.

Many aspects of the spiritual practice of Rastafarians are strikingly similar to those of other indigenous, spiritual traditions I am acquainted with, such as Yoga, Shamanism, Curanderismo, Huna, and Sufism, even many paths of Buddhism, with the keyword being practice. These paths, among so many others, will generally not label themselves as this or that religion. They will simply state their practice through the wisdom of their lifestyle. They all have one belief in common ... The Sacred Law of Impermanence.

"The wound is the place where the Light enters you."

~ Rumi ~

"Verily all things move within your being in constant half embrace,
the desired and the dreaded
the repugnant and the cherished,
the pursued and that which you would escape.
These things move within you as lights and shadows
in pairs that cling.
And when the shadow fades and is no more,
the light that lingers
becomes a shadow
to another light."

~ Kahlil Gibran ~
The Prophet

The Sacred Law of Impermanence

What is the Sacred Law of Impermanence?

Returning to the U.S. from the Caribbean, I was confronted with the nightmare of reacclimating to a life back where it no longer felt like home. My struggle to survive the emotional devastation after the loss of my mother returned, compounded by extreme culture shock. My life was sent spinning in many terrifying directions, circles that used to be timelines that I understood had all been erased. The pain turned physical, and there was no relief. I was beginning to understand that neither time nor distraction could change any of it. I would have to change me.

Seventeen years had passed after first having heard the word "Vipassana" from my Traditional Chinese Medicine class teacher. Vipassana is an ancient, powerful meditation technique that would allow me to continue my radical healing process. She had announced that she felt "frayed" and would not be able to teach the class that day. She told us that she had just returned from a ten-day meditation retreat. Of course, we wanted to know more about it, and she graciously shared her experience with us.

She told us that from the moment one first hears the word Vipassana, that is the moment they have begun their journey toward it. It took many years, much loss, and enough suffering before I finally registered and completed the ten-day, silent meditation retreat. The objective of the Vipassana meditation technique is to see things as they really are. That is where I learned about Anicca, the Law of Impermanence. Anicca means "change," and as we know, everything changes.

The promise of change is as cliché as we sometimes allow ourselves to become. So many common expressions of it come to mind. We casually say things like, "the only thing certain in life is change; the young become the old; you have to take the good times with the bad; the only thing we can be sure of in life is death and taxes." Rarely do we delve into the depth of their meaning. All change can introduce itself into our lives as chaos, even when we perceive the change as welcome. We instinctively know that the same gentle wave kissing the shore can draw back a heavy hand and, upon its return, smite everything in its path. The cycles of the Moon, the Sun, the transits of the planets … everything in life spins and moves at the effect of this dance of existence. Life is a book of changes, writing itself into the realm of common understanding. Our undoing is to fear it. We must know ourselves as the stillness in that unchanging eye of the storm. We are that place called Eternity … no form, no past, no future, no story, sharing the very Essence of the Creator.

"Nothing lasts forever" is another common expression. It is not a casual concept, nor is it complicated. When living in times of turmoil, chaos, and suffering, this is the good news. In the throes of earthbound joy, this news can cause great suffering, if that is how we choose to react to it. It is a gift to be able to coax the conscious and subconscious mind into reacting with a yielding spirit, to understand and accept the ebb and flow of life's circumstances, to respect the sacred Law of Impermanence. Most of us think we do not possess the ability to respond to change with the insight of equanimity, which is a choice of fundamental non-interference with the natural fluctuations of sensory experience. We often struggle to maintain full charge over our emotional reaction to life's changes without willful pushing or pulling, without attachment or aversion, without judgment or naiveté … no hump for any random emotion to ride. What a challenge it is to be able to gracefully yield to life's changes, willing to throw our surrendered hands in the air, on this wild roller coaster ride of existence.

We are required, for our highest good, to witness everything, see everything and everyone through the filter of Impermanence. We observe without judgment or fear, from the perspective of the changeless, eternal being that we really are. There is no permanent or fixed reality. All is fluid and changing. All is perishable with a reality of rising up as manifestations and passing away, rising up and passing away, only to rise up and pass away again. Our illusory reality is the flip side of the coin of Anicca.

Anicca is a Pali word that refers to one of the fundamental doctrines, the "Three Marks of Existence" in Buddhist philosophy. The term expresses the concept that all of conditioned existence, without exception, is in a constant state of flux. To be conditioned is to be dependent on or affected by something else, and the Buddha taught that all phenomena, including beings, are conditioned. The transitory nature of all conditioned things is the basis of life because all phenomena are in a state of unrest and continuous becoming. Time is circular, not linear.

Anicca means "inconstant." It is a paradox that refers to the relationship between continuity and permanence, as well as their opposites, change, and impermanence. Change is constant, which means that this state, while continually changing, also stays the same. Embracing the Law of Impermanence liberates us from needless suffering, for we accept the changes of life with grace, knowing that all things are transitory. Consider a timeline of photographs of ourselves from birth to advanced years. Imagine the baby picture next to the picture of the child, the teenager, the adult, progressing into old age. We ask ourselves, which one of the pictures is that of the real being that is photographed? The answer is none of them!

We are more than the images we express as ourselves. We are the sacred Creative Essence that emanated them. The only evidence we have of our changes would be the images we have somehow captured and preserved with the scent of the memories left behind. It is insane to believe that anyone remains the same for his or her entire lifetime. It is unwise to believe that we are those images frozen in time, on paper, which is also perishable. That includes the mirror images that even the mirror will not cling to.

Our perception of change and our reaction to it is what determines its impact on our life experience. When we transcend the mundane mindsets of average human beings, we step outside of the baggage of the personality trap. We are more than that. We are Timeless, formless, immortal beings. The personal faces of our many identities are merely the masks we wear as the body vehicle is guided along its destined path. As we embrace change, we change our relationship with impermanence. We understand that our culture's forever 21 mindset is causing great suffering. Impermanence is not limited to waning and decay.

Keep in mind that in our reflections on change, death, and loss, there is more than one kind of letting go. We can experience the pain of a death with the end of relationships, friendships, aging, illness, loss of livelihood, loss of property, loss of health, loss of sovereignty, and the loss of quality of life. It cuts like the reaper's sickle and can leave an indelible stain on our very soul. These kinds of heart-shattering losses are still the manifestation of Anicca.

I know it seems to make no sense to seek to reconcile such justified emotions and become objective, with neither attachment nor aversion. What kind of strength would it take to be able to do that? That is what this pointing is about. We are not our bodies. We are not anything that happens to or around it. There is an offering of a liberation, a freedom that can transcend or transform suffering. Impermanence expands to a continual becoming. When we focus our attention on it, observe it, understand it, and respect its sacredness, it becomes a healing balm for the sorrows of temporal life. To embrace Anicca is to embrace freedom from needless suffering.

The Law of Impermanence is the feared and dreaded enemy of clingy attachment/aversion drama scenarios characterized by the unwillingness to let go. We will surely lose what we seek to cling to. The flip side of the coin of attachment delivers the very sense of tragedy and unbearable pain that we are trying to avoid. The Buddha taught that because conditioned phenomena are impermanent, attachment to them becomes the cause for future suffering. We must release our fear-based anxieties and make impermanence our friend.

Scientific studies have shown that the act of observing produces a change in what is being observed. If we choose to observe "death" with a non-dual mind, respectful of the Law of Impermanence, we are offered a unique opportunity to alter the way it occurs to us. How we view death has a lot to do with our cultural underpinnings, yet no one can escape the tremor in the face of its patient waiting.

It is easy to entertain philosophies about death. But when it parks itself on our doorstep, we can be thrown into abysmal emotional turmoil, our faith and objectivity challenged and threatened. It is an awkward, fragile dimension to be cast into. We feel vulnerable and alone, we feel helpless and left to cope with the loss we have suffered, compounded by the triggering of crippling mortality issues.

The death of anyone or anything we value bites. We are expected to succumb to that pain as it emerges in a variety of emotional manifestations. Embracing the Sacred Law of Impermanence can initiate the healing process so that we may find peace again. It worked for me. On a roller coaster of change, I found within myself that which does not change … and I learned to cherish it.

I will not engage in a dissertation regarding the fundamental belief systems of any one path or religion about death, nor will I endorse any expression of spirituality over another in this text. The paths are many. The destination is One.

Death does not care what we believe in. Change does not care what we believe in. The Three Marks of Existence, according to Buddhist philosophy, address our conditioning regarding existence and death in times of suffering, loss, and grief. There is profound healing available in understanding that our suffering is not personal, just a reality of life. Anicca is just one of the Three Marks of Existence. I would be remiss to reference one and not the other two Laws. They are essentially connected.

The Three Marks of Existence

This is not a book about religion. It is a sharing of philosophies and secular meditation practices that, in my time of need, offered a profound healing after the devastating loss of my mother. Death and grief drift in the Ether of our being as a counsel and advisor, independent of our beliefs and opinions. Many religions and belief systems have spawned philosophies that have gone mainstream in diverse cultures around the world. Many contemporary traditions have roots in age-old mystical practices. We accept this medicine of the ancient mystics and healers with love and gratitude.

All things are characterized by the three marks of existence. The First Mark or Law of existence is Change … the Impermanence doctrine or Anicca. According to the Law of Impermanence, human life embodies the fluidity of change in the aging process, the cycles of birth and rebirth, and in the experience of loss. The Buddha declared that "Decay is inherent in all component things." His followers accept that conditioned phenomena can also be referred to as compounded, constructed, or fabricated. This is in contrast to the unconditioned, uncompounded, and unfabricated Nirvana. Nirvana is the reality that knows no change, decline, or death. Anything that is temporary is an illusion. All that is true reality is that which is not subject to change and does not come and go. We affirm that only the unchanging is real.

The Second Mark or Law of Existence is suffering, or Dukkha, unsatisfactoriness or unhappiness. As great as this gift of temporal life is, we cannot and will not enter and exit this Plane of existence without experiencing pain, loss, and suffering. This phenomenal field of our own perception offers no illusion of a pain-free worldly experience. It is characterized by Impermanence, and some form of suffering or Dukkha is the result of that. The Law of Dukkha is characteristic of the human condition, and here unsatisfactoriness manifests as the kind of suffering we experience when we lose a loved one or wrestle with our fears regarding the transience of our own existence.

The Third Mark or Law of Existence is Anatta or no-self, no-thing. It is the ultimate unfolding of the annihilation of the ego. It is the ego that clings with attachment to being defined by conditioned concepts and identities structured around the physical form. I have heard the "True Self" described as a metaphorical drop of water released into a vast sea. The drop of water is not diminished by merging with the sea, an entity of the same element as itself. Though it may seem that some of the self-hood of the drop of water was sacrificed, it is actually expanded as it becomes one with the vastness of the sea. It moves beyond the distinguishable boundaries of its expression as a form called a "drop" with no loss of identity. It is water, as much as it ever was. We are much like that drop of water, with our self-imposed boundaries, limitations, labels, and superficial identifications. As our subtlest level of Self releases into the vastness of the Origin of all there is, we merge and realize we have only become That which we were all along …The I AM.

The experience of union with the Divine dissolves the ego, and it becomes empty of the desire for individuated existence, unattached to personhood, becoming the Oneness with Ultimate Conscious Awareness. Becoming reabsorbed into the Point of our Divine Origin is the most exalted state of becoming One with the Ultimate in the realm of the Incomprehensible … the Unfathomable … the Unknowable … beyond language and names, as no-thing.

As we meditate on the Divinity of the True Self, the realization of "Self," as such, can cause the ego to feel threatened. It can feel like we are disappearing. To conquer the urge to drift back into delusion and perpetual suffering is to taste freedom and experience liberation. Entertaining the false illusions of the ego self is a powerful human instinct and one of the most potent sources of ignorance and pain. There is more than one way to transcend the bondage of suffering associated with the changes of inevitable impermanence. The dissolving of the ego triggers an awakening to the true nature of the Transcendent Self. The revelation of a Timeless, stateless state leads to the unveiling of our relationship with the Divine, as One with That Holy Essence … In the Self-Illuminating Triple Darkness of Negative Existence. We are the reed flute, and the Beloved is the Breath that becomes our Life Force. Those who seek God find Self. Those who seek Self find God.

> *I searched for God and found only myself.*
> *I searched for myself and found only God.*
> *~ Rumi~*

Understanding the Experience of Grief

My most visceral experience with unshakable grief was the loss of my mother. However, not all grief is associated with death. Some of the techniques and traditions that I found to be healing in situations of grief, loss, and trauma, are age-old, tried and true. These practices serve to establish and maintain equanimity within one's Self, to the point of alleviating the suffering that is a natural counterpart of existence in this realm.

I have had my share of traumatic experiences throughout my life, on every level. The holistic approach worked as a healing for me, even on the subtlest levels of grief and trauma. I was blessed to have been studying spiritual paths that offer a blend of bitter-sweet transcendence through secular spiritual practices. None of us get out of this life without the experience of a grocery list of horrors to transcend. Our struggles build the strength and perseverance required to maintain control over our own selves … our own lives … even in the face of crushing grief and loss. We all want liberation from the bondage of needless suffering. Know Self … No self. Transcend all that is not the True Self.

It is important to expand our perspectives and think outside of our own situational boxes. Allow for cultural differences among the countless expressions of the experience of grief. It helps to have a social support system in place of family, friends, spiritual, psychological, even medical professionals to aid in the process of healing. Reaffirming the Light of life while accepting its inherent shadows are two wings of the same bird. A shift in consciousness and perspective are required to fly. Meditation and energy healing have been scientifically proven to have a profound effect on the recovery process. It certainly works for me.

As we observe the practices of some tradition's cross-over, home-going rituals, and ceremonies, they may not even appear to us to be grieving. Sublime states of consciousness associated with the transcendence of grief can be occurring, unnoticed, before our eyes. It is also beneficial to generate our own culture of healing rituals and ceremonial traditions to acknowledge the losses we suffer and hold as sacred the resultant pain and grief. As we gather up the scattered pieces of our shattered souls, we affirm that life is good, *even now*.

<u>Losses that can provoke grief include, but are not limited to, the following:</u>
(not consecutively ordered according to the severity of impact)

- The cumulative effect of a pattern and history plagued by instability and continuous change;

- Unresolved feelings, losses, pain, unprocessed grief from past traumatic events and experiences;

- Death of a partner, loved one, or family member;

- Death of classmates or colleagues;

- Loss of a close friend;

- Relationship break-up and the arguments and discord that leads to it;

- Physical and emotional abuse in a relationship with narcissistic undertones;

- Loss of a loved one who is still physically alive due to addiction behaviors involving; drugs, alcohol, cults, personality and energy shifts, emotional distancing (ghosting);

- Loss of witness of life events, shared rituals, traditions, culture, and ceremonies (especially with extenuating circumstances);

- Waning of youth and vitality;

- Loss of health;

- Loss of mobility;

- Loss of former sense of personhood;

- Diagnosis of major health issue or chronic illness of self or loved ones;

- Unreconciled issues regarding abortion, miscarriage, fertility issues;

- Marriage;

- Pregnancy;

- Complications of pregnancy;

- Birth;

- Loss of intimacy;

- Sexual problems;

- Divorce;

- Relationship reconciliation;

- Custody issues;

- Graduation from school;

- Empty Nest Syndrome;

- Leaving home;

- Loss of home, property, status, reputation;

- Change of residence;

- Change of schools;

- Change in living conditions;

- Foreclosure;

- Bankruptcy;

- Buying a new home;

- New job;

- Starting a business;

- Pattern of frequent changes of residence, feelings of rootlessness, difficulty forming lasting relationships;

- Victim of sexual assault, physical/emotional abuse, domestic violence;

- Victim of random violence;

- Loss of freedom;

- Imprisonment;

- Loss of a pet;

- Loss of computer, crash, theft, malfunction, accident (no backup copy … yes, this belongs here. People, including myself, have literally lost their minds over that one);

- Losing driving privileges;

- Accidents and injury;

- Accumulation of bills, paperwork, doctor appointments, shared plans and activities, responsibilities, and chores, are now experienced solo;

- Loss of photographs or other irreplaceable items;

- Loss of job, demotion, change of job or livelihood, retirement;

- Problems with boss or coworkers;

- Change in job description, work hours, work environment;

- Crisis of faith;

- Loss of approval;

- Loss of the essential belief systems surrounding trust and safety;

- Dark night of the soul, associated with enlightenment;

- Excommunication or drama related to religious or spiritual groups;

- Exclusion;

- Bullying;

- Social Media bullying, arguments, and attacks;

- Exposure to an unceasing barrage of news programming;

- Loss and separation due to migration, climate change, war, persecution, oppression, economic and political upheaval, violence, organized crime or delinquency, social unrest, disappearances, strikes, protests, loss of security;

- Loss and separation caused by clashing political or religious ideologies, issues of class, race, even diet when someone chooses a meat-free diet;

- Judgments, discrimination, bigotry, and life-endangering violence caused by gender identification and orientation;

- Holiday triggers;

- Remarkable personal achievement or failure.

Forms of Grief

<u>Normal</u> – Lose this term, "normal." There is no such thing. Normal according to whom and compared to what? The response to grief and loss is unique to every person experiencing it. Associates in the familial, social, and professional circles of the grieving individual are often at different stages of the healing process, and we might find ourselves feeling left alone and face down. Tolerance is important as we adapt to new emotional realities. Even the word "recovery" is inappropriate. Some things are not possible to recover from in any typical way. To what standard does one hold the concept of "recovery?" What does "recovery" look like from one individual to another, when there are many unique manifestations of the grief response? One's personal perception of the loss determines the length and intensity of the suffering. It could manifest as a prolonged or chronic response, which may require professional holistic treatment. The energy field of grief creates a perfect storm of needless, seemingly endless suffering.

<u>Common Manifestations of the Experience of Grief</u>:

- Symptoms such as sleep disturbances, nightmares, ruminating, distressing thoughts, depressed mood, social isolation, and/or severe anxiety;

- Feeling like you're losing your mind;

- Brain fog, PTSD, ADD, delayed or impaired response time in regards to the process of decision-making, rationalization, and problem-solving;

- Despair, depression, rage, loss of trust;

- Possible unresolved guilt issues or remorse for not having 'closure';

- Lethargy, apathy, ambivalence, lack of motivation, emotionally numb, and unresponsive;

- Dazed, ongoing shock, surreal other-worldly feeling and ungrounded;

- Fight/Flight syndrome, compelling need to escape;

- Chronic illnesses and a weakened immune system;

- Feelings of social anxiety, social isolation, separation anxiety, alienation;

- Fear, panic, nerve and grief attacks;

- Feelings of aloneness, frustration for being misunderstood;

- Loss of shared memories;

- There is no denying that the intense energy field created by the emotion of grief can create a portal into the invisible realms. Extreme emotional states are known to be a trigger in the experience of mystical phenomena. The pursuit of what is lost removes us from present reality and takes us into a parallel dimension where the suffering is not occurring. That could feel like a relief … until we find out that we may be stuck there;

- Spontaneous crying, emotional breakdowns in response to triggers;

- Insomnia, lucid dreaming of the event;

- Physical and emotional fatigue;

- Neurosis (psychological problems);

- Shock so extreme it feels like an Out of Body experience;

- Disbelief, preoccupation, and rumination over thoughts of the event;

- Hallucinatory, mystical, otherworldly feelings and experiences;

- Feeling ungrounded, spacy, unable to concentrate, inability to concentrate;

- Feelings of meaninglessness, left without a defining point of reference, lacking purpose in life;

- Social withdrawal and avoidance behavior;

- Exaggerated response to inconsequential stimuli;

- Feeling numb, emotionless, traumatized, confused, disoriented.

Anticipatory Grief – When a loss is anticipated or predictable, such as a long-term or terminal illness, there is often a difference in the grief response. There is more time for closure, more time to prepare for that which cannot be prepared for. We find ourselves dealing with the suffering related to the anticipation of the loss and the suffering related to the loss itself. We must adapt to morphing roles and challenging changes in relationships in family, professional, and social circles. It is reasonable to expect feelings of loss in the event of a long-term illness, loss of freedom, security, or mobility.

Abbreviated Grief – Often, surrogacy is used to fill the void left by the loss of a loved one. With the ease of a stage play stand-in, someone or something immediately slips into the role of the absent lead actor and offers the illusion of a quick recovery. It is a common behavior in the avoidance of extreme suffering. An unusually short grief response can occur when emotional bonds are weak.

Masked Grief – Manifestations of masked grief include a host of physical symptoms and deteriorating health. What makes a 'masked response' unsettling, is the fact that the individual is not really conscious of their own behavior, or able to identify the root of it.

Distorted Grief – A distorted grief response is characterized by unusual, disturbing, and self-destructive personality changes. It is marked by destructive, violent, hostile, confrontational behavior, and may manifest in uncharacteristic, inappropriate preoccupations. When the energy of grief is found to be unbearable, it is often veiled as anger to maintain the perception of having the strength to survive the loss. The typical stages of grief can either implode or explode as surges of rage, causing further suffering.

Absent Grief – A person who responds to loss by the withdrawal of presence seeks to disacknowledge the reality of what has happened. Shock and denial may camouflage the suffering of grief. This is especially prevalent in cases of sudden loss.

Disenfranchised Grief – When the nature of the perceived loss is in any way culturally stigmatized or the subject of scrutiny, controversy, or judgment, the grief process is compromised and denied the opportunity to heal. When there is any form of ambiguity or vagueness surrounding the perceived loss, a deep emotional response seems somehow invalidated.

Chronic Grief – There is no way to determine how long is long enough to grieve after a perceived loss. However, the condition could be considered chronic if the period of grieving continues indefinitely or intensifies in such a way as to compromise the sufferer's life experience. If there are no signs of the tides of suffering receding, aggressive measures should be considered.

Inhibited Grief – When no apparent signs of grief have presented in a reasonable amount of time, this delayed grief response can manifest in the onset of an array of physical, psychological, mental, and emotional maladies, new habits, and eccentric transformation. Transformation is not to be confused with transcendence. The suppression of the grief response can result in unpredictable psychosomatic drama and the eruption of subconscious hyperactive emotions. It can be used as a safety mechanism to maintain control over the painful and volatile compressed energy.

Traumatic Grief – There is no way to predict or prepare for shocking, sudden losses due to accidents, crimes, suicide. We no longer feel safe or secure in this new world into which we've been violently thrust. Our trust in life is shattered. We irrationally fear for our safety. We feel threatened, no longer having confidence in our ability to protect ourselves. When the nature of the loss is perceived to be sudden, shocking, terrifying, violent, or horrifying, the trauma can be severe enough to render the grieving individual completely dysfunctional. These are critical warning signs of the necessity of URGENT treatment.

Exaggerated Grief – It is regarded as an 'exaggerated' grief response when sadness and pain result in isolation due to the inability to manage it. The suffering becomes so overwhelming that the person is completely debilitated and unable to function in life. The intense suffering worsens over time. Exaggerated grief response often manifests as nightmares, drug or alcohol abuse and diverse addictions, thoughts of self-harm or suicide, violent speech and behavior, extreme paranoia, and in extreme cases, the development of psychological and/or psychiatric conditions.

Complicated Grief – Many classifications of various types of grief (Chronic Grief, Delayed Grief, Distorted Grief) fall under the umbrella of "Complicated Grief." The psyche is shattered, the aura is ruptured, the energy field becomes magnetized to attract, and become trapped in the binding energies of anxiety and depression. This level of grief is aggravated by complex family issues and situations and clashing shared grief response.

Collective Grief – One symbol for Collective Grief is a flag flying at half-staff. Collective grief can be shared by groups that have no flags to fly. Any community, nation, race, religion, belief system, gender, or socio-economic group can experience Collective Grief. Globally, with the event of natural disasters, war, political upheaval, or any other tragic world event, Collective Grief may follow indefinitely. The collective trauma suffered by millions, in historical atrocities such as slave trading, holocausts, genocides, colonization, burnings, and horrific acts of terror, has been documented and studied. It is a scientific fact that the descendants of the people who suffered these atrocities are affected by the trauma and grief stored in their genetic memory for generations to come. Healing the extensive damage can be a challenge, yet it is encouraging that diverse traditions are emerging as energy workers to help manage the healing process. New cultures are forming around the mission of healing from the past and creating a more wholesome future, through the choices we make now.

Cumulative Grief – When losses have been piling up over a period of time, one more loss can be the proverbial straw that breaks the camel's back. A grief response of a person who is overwhelmed by a series of painful losses may present as extreme and dramatic in nature. A torrent of emotions is unleashed over residual energies of "attachment." This grief overload creates a domino effect that can literally disassemble a previously well-structured life.

Sometimes I wonder why I ever thought I had the authority to write a book like this. I write fiction. I am a poet. This was a journal that evolved into a textbook, hardcore research, and editing … not much wiggle room for poetic license. This was not the book I was writing. I was working on a different book about how to erase time … oh, and death. My poetry was mostly about death. I loved the study of Eastern mysticism and healing practices. I knew all about chakras, and I knew how to use them. What I didn't know was that every one of them was about to be crushed … at my most confident stage of "enlightenment," and I would have to find the strength to dig my way out from under that debris … Intact. Little did I know

… This level of emotional wreckage is only one of the many gateways to the "concept" of True Enlightenment.

We Are Bodies of Light

In my attempts to heal from grief and loss, my journey turned into a fascinating study of everything I could find to help me come to terms with the Law of Impermanence. I suppose my goal was to become as comfortable with non-physical existence as I am with the physical. I totally immersed myself in the study of the reality of the non-physical Self. I have been rewarded for embracing the study of Light and the Source of it, as it relates to Self-Realization. I have come to understand the experience of a less than subtle shift from worldly matter to the reality of the beings of Light that we are.

I speak of Light as an energy, a vibration, a frequency. We came from The Light. We are made of that Spiritual Light, and into The Ultimate Light, we are reabsorbed. I realize now that any perception of our separateness from that Light is pure illusion. We will all one day shed the burden of our physical forms, and yet continue to exist as a body of Light, dissolving into Pure Consciousness. We will all return to the Original Formless Essence, Creator, and Source of our emanation.

The Light body is sometimes called the spirit body. Some call it Ether. Some refer to it as the Soul. These are only verbal attempts to describe that which is Unknowable, that which renders mere words vague and empty. One thing most attempts to describe that which cannot be described have in common is that there is a form of Light generally associated with the viewing of our non-material form. This Light or Light body is an indwelling presence as consciousness, that is more relevant to our temporal life than the physical body. It is the energy field in which the physical body manifests. Even though there is Divinity about this Light that we are, we humble ourselves before Ultimate Light, knowing we did not create ourselves.

The needs of our Light body must be respected as much as the needs of our physical self. It must be nourished just as the clay body must be nourished, or its Light will be left diminished and starving. All that will sustain it is Light. To attempt to nourish it with anything other than Light, one way or the other, will lead to energetic damage and ultimate demise of the other bodies. That is why the realization of the existence of It becomes the recognition of the Eternal beauty of It, the immortality of It. We will affirm that we are It, in Essence, opening a portal of consciousness through which we may enter into the transcendence of the container without breaking it or escaping it through physical death.

We are the Light we seek, and we must have a clear understanding of its accompanying shadows. Rumi has referred to our transient, conditional manifestations as foam upon the ocean of Time and Timeless, appearing, disappearing, and reappearing as Light and shadows. If we accept and understand our Light and accept and understand our shadows, as we accept and understand both the sea and the foam, we are drawing closer to our personal *hereafter. Here, after* the demise of our ephemeral, perishable self, and our emergence as our transcendent, immortal "Self," no longer at war with ourselves or one another. We will then be free to see ourselves through the same filter of Love as the merciful, forgiving Consciousness of the Source of all creation. We can choose to see ourselves and one another that way now. We are free in our embrace of the beauty and purity of the Breath and Light that we are as the driver of these forms fashioned of clay, the vehicles of this magnificent journey of ours.

Our Light Body understands its relationship with us, mere clay creatures, transformed by Will into individuated, intentional beings. The shadows cast upon our spirits by the attributes of our clay forms are a natural part of our creation. We must embrace our shadows with the same Love as we embrace our Light, understanding that the Light is real and the shadow is temporal, therefore it is not real. If we wish to be known as more than a clay and water clod of mud, we must expand our consciousness to understand that the primordial contradiction of flesh and spirit can thrive in glorious union. It can just as easily become a disastrous, relentless, personal holy war that knows no winner. The greatest of all wars is the war that rages within our multi-dimensional being, between our higher and lower selves. Our Light is often held hostage by our shadows. We must use the understanding of our Higher Self as a tool, a weapon, and a shield, in winning the daily war inherent in the seeming contradictions of our very existence.

To approach the study of healing the Light Body, it should be understood that it affects the healing of all other bodies. The first step is to understand what it is. Since it is made of Light, the laws that define and govern Light would naturally apply. It has a subtle density, to the point of aspects of its existence being debatable. It is in perpetual motion and travels at phenomenal speeds. It has a fluctuating vibratory rate. It can touch as well as be touched, even though scientists often avoid that conversation. As we consider the natural properties of Light, we are considering the natural properties of a form of our Essential Self ... but still not the subtlest.

What is The Light Body?

From beyond the textbook concepts of our realization that we are bodies of Light emerges a rich body of experiential evidence of that reality. However, it is seldom that such accounts are shared with others for fear of being ridiculed, rejected, and considered insane. At the risk of sounding like an "I see dead people" movie, I share that I have had one such experience. It was not induced by any type of séance, drug, ritual, mystical knowledge, or longing.

Many years ago, someone quite dear to me passed away suddenly … violently. The news was shocking, crushing, and heartbreaking. It felt like the whole world turned to gray clouds and dark shadows. A beautiful life snuffed out … gone … dead … until about seventy-two hours later. I was given a message by him, the essence of which was that Love is stronger than that illusion we have bought into called death. I had never seen a Light body before, nor would I have ever been interested in seeing one, at that, or any other stage of my fixed, linear consciousness. I had consciously chosen never to contemplate such things. I would have never even considered being drawn into a conversation about ghost stories. I would have thought it grounds for calling security if someone had attempted it. But there he was, in front of me and the windshield, as real as ever … just made of some strange manifestation of Light I had never witnessed before.

That beautiful but solemn afternoon, I was traveling up Pacific Coast Highway with family from an ashram where we had offered prayers for him. My mother was sitting behind me in the back seat on the passenger side of the car. She later told me that she "felt something in the car" and had intuitively reached forward and quietly locked my door. She said she had not actually heard or seen anything. She said she just "felt some strange and overwhelming presence or energy." It must have been at that point that the consciousness of my Self was no longer in the car. At one point, I experienced traveling outside of my body. Something of some other-worldly energy was there present with me. He told me that he just wanted to let me know he was "alright," and after repeating that a couple of times, he turned his attention to something or someone behind him as if he was being called. With one last assurance that he was alright, an expression of pure bliss swept across his face. At that point, he was drawn back into the direction of whatever he had seen behind him, just as suddenly and mysteriously as he had appeared. I eventually found out that I was not the only one who had seen him and been delivered the same message.

I did not take it well. I cried out to pull the car over, trying to exit it before it came to a complete stop. Once the car stopped, I struggled to release the lock on the door, jumped out, and fell apart. I just sat there on a big stone, shaking, crying, and rocking back and forth, in shock, trying to console myself. I was afraid to tell anyone what I had seen, heard … experienced. I couldn't face the fact that it had actually happened … and to me! At that time, the thought of something like that happening to anyone was a plane that would have to keep on flying because there was nowhere for it to land in my consciousness. I had absolutely no belief system to support that something like that was even possible. I did not believe in it. I didn't want to hear it. My goal was a "normal" life. Yet, I could not deny what had just happened, even though I didn't understand it. I was not grateful for that experience when it happened, but I am now. Had it not been for that, I may have never paused my one-dimensional life for a moment to pursue the studies that caused me to ultimately embrace truth, with trust and faith. I never intended to share this story in this book, but I can't write about what some call the "theory" of the existence of a Light body if I am unwilling to share that I have seen one myself.

It was that experience with a Light body that caused my path to exit the "doing lunch" at the mall of denial mentality. After that, I had no choice but to engage in a study that would become a calling in my life. I felt I had to learn everything in the Universe to bring some level of normalcy to that experience. I had never witnessed a Light body before that one. I have not witnessed one since, in that form of density. I had never sought to and do not seek it now, even though I know it can happen on many levels of manifestation.

Since then, I have witnessed many appearances of Light bodies as orbs that resembled shimmering bubbles or spheres made of Light, some with an apparent consciousness about them. One day, my son was standing in the kitchen, not doing his chores. I asked him why he was in there playing with bubbles instead of taking his turn to do the dishes. There were five glistening orbs of light about the size of a small fist floating, dancing around his head. Then I saw a spray of light that looked like fireworks, beads of light descending like falling stars, rain, snowflakes, or like decorative Christmas lights I've seen. Very confused, he looked at me and told me he couldn't *imagine* what I was talking about. Fifteen minutes later, I received a call that my father had passed away fifteen minutes prior. I don't feel that the reality of this, or any other manifestation I have witnessed, is threatened just because someone may choose to have an opinion that what happened had no spiritual significance. It is not relevant to me that someone may or may not think I imagined it or that it was a coincidence. What I witnessed is just the tip of an iceberg of expressions of our complex existence. There is nothing mysterious or unnatural about it.

Ethereal manifestations of our many forms can appear as shadows or flashes of light. They visit in our dreams, ride our thoughts and meditations. However, we do not have to waste vital Life Force spinning around every single phenomenon we witness or make a religion out of it. These things are to be expected in a world born of the same energetic drama and are never necessarily meant to be understood in a linear context. If we waste our energy bowing down in worship before spiritual phenomena as a fixation, we will lose focus on our primary objective, Self-Realization. In the study of Self, we will find that we *are* a phenomenon. A meditation of Self-Inquiry leads with the most compelling question of all, Who am I, really? Behind the last mask of density, we will find all phenomena becomes commonplace and normal by the standard of the reality of the Higher Self.

There are many ways to experience a Light body. It is not always associated with the occurrence of a physical death. In deep states of meditation or among those who are familiar with astral travel, remote viewing, bi-location, or myriad other studies and practices, the Light body can be observed without the death of the physical body.

I was fortunately blessed with many remarkable spiritual teachers in Hawaii. In one of my meditation classes, I was guided into a profoundly deep meditative state. My son, who was about three years old at the time, was sick the day of the class. My mom encouraged me to go on to my class, saying that he would be fine with her. During the guided meditation, I found myself becoming distracted by worry and concern for my son. I was able to pull myself back into the meditation and resist the distraction. That afternoon when I returned home, my mother was worried, asking if I was okay and if anything "strange or unusual" had happened. She was disturbed because my son had been nearly hysterical, screaming from room to room through the house, "Mommy is dead. My mommy is dead." He said that he had just seen me but that I was a ghost, so I must be dead. When I returned, he was quite relieved to see me intact.

My teacher told me situations like that were common in his classes because people tended to go "so far out of body" during his guided meditations. He told me there are many forms and manifestations of this type when astral travel occurs spontaneously. It is often an unconscious projection or expression of the meditator.

It was not the first time that it was reported that a Light body double had been seen and recognized in another location by someone known to the meditators. The difference between that type of Light body encounter and one of someone known to be deceased is that there is what is called a "silver cord" that connects the astral body to the living physical body, but after death, this cord is eventually broken. There are many forums available where people can feel safe to share such spiritual experiences and receive information and help with understanding them. Many people, including our family or friends, are just not available for such a conversation, and I understand why.

The consideration of the Light body in this text is to inspire a cause to relinquish our attachment to our conditioned identification with the physical body as being our only or even primary label of self-concept. This does not qualify as a ghost story. If you see an apparition, one would classify as a "ghost," that is still not the Essence of the being that has been seen. Our study begins in the realm of subtlety, which cannot be seen using common vision.

So profound is the fear of death that even a ghost story brings more comfort than the truth of who we really are as Timeless, formless beings. The fear of death is connected to survival mentality, the fear of not existing anymore. Reaching for ghosts is still a way of reaching out to exist as something that can be seen in some "form." Beyond the dimension of that "ghost body" or visible Light body, there is pure consciousness, pure awareness, seeing but not seen. That is the most sacred state of being. The Light body is an expression of the essential self, but given its density, it is still not the Essential Self. If you can see it, it is not in its least dense state as pure awareness.

The I AM is the invisible Essential Self that precedes and survives the physical body. It operates in cooperation with, as well as apart from, the physical body. The Light body can manifest clearly enough to be seen in some form for a time and reason. As with all manifestations of phenomenal forms, it will pass away into the energy from whence it arises. It has no form. It does not suffer. It does not fear death. It was never born. It cannot die. The energy into which it passes away is the energy from whence it emerged. We are That.

I am not a scientist. I was always told to write what I know. I know I have witnessed a discarnate Light body after the death of the physical body. I know I have been witnessed as a discarnate Light body due to a spontaneous Out of Body experience during deep meditation. I have experienced contact and communication with those in the form of a Light or Essential body. I would like to venture beyond any attachment to these phenomena because density is really just a matter of our own perception anyway. Things of this world that we believe to be solid are not really solid. Everything is energy, even apparently inanimate objects, even ourselves. When we grow to accept ourselves as who we really are (energetic manifestations in many states of appearance), we will be able to embrace the True Self, subtle, and void of form, as a natural part of our reality.

In the rising of the Light body from its vehicle and cage, the question becomes: Where does it call home? The Light body can coexist in the invisible realm among dense bodies of matter without being noticed. Once having emanated the shell of dense matter, the Light body often feels as though it is trapped in a prison when it is not energetically nourished. We concern ourselves with the nourishment of the physical body, often with no thought of the nourishment of the Light body. We literally starve it to death by denying it the Light that sustains it. In the process of this torturous act of negligence, resulting in suffering, disease, and ultimately death, the physical body is also broken down in painful, dangerous, and unpredictable ways. So, the question remains: How do we sustain it, and where does it call home?

The Light body and the other bodies of the human body system are sustained by proper care for their energetic counterparts. The aura is one such counterpart and can be cleansed in many ways. The diagram that follows this section is an overview of the human body system. The cleanliness of the physical body, internally and externally, is essential to the electromagnetic energy field or aura that surrounds the physical body, and the seven primary energetic vortices called chakras. It speaks to our spiritual, mental, physical, and emotional well-being and healing as we groom ourselves to become the sacred space we are capable of being. Our objective is to increase our vibration through study and spiritual practice and avoid anything that will pull our vibration down, sometimes lower than that of the animal kingdom.

The things we study, the things we eat, the company we keep, and the energy of our thoughts and actions, are all the same things that cause our energy to vibrate at a higher frequency, regenerating and nourishing the Light body. We can choose to build a new, regenerated body of Light. Our thoughts and emotions can be purified and transformed, seeking and finding a higher vibrational level. As we turn within, we ask one question: Who am I? … we seek and find the indwelling being of Light that we are and treat it as sacred space. Fear falls away. Suffering falls away. Even death falls away.

I take this privileged opportunity to share the pointings that redirected my energy and caused me to see with clarity, the first step toward healing. Mystical Meditation can reveal our inner Light and nourish us with the remembrance of who we really are. With the heart of a child, the "I in I," the I AM, all that we are, can go within and find there, the greatest Love of all … in the mirror of the Timeless … in the mirror … Faceless.

The Body System

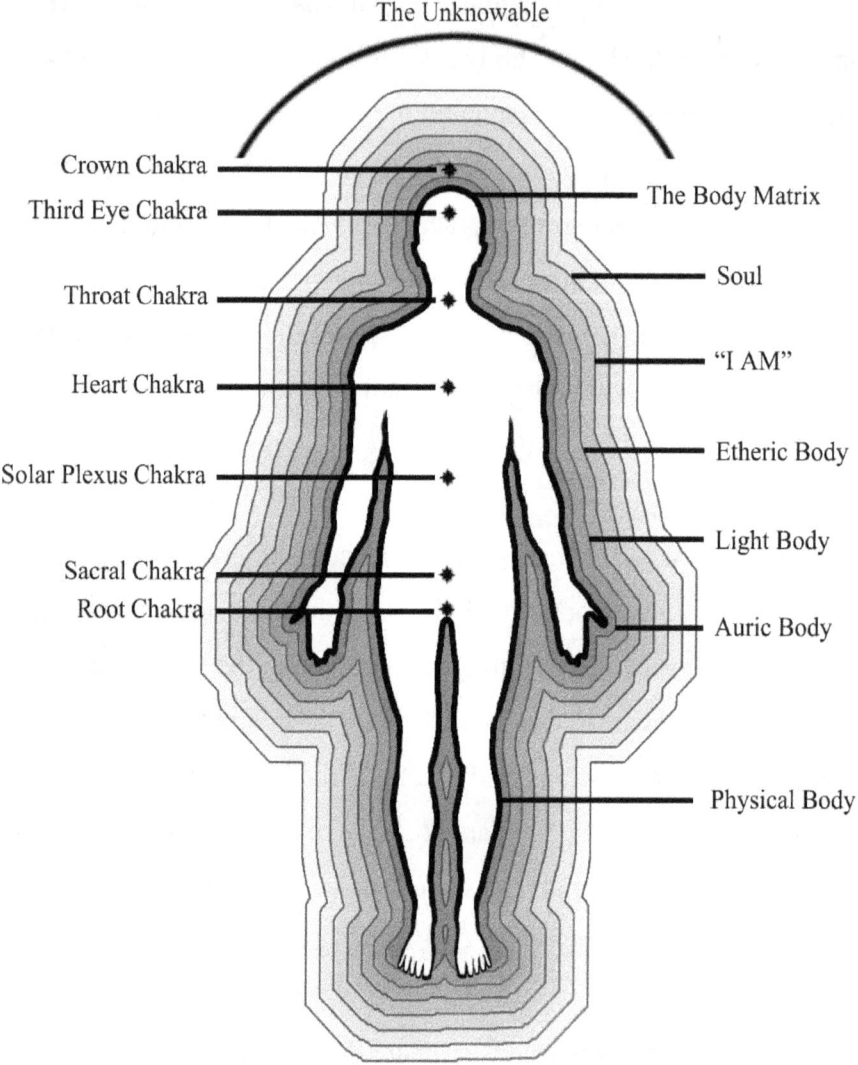

The multifaceted body matrix is a system that knows no boundaries or borders. They are interconnected and can make a dominant manifestation for their own time and purpose, even while still connected to the physical body.

This diagram is a representation/approximation and in no way indicates actual or exact locations of the "bodies" of the Body System.

The Body System

The ability to utilize all aspects of our True Being, particularly our energetic frequencies, is important as we continually evolve into a perfect vessel for the Spirit of the Natural Mystic … That Sacred Indwelling Presence … a Spark from The Original Flame. Our Mystical Meditation discipline begins with our decision to become a desirable container through which The Creator chooses Its Expression. This process involves every aspect of our being; spiritual, mental, emotional, and physical. We are not one body. We are many bodies, variously layered in many forms, rising, fusing into Oneness, seeking balance and union. We must give each aspect of our many selves their own domain of significance in our lives. Our many bodies must be cleansed and healed with Light and Love.

The Light/Subtle Body

The soundest advice I can offer in approaching mystical studies is, Know The God. Be conscious that we have come into this incarnation with the responsibility and challenge of getting out with our Eternal souls intact. The soul is all we have and all we are. Our connection to the Divine One is the Light Energy of our immortal soul. We must see ourselves in the big picture that extends beyond our physical form.

I cannot imagine a more chaotic, empty, and lonely life, than the feeling of separation from The Creator. In my references to "The God," I speak of the Love from which we all emerged. I say "The" God to distinguish The Creator God from lesser gods, for there are many. Our sacred connection with The God transcends Earth Plane precepts and concepts. It is inclusive rather than serving to divide and exclude. Before blindly embracing any spiritual practice served up by mortal beings, we must consider the source, consider the cause and effect, and consider the consequences. The spiritual must bend to The Greatest of Spirits, That Which

Created it all. We need no intercessor or interpreter. We are One with That. Allow the Frequency. We are That. The subtle body is The God Essence that we are. There is something Divine about us.

The Mental Self

The mental process plays a major role in making meditation work as we fortify the Light body to become a powerful warrior, fearless on the battlefields of the mind's relentless struggle to make things permanent that are not. It is within the higher frequencies that our strongest meditations and prayers for healing occur. The first thing we must understand is who we really are. We are not our minds. We are not our bodies. Who we really are is what observes the mind and all of its myriad changes. It is within the hidden chambers of our minds that we may access and process the knowledge of who we really are.

We must exert an effort to reprogram the conscious and subconscious negative messages we give ourselves. These are conditioned, programmed belief systems that we may not even be aware of, sabotaging our best efforts to survive the un-survivable. If it is love that we want to manifest in our lives, and deep within us there is an abyss of toxic, negative beliefs about love, our fear will be more powerful than our longing. We cannot expect positive results from our strongest conscious efforts to manifest love in our lives if we don't believe in love. If our relationship with money is guilt and fear-based, we cannot expect our efforts to override our subconscious negative belief system.

Affirmation, prayer, meditation, and chanting help us to channel our wandering thoughts into a single stream of energetic intention. These positive thought-forms summon our intentions into manifestation. A pure and focused thought-form can assist effectively in magnetizing our own electromagnetic force field to attract our conscious and subconscious desires, in accordance with Divine Will. It is, therefore, a spiritual mandate that we are very sensitive in detecting and banishing negative thought-forms that may be projected from within, or from an external source. It is equally important to reinforce positive thought-forms that work in favor of manifesting our highest good.

The mind can be a powerful ally or a mean spirited, fickle bully. Our own minds can be the most dangerous psychic attacker we will ever encounter. That is why there must be time set aside to silence it so that it can rest and heal, or it can cause damage to the entire body system. Sometimes the mind longs to be liberated from its vain, petty preoccupations so that it can return to its natural, peaceful state of surrender to the I AM, the Essential Self.

The Emotional Self

Studying Mystical Meditation impacts our emotional stability in a positive way by offering a sense of sovereign security in spiritual practice. We learn to take full responsibility for all aspects of our life. Some people really are better off being a part of a consistent support group or circle that offers a forum to vent, heal, and be understood by people who are, themselves, coping with loss.

Some chose to be loners while coping with grief and loss, rather than associate with people who would unintentionally introduce triggers that would slow the healing process. Though it is a fact of life that it fluctuates, there is an emotional balance that must be kept. When depleted, energetic balance can be restored by constantly cleansing our own emotions of the spiritual burden and heaviness of guilt, jealousy, envy, anger, and hatred. Forgiveness, whether it is deserved or not, is important to maintain positive energy. The emotional must yield to the spiritual because unstable emotions can cause "grief attacks." A grief attack is much like a panic attack but is directly related to an emotional response to specific triggers.

The Physical Self

The part that the physical self plays in walking the path of the Natural Mystic is often ignored and considered unrelated. Our physical condition can either make us a fit or unfit vessel for the flow of creative, mystical forces. To facilitate the safe and effective performance of prayer and Mystical Meditation, we must give proper attention to certain aspects of our physical health.

Pharmaceuticals and over the counter medications must be used with caution. The side effects of certain drugs can cause energetic damage and create auric ruptures, opening portals into our consciousness that are not easy to close. A perfect storm of discordant elemental energies can leave us vulnerable to all manner of physical, mental, spiritual, and emotional trauma.

Tai Chi, certain systems of Yoga, Chi Gong, or sound disciplines of personally compatible forms of meditation and exercise are helpful in establishing the groundwork of mystical practice. Many mystical and spiritual disciplines promote the maintenance and well-being of the body's seven major energy centers, the Chakra System. This text offers exercises that are helpful in that effort. A holistic approach … mind, body, and spirit, can facilitate a healing that can cause a radical and positive shift in energy.

We must not underestimate the transformational potential of the energetic exercises recommended in this and many other spiritual texts. Our goal is to strengthen our energy centers, maintain a healthy aura of protective Light, and energetically close portals through which we may be invaded or occupied. Our concern about the care and maintenance of the health and well-being of our many "selves" is marked by our well-rewarded sacrifices as guardians of the Temple of our Creator.

The use of consciousness-altering chemical substances, legal or illegal, is generally not recommended in most common spiritual practices. It can leave us wide open to energies and forces we may not have the experience or strength to be able to manage. Even on spiritual paths that do use substances that will alter consciousness, it is generally practiced in a prescribed, supervised, and sacred manner. It is always advisable to consult both spiritual and medical experts to determine what best serves our individual physical and spiritual needs.

There is an army, visible and invisible, of Divinely commissioned guardians to guide and protect us on our journey through this life, with all of its Light and shadows. There are accessible states of consciousness that exceed the capability of any drug or consciousness-altering substance known on this Plane of existence. Access to these realms can be spontaneous or induced. I have personally experienced both on more than a few occasions. These experiences were so profound that I have no words to describe what happened. There are no set rules, only amazing rewards for our longing, on our sacred quest for the Unattainable.

The Soul, The Ether, The True Self

The soul is the least dense of our being. It, like its Source, can only be expressed as Silence. This silence is not the silence of the absence of sound. It is a silent awareness that is a spark of the Flame of the Ultimate Essential Being, That which created all.

The soul has no form or substance in the way that beings of the spirit world may have. Even though that is true, it is not beyond manifesting a form to be perceived for whatever time and reason. It cannot be identified by the same standard as an incarnate being with an endless list of archetypal and personal qualities. It cannot be bought or sold. If it finds itself feeling fractured or scattered by some traumatic event, it can be mystically gathered up and retrieved, becoming stronger in the broken places.

It is the drop of water that embraces the ocean and ultimately becomes it. That drop can feel either diminished or enhanced. It can feel as though it disappears in a vast sea of its own element. It can claim a higher understanding, as the sea in all of its vastness. That is the choice we have. Do we cling to a multitude of self-defining identities in the face of the opportunity to become One with the Source of all existence? Or do we engage an ego fueled argument as a wave rising on the ocean, declaring sovereignty?

The soul is not something that I feel inclined to speculate on, as though I am able to define it. All is speculation because none of us can say that we really know. It is of the realm of The Unknowable. It does not belong to us. We were manifested by way of it, individuating as us, emerged from the Source of all.

How Grief Affects the Aura

The Aura is a luminous, astral substance, which creates an energetic force field emanating from, and surrounding the human body, much like the glow around the flame of a candle. This force field can reveal the spiritual, mental, emotional, and physical state of an individual, to those who are sensitive enough to see and read the human aura. Whether or not we are consciously aware of it, we sense and are affected by our own auric energy, as well as that of others. It is the environment of these emanations that we tap into to extract energy needed to replenish and nurture the entire body system. It is also the environment that we tap into to cleanse its energy when it has been affected by disruptive forces outside or within.

The Law of Impermanence reminds us that everything changes. Nothing stays the same. All things come and go. Only the imperishable is real. When the naturally occurring changes of life feel overwhelming, we can be sent into unbearable states of grief, anxiety, depression, and physical illness. The energy of these emotions can damage or pollute the aura and cause a shift of consciousness, mood swings, and a general reversal of good fortune.

The aura can contain impressions of symbols and pictures that display very specific evidence vital to determining the extent of the damage that requires healing. These images often manifest as variations of the seven-color spectrum of a rainbow in the aura's celestial Light show. The pain of our emotional state, our thoughts, our feelings, can take on a life of their own. They can occur as parasitic, ethereal garbage, trapped as litter, in a fading and cloudy aura. The energy drain can expand to affect everything and everyone in close proximity to the person who is emitting the toxic energy. We literally turn into a magnet for a negative experience of life. The pain of our suffering is as sacred as our healing and should be treated as such. Our tears are as sacred as our laughter. We cannot avoid suffering in life. Avoiding the natural suffering of life is no more an option than challenging The Law of Impermanence. It is the price we pay for existence. It is the price we pay for love. When we heal the aura and its energetic counterparts, we are taking responsibility for our own emotional healing and growth.

The energetic field of the aura creates a "charge," or current, that can affect the practice of meditation and prayer, under the best of circumstances. This energy can be transferred between people as well as objects. In certain forms of meditation, crystals and other semi-precious stones, charged with positive energy, are used as a catalyst to boost the force and depth of the meditation. These stones are charged with astral material associated with the essence of the individual who charged it. Objects carry a vibration, and the meditator taps into the frequency, much like scanning the band of frequencies on a radio, to find a clear signal and a channel with music agreeable to our personal preference. Energy is gathered by relaxing into the clearest possible channel, and listening to the subtle voices we will learn to distinguish from those of our own thoughts.

Energy is channeled in practices such as the *charging* of Holy Water, anointing oil, candles, and other objects. Energy is transferred and shared on contact, in a common energy field. It can be a factor in the discomfort felt in the presence of some people, and the pleasant feelings experienced in the company of others. It is why certain people with a "green thumb" are better at growing strong, healthy plants than others. The energies of some people are more conducive to nurturing the life force of plants than others.

Certain colors tend to be associated with emotional states of mind. These colors demonstrate a correspondence to the colors of the chakra energy centers and their representative energies. However, there are no hard, fast rules about the interpretations of the colors of the aura. People have their own unique emotional reaction to, and interpretation of, these colors, which may differ from textbook correspondences. Which is right? Your intuition will give you the best information as to the meaning of the colors and impressions of the aura.

The aura can be charged or magnetized by the energy of our emotions to either attract or repel many of the experiences of our lives. Through proper physical and spiritual care, the aura can be magnetized to protect us from spiritual and physical damage. Before entering a meditation, and as a part of a generally healthy spiritual practice, visualize your aura surrounding you as pure white Light, a brilliant illumination that continually grows more intense with the rhythm of the breath and heartbeat. Envision yourself comforted by the Pure, Radiant White Light of Divine Protection, Healing, and Love, as a shield against the damage of emotional trauma. Visualize yourself encapsulated in an egg-shaped body of Light, which extends several feet from the physical body. Nothing penetrates this powerful barrier, except that which is Divinely Ordained with Permission to do so. These visualizations are empowered by prayer and remembrance of The God as our Protector.

It is important to the effectiveness of spiritual work to restore balance to an aura devastated by grief, that we control our environment as much as possible. We must not pursue exposure to repeat offenders to our efforts to regain our emotional balance, once we have identified certain situations as toxic triggers. If you want a scab to heal, stop touching it. The aura is magnetic in nature and very sensitive. It must be well maintained, and a part of that maintenance is to avoid substances that are generally known to be toxic to both the physical and Light body. It is important to avoid the damage of bad habits we may develop as we seek emotional comfort. Substance abuse has many manifestations, such as alcoholism, drug addiction, eating disorders, even extending to sexual dysfunction, our choices in music, entertainment, and thrill-seeking behaviors. There are certain vibrations, even lighting, such as fluorescent and strobe lights, that are very damaging to the aura, and can affect our emotional and physical health. This energy can literally take on a life of its own as "thought-forms" that can attach themselves as astral material to the aura, creating negativity that can ultimately lead to attracting misfortune and poor health, on every level of our being. Many emotions, even love, though positive in nature, can be damaging when the object of this undesired attention does not welcome the invasive energy.

It is important to develop skill in the verbal expression of emotions and seek to communicate with an effort to resolve emotional conflict in a timely manner. We must seek spiritual guidance with regards to the virtue and mandate of forgiveness, as we exercise humility and compassion in the expression of our volatile spiritual and emotional energies.

Suppression of grief does not guarantee that it is under control. Denial of grief can cause an escalation of this normally occurring emotional energy. A critical mass scenario is created, building to an explosion or implosion, equal in intensity to the degree of suppression. These energies can be seen in the colors and images floating around the aura of an individual. This can occur when one is obsessing or brooding over any particular thought, either consciously or unconsciously. The energy spins and gains momentum. Intention directs this concentrated emotional energy. Anger and resentment can show up in the aura as a dirty red hue. Grief shows up as cloudy gray or shades of brown. Fluctuations in our spiritual, mental, emotional, and physical condition can cause discoloration of the aura surrounding us. These colorful illuminations can be seen or sensed by those who possess that spiritual gift. We all can be trained to see auras, or it can happen spontaneously.

It is a spiritual imperative to devote our energy to the study and implementation of methods of insulating ourselves from invasive triggers. It is a common occurrence that strong emotions scale the fences of the energetic boundaries we set in place to maintain normalcy in our lives. They can attach themselves as attacking thought-forms that can activate a spontaneous grief attack. Those who can see a grief-tainted aura can identify cloudy, shadowy, holographic images ... dark light, mottled by the litter of floating Astral Plane garbage. The energy of fear and guilt rank high on the list of what makes a person an attractive subject and increases the effectiveness of the negative, attacking energies.

The experience of extreme, traumatic grief can result in a damaged and unclean aura, a precursor to physical illness, as negative energy penetrates both the aura and the physical body. The human energy field, or matrix, is the seed from which the physical form has grown. The formless Self existed *prior to* the physical form. That fact explains the phenomenon of phantom limbs of amputees who continue to feel sensation in a limb that is no longer a part of their physical body. Those who possess the ability to see and read the energy field can see these limbs. Traditional Chinese Medicine (TCM) approaches healing at the origin of disease, rather than merely relieving the symptoms of it. Practitioners have been known to treat organs that have been surgically removed because they recognize that the organ is still there on an energetic level, and can still be the source of illness.

The symptoms of maladies that result from these conditions can range from an inability to concentrate, all the way to going barking, stark raving mad. Thought-forms can attach themselves, but they are perceivable intuitively. If you are aware of them, they can be banished. If you are not aware of them, they can influence your decisions, concentration, and behavior. These negative thought-forms, entities, and energies, literally feed upon the energies of fear, guilt, and anger, using it in much the same manner our physical bodies use food for nourishment. A sound clearing or cleansing ritual is an effective way to release these energies, before they turn us into a magnet, attracting the experience of being ambushed by debilitating grief scenarios that increase our suffering. They can manifest as interference in our relationships with other people. They can manifest as interference in our relationship with our Self. They can throw us under the bus of sorrow with the feeling that the pain will never end.

Grief seeks to drain us of vital Life Force energy and can deposit spiritual parasites into our aura. It becomes important to replenish our energy resources after having been depleted of energy. We must seek restoration from positive sources rather than any random source available. Reaching out indiscriminately, trying to fill that type of energetic emptiness can lead to bad habits, substance abuse, and cause further damage by leaking vital energy through ruptures in the aura. Incorporating methods of healing into a daily spiritual practice provides protection from those who are either consciously, or unconsciously, corrupting our positive energy.

Care must be taken in cleansing the residual auric debris caused by encounters with grief triggers and the subsequent pain experienced in their wake. After they leave us drained, a salt bath, or smudging with sage, along with life-affirming prayer, helps restore balance. Some people replenish low positive energy levels by hugging trees, gardening, swimming, or being immersed in the ocean if that option is available. Taking a nature hike, exercising, and horseback riding, even listening to certain types of music can have a cleansing and balancing effect. Ancient practices of Tai Chi, Qi Gong, and breath control meditations are helpful in rebuilding our energy levels.

Another method of revitalizing positive energy and recharging the Chi or Life Force of the person, the home, and work environment, is the study and practice of the ancient mystical science, Feng Shui, the art of placement. It extends from the ideal placement of furniture in the home or office to intricacies of the architecture of the building. The Chi energy of the home or office is enhanced by elemental, symbolic, and mystical cures to any energetic obstructions and interferences. The goal is to provide a healthier flow of Chi energy in the home and work areas while keeping our positive vibrations and overall well-being at optimum levels. This can be assisted through the use of aromatherapy, flowing water, lighting, colors, crystals, mirrors, flowers, and plants, among other remedies.

Never lose touch with the most basic truth, *the power of prayer exceeds all else*. When we feel depressed as frictional emotions try to penetrate our energy field, one way to immediately protect ourselves from them is to cup our hands close to our mouth, catching the breath of intense prayer. Concentrate on the approximate area of the Heart Chakra. Perform an ablution (cleansing) with the breath of the prayer affirming the nonexistence of anything but The One God. All else must concede. Nothing exists but The God.

Healthy Aura

Aura Affected by Grief

Polluted Aura

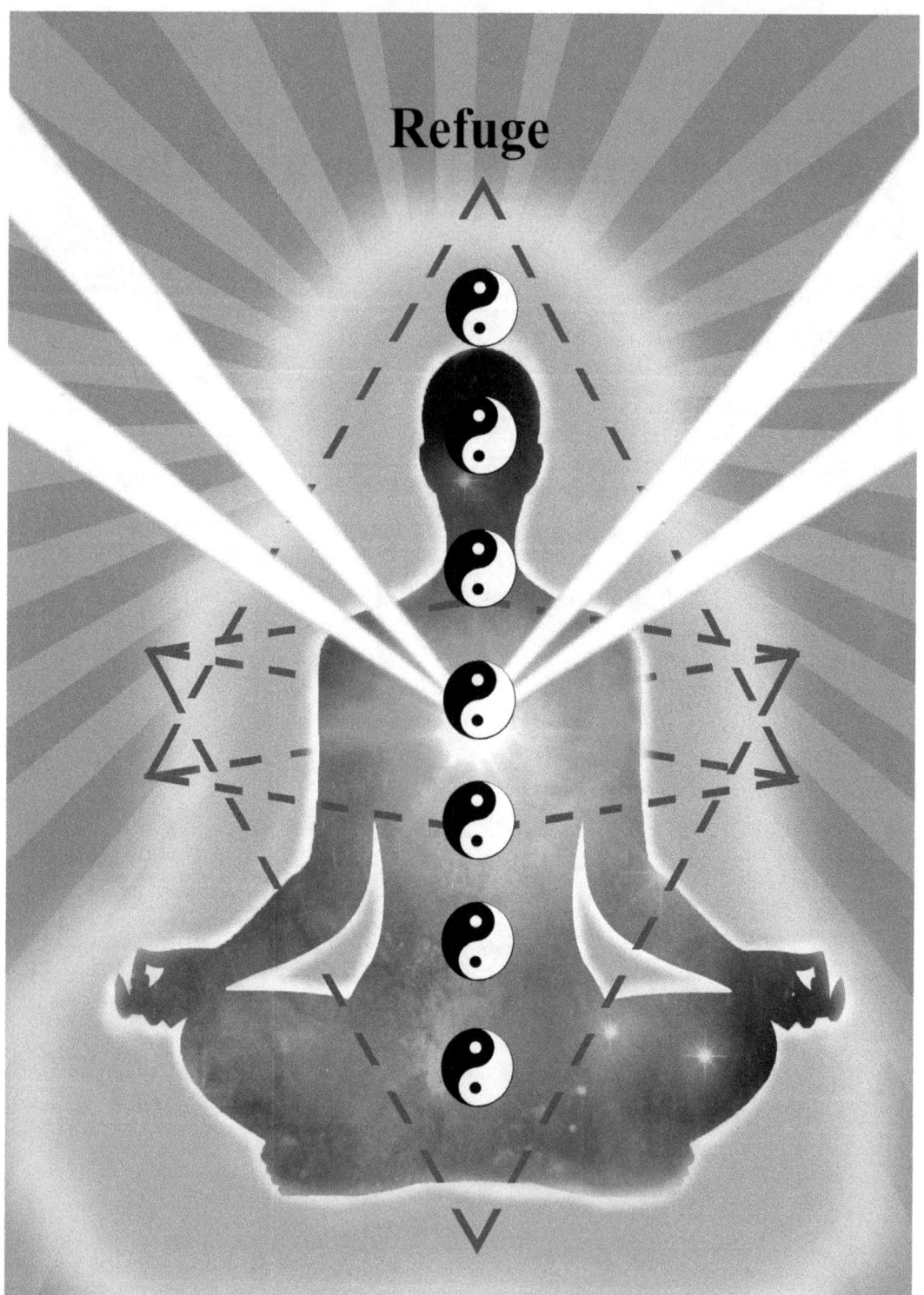

What is Death?

NAMELESS

Everything
happens for reasons
we are blinded to
in present tense
exalted by in tenses past
words inscribed
on walls of that which was written
knowing our only significance
is given by The Hand
that wrote it

All we can do
is allow
our body
of emotions
to be the pen
our souls use
to write our story
across time
in smoke
on dervish magic mirrors
correctly spelling
our names
and the words
of that story
shall retain the magic
of the very first
Om

We leave footprints
in sand or cement
knowing we are the wind
the heavens sent
to blow them away

Ours is the breath
that extinguishes flames
of candles we burn
as we wait our turn
to know we are one
with the One

We are casters of shadows
we leave behind without a trace
We are that
which erases all
from cosmic canvas
replaces all
with brand new dreams
etched in Ether
born of Light
into clay

We are bodies
of water
We are that
which contains them
We are the blaze of fire
that reminds us
we are ash
We are the air
which sustains us
the Earth
that last tastes
the flavor
of our Essence
and swallows
us whole
beneath feet
six deep
but repeats
our name
as we walk
with time
until time has
no end
and the mind
of time
remembers
that we were here
and why

Death: The Final Illusion

The definition of death is the "end" of the Life Force of the physical form. How can we call it "death" when we rise into a condition that is *still* "life," just life in a different form, the original formless state of who and what we really are? We engage a conscious choice of not seeking to chase death for closure, nor chase life with attachment, with no craving, or aversion to either. We, in our formless state, become the observer and witnesses of what is. That includes the demise of the physical body.

We possess the potential for having the wisdom to know that we need not attempt to erase our fear and loathing of death as our temporal reality. What we do instead is seek to heal it. We can choose the liberation of exercising our Free Will to face our own mortality and immortality fearlessly. We pray that we may be blessed to resist wasting our Life Force for even one moment, living in dread of the inevitable. We are promised that we will all taste this mysterious elixir we call "death." By the Grace of The God, we will yield, we will surrender, and we will succumb, with the same appetite for satisfaction that we tasted life.

Our ultimate goal is to expand our perception of self to include all aspects of our being, seen, and unseen. Among our many bodies, our Light body stands out as the essence of the spirit of the I AM that we are. The Light body arises in the field of the Ultimate Consciousness as Light issuing its manifestations through the prism of Divine grace. As these colorful appearances of forms, we dance on this stage, in this elaborate theater, then drop the costumes and characters and go home.

The healing of the Light body of consciousness is a microcosm of the healing of all creation. If the healing we seek is for purely vain, self-serving reasons, it is an empty pursuit. A worthy objective is to rise above our own personal ego and conquer the sin of its vanity. When I speak of "ego," I am not talking about the personality flaw of vanity and the arrogance of "ego" that accompanies that brand of narcissism and conceit. It is the I, me, my, mine mentality of a small, limited self-concept, composed of a million labels adrift in a sea of false identities. If we wear a wardrobe of masks long enough, we eventually forget who we are beneath them and become a ghost waiting to happen. The goal of the ego self is to distract us from the reality of who we really are as an eternal being and replace it with a fearful, desperate, insecure creature that begins at birth and ends with death.

The flip side of the coin of Self-Realization is the experience of "Ego Death." We view ourselves as pure consciousness. As we evolve, we see our Higher Self in its radiant glory, as the essence of who we truly are, with or without the physical container we identify as self. The ego self becomes "slain in the spirit" as we journey to the awareness of the Higher Self. We are then empowered to see from a different place of seeing by changing and refining our perceptions of self, others, and of existence itself.

The Light body is not the least dense of our many bodies and is not necessarily subject to the laws that govern matter. From the point of Origin, the Light body emanation changes into the denser bodies that all express our unique energy. The health of the subtle Light Body manifests in and through all of our other bodies, extending to and beyond the physical body. The sustenance of the energetic Light body results in either vibrant well-being or the appearance of disease and decay.

To know our Essential Self as the Light body that we are, we access and experience a *becoming* of that Light, fueled by the choices we make. It is a challenge for us to not confuse ourselves with the clay shell that contains and imprisons us. At the point of our departure from the "container," we, "the contained," continue to exist. How we view this transition depends on many things like culture, conditioning, religion, and background. Our level of acceptance of the inevitable depends upon our perspective. We have the power to change our perspective if it does not serve our Higher Self.

Meditation and Ego Death

Meditation can be a bridge between false perceptions of reality and Ultimate reality. THE TIMELESS NOW features the *I Transcend My Ego Self* meditation, a guided meditation that begins an exploratory voyage through the wisdom of the ancients and beyond the door of the fear of death. The journey begins with how we perceive ourselves on the other side of the Self-Inquiry that begins with the question, "Who am I?"

As I stepped into becoming the answer to that question, I AM … the revelation had begun. Self-Inquiry is the fixing of one's focus on the inner reality of Self, or "I," as pure awareness witnessing the body vehicle. It is the dismantling of conditioned structures that seek to define the self in one-dimensional and purely physical terms. To hold our attention on the witness as "I" offers the freeing opportunity to experience the true, formless, Timeless, Eternal Self.

Through Self-Inquiry and a study of the Universal Law of Impermanence, I sought the fluid state of Self-Realization, wherein we embrace the sacred transition from what we call "life" into an unknown territory of Life beyond life. Meditations of this and many other types can free the non-physical Self from the physical self, enough to produce the experience of an altered state of consciousness. An experience of being pure awareness or nirvana can free one from the perpetually spinning Karmic wheel of life, death, and rebirth, if only during the Timeless moments of the meditation. It may be a state we find difficult to remain in, but at least it introduces us to an energy we can evoke and revisit at will. The Sanskrit word nirvana refers to the extinction of all concepts and identity and the subsequent state of bliss. It is known by many different names from many different traditions; Satori, Kensho, Moksha, Paradise, Fanaa, Sacchidananda, and Samadhi are only a few.

A taste of this ethereal state of consciousness can even occur spontaneously. I have experienced it. As terrifying as it was to me, when I realized I had looked deeply into the eyes of Impermanence, I was released into a state of Ego Death or "being slain in the spirit." I disappeared to myself as if I had fallen through a hole in Time. I died to my ego self. Awareness embraced both nothingness and expansiveness, releasing me from all concepts of suffering.

The *I Transcend My Ego Self* meditation allows us the perspective of the observer of our own sacred transition. We are able to realize that change can be a terrifying passage or a welcome reprieve. It depends on how we choose to experience the fact that we are not the body. Even when the body falls away, we are still there as something that does not change and cannot die. We meditatively transcend our attachment to the physical body vehicle at will, in total embrace of the essence, the consciousness that we really are. The Light body accepts the bittersweet shift of perception as the formless Self merges with the Ultimate reality. It patiently waits for the soul's return with loving, open arms, even for the brief visits in meditation and prayer.

Who am I?

"Who am I?" is a question of transcendence. Being that our most essential Self is Spirit, it is reasonable to experience the domain of The Holy Spirit, The Holy Ether of The Creator, through which we experience spiritual strength and resilience. We do not have to understand it or turn it into a religion to have a healing relationship with it. Through prayer and diligent meditation practice, we exercise the muscle of complete submission to The Will of The Divine. When we choose to live a surrendered life, we are rewarded with courage, sufficient to quell the sense of foreboding that will naturally wrench our egos at the thought of the world we have come to know without us in it. That thought sends shudders of paralyzing fear through to the core of the being of a mind conditioned by fear and attachment to identification with physical forms. We begin to understand that we were in the picture we see of this world before we were born into it, just not in our present form. So, the question is, "Where were we?" When our faces are erased from the canvas we call the mirror, where will we be then? But, particularly, are these "places" really so distant from one another? Are they "places" at all? We are the designers of temporal reality and seek to define a distinct past, present, and future. We have the power to engage a filter that refines our reality to the point of fluid redefinition, all variances merging into the all-encompassing now. Who we really are is Timeless, unchanging in this changeful world.

Let Go

Our goal is to meditatively let go of our attachment to the physical form and mundane realities that lead to a fear of death that is so overwhelming it disturbs our experience of life. As we perform this intense spiritual contemplation, we train our mind's eye to look into the mirror and not see the vehicle, and look into the eyes of eternity to see our souls. The vehicle comes, and it goes. The driver, our soul, that eternal, formless being who we really are, does not come and go. It does not die. We are energy, and energy cannot be created or destroyed. As our essence, we existed before we entered the body vehicle, and we will not cease to exist without it. With this profound insight, we can take responsibility for the health and well-being of our essential Self as a Light body, and see the positive results of our efforts manifested in the quality of our lives. We seek to concern ourselves less with all of the persons, places, and things that come and go. We find that which does not come and go, that changeless space; the Eternal Being; who we really are, and focus on that.

Our Blessing

The Universe becomes our playground, but not our toy. This is not a game. I do not recommend a mere cursory study of the practice of Mystical Meditation. To ignore its complexity is to miss the benefits of its simplicity. Practice and commitment can evolve into an abundantly free spirit, able to navigate the whirlwinds of circumstance. The goal of this text is to encourage the acceptance of our responsibility as builders of our innermost sacred temple, that we may retreat there from the linear, superficial values that often serve as obstacles to our transcendence into the consciousness of the Eternal.

Beginning with this spiritual study and work, we are reaching into the archives of the mysteries of the ancients for tools that will help us on our path to peace of mind. These tools are used with spiritual authority and responsibility. They are tentacles used to plug into age-old systems that can allow the transmission of truth and guidance. We seek to manifest the Desire of the Divine Oneness upon the unique design of our destiny.

We seek to respect, love, nurture, and energetically sculpt our formless, imageless Light body, into the awareness of the perfection, the connection, the Eternal I AM that it already is. We accept that we are shape-shifting Lightworkers in this time of spiritual awakening. We are beings of conscious Light in Timeless Oneness with the Eternal Essence, whether we realize it or not.

At the crossroads of my spiritual journey, there were helpers. At every twist and turn along the way, there was guidance, seen and unseen. The highest aspiration is to be a pointing for others. The path reveals more than the destination. The path is the destination. The embrace of the Sacred Law of Impermanence allowed me to accept that pain is the flip side of the coin of joy. It evolves from a practice into a spontaneous way of being.

Death: The Archetype
Removing the Veil

There are few reasons that any human being actually looks forward to a conversation about death. If we cannot fathom the most essential part of our being experiencing and enjoying freedom outside of the elaborate "cage" of the physical body, we will not experience true joy living inside of it either. Without exercising the muscle of transcendence, at will, the quality of life can be diminished to the degree that it may become unbearable to live because of the bondage of our fears and suffering.

An attempt to examine the meaning of death depends upon many things, one of the most influential being cultural conditioning. Many Eastern-based cultural ideals differ greatly from Western ideals, so much so that death is viewed as an entirely different experience. One declares a bittersweet victory, and the other descends into dramatic mourning. There is no such thing as death. How does one begin to apply definitions and traditions to something that does not really exist? Our individual experiences around the subject of the sacred transition of death are as distinct as fingerprints. For some, it is a return. For some, it is a new beginning. For some, it feels like the end.

On this subject, I will share with you in this text excerpts from my book, FACELESS: THE SACRED RELATIONSHIP and LIMITLESS: MADE OF LIGHT, for deeper insight into the energetic shape-shifting around the archetypal, personal, and mystical perceptions of death. In our meditations, we are focused on the transcendence of the ego self. Once we release our attachment to identifying ourselves as the body, it will begin to heal our fear of death.

An Archetype is a model, prototype, or pattern of behavior common to all human experience. There are many. They are every mask we will ever wear throughout our existence. We will not study these masks to become them. We study them to understand how to heal them and even remove them at will to experience ourselves as who we really are. FACELESS: THE SACRED RELATIONSHIP is a comprehensive mystical guide to Archetypal Healing available from *dreamuniversalmedia.com or amazon.com*. From LIMITLESS: MADE OF LIGHT, I share *The Shadow of Death,* and from FACELESS: THE SACRED RELATIONSHIP, I share *The Tower Archetype*. The energies of *The Shadow of Death* address loss on a spiritual level. The energies of *The Tower Archetype* relate more to the loss of material things. I share this here for deeper insights into archetypal energies relating to our spiritual healing as we seek to embrace the Sacred Law of Impermanence.

The Shadow of Death: The Archetype is an excerpt from LIMITLESS: MADE OF LIGHT, our companion manual for Archetypal Meditation.

The Shadow of Death: The Archetype

The Reaping

Long before he visited me, we passed one another at the crossroad. He taunted me. He haunted me. "You had better do what you came here to do," he mocked me. He beckoned and whispered. He opened his arms ... welcoming me. "Come with me. Take my hand. Rise out of the land of dreams and flesh. Free your soul to fly into eternal reality. I will lead you there into the Light
to play among the angels.

Don't be afraid. Trust me.
I, too, am an angel loved by The Divine One, for I am the one that frees you to melt into the warmth of That Embrace."

Shrinking from his invitation, paralyzed by fear of the unknown ... the unseen, I desperately cling to the dream. I frantically hold on to the illusions of the temporal Plane, rejecting my ascent into Spirit. He lunges in my direction, grasps my reluctant last breath, and shouts, "NOW!
Who do you think you are?"

I call out to the Light as It embraces me ... quench the thirst of my parched and weary soul with the waters of time without beginning or end. I sigh, relieved of the gravity of flesh ... embarrassed to have feared him ... I smile.

Spirits rise from the Temple of manifestation
Light beings dance from Plane to Plane
to the enchanting anthem
of their cosmic domain
ascending to all that is real .... finally .... finally free

Profile of The Shadow of Death's Cyclical Archetypal Influence

The illusion of death manifests as the demise of the physical body. At the junction where science and philosophy meet, what happens next is quite subjective. We are free to believe whatever we choose to believe. If we choose to see ourselves as finite, limited, purely carnal beings, we can do that. However, philosophy and evidence agree that it is a sign of our soul's travel to another realm. We may expand on that and see it as our soul's return to its Divine Origin free of the individuated concept of self. The physical form in all of its wonder lives as a dream on the stage, in the theater of corporeal reality, while the spirit world watches and remains our original and ultimate reality.

It is typically the Western cultural belief system that causes our deep fear and dread of death. With nothing but fire and brimstone or milk and honey to look forward to, we view death as a horror story. In many other cultures, there are very different attitudes regarding the subject of death. From his Eastern perspective, famed Persian poet and mystic, *Omar Khayyam* shares in *The Rubaiyat*;

> *I sent my soul through the invisible*
> *some letter of that afterlife to spell*
> *By and by my Soul returned to me*
> *and answered, "I Myself am Heaven and Hell"*
> *Heaven but the Vision of fulfilled Desire*
> *and Hell the Shadows from a Soul on fire*
> *Cast on the Darkness into which Ourselves*
> *so late emerged from, shall soon expire*
> *We are no other than a moving row*
> *of Magic Shadow-shapes that come and go*
> *Round with the Sun-illumined Lantern held*
> *in Midnight by the Master of the Show.*

In the face of death, as in the face of Life, intense prayer, and meditation, remembrance, and affirmation, will keep us centered and grounded in the remembering of who we really are. Most religious, philosophical, and spiritual paths offer Light in this dark hour of departure. Some embrace it in celebration of life. *Affirm ... I will that Thy Will be my will and our Wills are One ... I will Thy Will in my life ... Thy Will in my death ... be done. My life and my death belong to The Eternal One.* These words of comfort and surrender to the Most High bypass negotiating, bargaining, or fighting for an outcome that is not within our jurisdiction to effect change upon.

We are given Free Will and authority over our fate, but not our destiny. Our destiny rests in the most capable hands of the Most High, All-Wise, and Almighty. It would be vain, if not insane, to seek complete knowledge and control over that which is beyond our limited understanding or authority. Death is the Ultimate Mystery. Death is the Ultimate Secret. We can only study and speculate. Beyond that, it becomes an issue of belief and faith.

It is a spiritually dangerous position to take, to attempt to defy or manipulate the Will of Divine, imposing our personal will upon a situation we may be facing, or performing interventions in the lives of others. It is an extremely unwise decision to engage in a battle of wills with That Which Created all. We cannot be so confident that we have the wisdom to know the difference between the things we can change and the things we cannot change. This is why prayer, meditation, and the intelligence to live a surrendered life, become so important. We need continual spiritual reinforcement when dealing with issues so emotionally charged that we might lose our objectivity, not to mention our faith and trust in Divine Providence and Intervention.

Except by Divine Intervention, every decision of our lives, both conscious and unconscious, is a step on the path toward fulfilling our soul's destiny. A Force more powerful than we can imagine governs this, and the consequences for interfering with it would be as disastrous and as pointless as trying to break a fall mid-leap. A destiny, as opposed to a fate, is already set into action long before this and other physical incarnations. These are the contracts between our Soul and its Divine Creator. Who are we to seek to break them, caught in the throes of the desperately manipulative nature of our physical form?

Life asked Death,
"Why do people love me and hate
you?"

Death replied,
"Because you are a beautiful lie and
I am a painful Truth."

~ Unknown ~

OUR GLASS

To whom
shall I beckon
with outstretched
hands and say
"Come with me?"
When the last
grains of sand
in my hourglass
sift through
the short
narrow
time tunnel
of my life
who, then,
would say,
"I will?"

Herein lies
my final truth
I was born
into this life
as spirit, alone
and as spirit
alone
I will leave it

Yet, there is no lonely soul
that is one with the Creator
A soul at peace
in its solitude
is only closer
to the beginning
closer to the end
and thus,
much closer
to The God

~ JAI ~
Smoke & Mirrors

The Tower: The Archetype, is an excerpt from, FACELESS: THE SACRED RELATIONSHIP, an advanced guide for Archetypal Meditation and healing. I share this here because the energy around loss, separation, death, and grief corresponds with the energies of The Tower. It is not personal. It is a fact of all life.

The Tower: The Archetype

I face ... I embrace

THE WINTER OF MY BEING

Spring has evaded me
as a flash of Ether
in my peripheral vision
in faint whispers
of its passing
gone
as though
it was only
my imagination
that it ever
happened at all

Summer has escaped me
slipping through
my desperate fingers
like tainted sand
of South Coast beaches
back to the Earth
gone
as though
it was only
my imagination
I ever
held it at all
Autumn taunts me
from behind her colorful wings

fiercely rushing toward me
sweeping my reluctant soul
toward the winter of its being

Upon me
the chill of time
and its swift passing
Upon me
the will of time
and its relentless dashing
in the face
of unpromised tomorrows
as though it were not afraid
as though it would be kind
as though it would not find
me waiting all alone
for you
like the seasons
fading into yesterdays
with fresh promises
of springtime
and the joyfulness
of summer

Gone
as though
it was only
my imagination
you were ever
here at all

Gone
as though
it was only
my imagination
that I ever
knew you at all

Now the frigid wind
of winter
sweeps my
lonely heart
into the winter
of its being

Profile of The Tower's Cyclical Archetypal Influence

The Tower never feels like good news as its door opens into our lives, yet it is not as bad as it may seem. There is no mistaking the energy of The Tower when it shakes our lives up so thoroughly that we feel like we've crashed and burned. The sound of the first domino falling gets our attention. After the drama, we finally collapse in exhaustion from stomping out brush fires. We hang in limbo waiting, as one by one, piece by piece, they all have fallen at the speed of light until finally, we find ourselves hip-deep in the rubble of what we once knew as our lives. There may not be any pieces left to pick up. The shock alone can feel like the end of the world ... consumed by the flames of The Tower. When the flames of The Tower rage, leaving nothing in their path of destruction, we must remember the Sacred Law of Impermanence. Nothing lasts forever. Pray for the strength to survive and transcend it, grasping its valuable lesson, rather than praying for it to go away. The Tower will burn off all that is not the Essential Self.

The blazing mental images one may conjure of the archetypal influence of The Tower are formidable. When The Tower strikes, it is invariably performing a cleansing, a purging, that is long overdue. The clutter of all that we neglect to sort out reaches critical mass, igniting the fire of its own destruction.

Mars, the warrior planet, rules the energy of The Tower. Much like the archetype of Death, The Tower speaks of major letting go and heart-wrenching goodbyes. The Death archetype issues in these changes on a spiritual level. The Tower energy brings a similar transition on a physical level. The key words describing The Tower are the great falling apart, the necessary purification.

The Tower portends decay, destruction, and loss in many areas of life. It can mean the falling apart of families, friendships, physical health, jobs, and careers. Zen-styled doctrines suggest an aspiration to simplicity and nothingness brings peace. The liberation of a simpler life often has more to offer than one full of complications and frills. Those who appear to be destroyed by a fall from The Tower are actually being liberated from the bondage of a life so geometrically structured that it turned into a prison. It was their distrust of Divine Providence that caused them to cling to the illusion. There is no need to die to the world of matter to be able to live as a fulfilled spiritual being. The magic and our test is in our ability to balance the two.

Western society has, in many ways, promoted and rewarded our descent into mere geometrical figures, into square pegs, no longer fitting into the round holes of spirit, no longer flowing smoothly with the currents of the Universe. Modern technology has advanced to the extent that human beings have been reduced to nameless, faceless serial numbers on plastic cards in electronic files. We are sorted, stored, and waiting to be deleted. Depersonalization has taken on the energy of attempting to render humanity obsolete and has given birth to conscienceless, predatory monsters that ravage natural order and challenge Cosmic Law, seeking instant gratification of their ever-increasing physical and material appetites. When unconsciousness of the spirit of Self and others prevails as a way of life, The Tower is close at hand, and the gates to our spiritual freedom are either set further in the distance or brought to our doorstep. It can represent the trials and tribulations that make us worthy of true freedom.

When The Tower burns and crashes at the feet of our well-structured lives, bringing separation and loss, it is the voice of Spirit trying to get our attention in whispers, turning into screams. It is the Universe's less than subtle attempt to effect change upon the stubborn core belief systems that bind us to the illusions of matter. There is something within that we have chosen to remain in denial of, something that has to be purified or burned off. It is the natural process. It is not personal.

When we identify the energy of The Tower sweeping through our lives, we must let go and trust in the Infinite Wisdom of The God and cling only to the Timeless. That which is not ours no one can give to us. That which belongs to us, no one can take it away. Most self-destructive is indignant resistance, struggling in vain to mitigate the damages, clinging desperately to all that is scattered to the winds of change … The Law of Impermanence, Anicca.

The poem, *Winter of My Being*, is shared here as an expression of The Tower from my books, SMOKE & MIRRORS and FACELESS: THE SACRED RELATIONSHIP. *Two Storms* was written in the face of an approaching Tower archetypal energy. *The Winter of My Being* was written while sitting among the ruins of my own life, consumed by the flames of yet another Tower. This cyclical archetypal influence is never welcome, but it always visits with an opportunity for spiritual rebirth.

TWO STORMS

Rising … The Sun touched
the cold Earth and
left it warm
The quiet night
prayed for daylight
in the calm before the storm

Two storms approached
with destruction and grief
leveling everything in their path
killing something in me

There was no place
to run for shelter
no door opened
when I needed
to run in
Two storms
exploding
and imploding
one outside
the other within

The wind was blowing fiercely
outside and in my mind
violently tearing my world apart
leaving innocence behind

Debris is scattered
Everything is destroyed
Now I must face the issues
I've been trying to avoid

I could allow my emotions
to get the best of me
and end up lifeless and uprooted
like the fallen trees
or I could keep on walking
making the best
of what is left
having faith

in the Divine and
believing in myself
I will hold my head up
seeking shelter, walking on
and though the tune
is a bit off-key
still try and sing my song

The storm is now over
but the damage is done
I turn from gray skies
in hopes that the Sun
will light my path
to a new way to run
making new the dreams
to which I once clung
The storm
in my mind
subsides

    The Tower can be more painful than death. However, *nothing lasts forever*. If the good times don't last, the bad times won't last either. In such times of need, we are challenged to trust the Universe and its perfect plan for our lives. From the ashes of our demise, we will rise again, unattached to worldly desire ... able to see a wondrous forest rather than just a single tree. These are the wings of freedom. We will fly again.

Do Not Stand at my Grave and Weep

Do not stand at my grave and weep.
I am not there. I do not sleep.
I am a thousand winds that blow.
I am the diamond glints on snow.
I am the sunlight on ripened grain.
I am the gentle autumn rain.
When you awaken in the morning's hush
I am the swift uplifting rush
of quiet birds in circled flight.
I am the soft stars that shine at night.
Do not stand at my grave and cry.
I am not there. I did not die.

~ Mary Elizabeth Frye ~

This beautiful poem was penned on a brown paper shopping bag in 1932, to comfort a friend grieving for the passing of her mother. It was written by a woman who had never written a poem before. She said the words "just came to her" in her contemplations about life and death. The poem was never copyrighted or published by her, and was offered freely to be commonly read at funerals as a comfort to the grieving. It is known for having a mystical healing effect on the bereaved. I share it here to affirm the dissolution of biting, stinging concepts of goodbye, of death, of separation, and change.

We change the things we can. We cannot buy, beg, borrow, or steal time in this form, in this temporal framework … not for ourselves, nor for our loved ones. Our first mandate is to know Self. To know Self is to love Self most intimately, as a product of our own creation; as an emanation from a sacred thought-form; as a portrait painted with love for Self, brushing with every stroke, new life on the canvas of time. In the portraits we have rendered of our friends and loved ones, we have stroked their images with ardent intentions of our own. When it is time to let go, we turn to water, melt without form, contort our energies into fetal position, hollow out, and follow these images into the cemetery as if that is really where the journey ends. When it is our time to rest, know that if someone were to visit the graveyard to let everyone out, intact, we would all be scrambling about looking for our things, screaming I, me, my, mine, mine, mine. We would instantly begin our counterfeit reality show again, void of the realization again, that all is transient. All is illusory.

As we, and those we love, awaken into Eternal Reality, the feelings of loss on this side of the veil of materiality can be incomprehensible, even unbearable. Take all of that love that we can no longer give to those we have loved face to face, and still love them, faceless. We must take all of that unconditional love and affection and give it to those who need it as much as we do.

When my mother passed away, I was fortunate enough to have already been involved with a local orphanage and had bonded with many children there who were classmates of my children. I remember being amazed by the resilience of those children and their ability to smile even after the worst had happened. I knew that one day I would have to find what they had managed to find in that place that is not called strength; not called a void; not called hell. They had to learn to go within and never forget that their lives still mattered. I knew my day had come when it arrived, the day I would have to do the same thing. I would have to go within as my mother had always told me I would. That is where freedom awaits our awakening. There is where we all live as one in the Timeless Now.

The Emotional Impact of Grief

The power of a negative or fearful thought-form is so strong that it is dangerously capable of setting into motion a self-fulfilling prophecy. It can bring into reality that which we most dread, based on nothing but the energy of our fears and misinterpretations. Death is all we are sure of, and the fear of it can paralyze our dreams and rob us of the lives we were meant to live.

One of the strongest connections we have with one another is the witnessing and sharing of one another's lives. When we must face the reality that our loved one will no longer be there as a witness to our lives, there can be feelings of disassociation from the self, as though the meaning and purpose of life have been diminished. When we consider the loss of the physical form, there can be great sorrow experienced at the thought of lives, once connected, not being witnessed or shared anymore. It can lead to feelings of no longer existing, with memories that haunt like ghosts and feelings of becoming a mere shadow of our former selves. That is what much of the unforeseen, but predictable, life-long impact of grief is about. There is comfort in knowing that our lives and the lives of our loved ones, with or without a physical form, will always be witnessed by the Eternal All-Seeing Eye of The One God, Creator, and Sustainer of all. When we lose someone we love, it helps to accept the Creator is our Eternal Witness.

Either by requirement or by choice, we are given many opportunities to return in other physical or non-physical forms, for the completion of unfinished business and spiritual growth. This is not to encourage an attachment to, or celebration of, the return to the physical through reincarnation. How can we even call it a return if we have never truly left? In the context of The Timeless Now, how can we focus on past lives or future lives when all of those tenses are One? The primary objective is to transcend the desire for remaining in the drama of the life/death continuum, evolve, and *get off* of the treadmill and ever-spinning wheel of reincarnation.

I do not recommend focusing too much attention on concepts of reincarnation, the Light body, and the spirit world as a way to invalidate or avoid the natural grief process. The avoidance of the necessary stages of healing grief can result in a subconscious, dangerous, and unhealthy relationship with the energies of both death and life. The experience of grief is critical to acceptance of the inevitable with grace and dignity. Dr. Elisabeth Kübler-Ross is well known for her account of the five stages of grief in her book, *On Death and Dying*. For a person who is given a terminal prognosis and for those who are losing or have already lost someone they love, the process of healing can follow somewhat predictable transitional stages.

The stages Dr. Kübler-Ross identified are:
- Denial
- Anger
- Bargaining
- Depression
- Acceptance

There is no truly predictable reaction to the loss of a loved one or the overall way we view the inevitability of death. Our reactions are unique and diverse. For some, there is numbness and disorientation at the thought of the impermanence of our present physical reality and that of our loved ones. When these sabotaging thoughts occur, we must completely surrender our linear minds to the Will and Won't of The Divine One. My anchor and bridge were a string of prayer beads I kept wrapped around my wrist. Every time a painful thought surfaced, I would chant it down in my mind by performing repetitive prayer. Healing affirmations helped to keep me centered and grounded. We must know that the seen and the unseen are equally real. We cannot die. We cannot live until we accept that as the Eternal Truth of who we are.

I encourage you to read the poems regarding death from my book of poetry, SMOKE & MIRRORS, as a healing that may bring comfort in the event that death brings its trials to your doorstep as it has mine. We are challenged to accept it from a spiritually evolved perspective. The most comforting reminder is that death is not the end, but a beginning, a birth into the world our Soul knows as home. It represents our departure from the material world of illusion, celebrating our birth, our ascent back into the spirit world, our Origin, and Ultimate Reality. It is so hard to say goodbye from this side and find the spiritual strength to endure the pain of missing the physical presence of our family, friends, and loved ones until we meet them again. Only Divine healing can give us the strength to go on. To That, we surrender our pain to have it transformed into faith, strength, and perseverance. We will survive … even this.

Is It Even Possible To Kill One's Self?

As I started to write this book, I was amazed at how death began to reveal dimensions of its mysteries to me in so many ways. I had a bizarre experience one afternoon around Christmas time, at work in a Los Angeles hotel. Alone in my office, I noticed it was quiet in such a creepy way. An eerie chill filled the room, and I felt as though I had stepped into someone else's horrific vision. Something or someone was showing me the final scenes of a sad and troubled life. I felt as though I could hear the last conversations between herself and her demons. I typed everything I heard. I saw a woman in the vision, vivid enough to describe her to someone who had worked there for many years and remembered her story. It was worth the risk of this disclosure to find out that I was not the only person who had felt her presence. She had worked in an office on that same floor for years, and no one really knew her. She stopped showing up for work. No one missed her until word arrived that she had committed suicide. She had been seen by some over the years, wandering the hallways of the hotel. From her communication, I was given visceral impressions of the great disappointment that follows a choice like that. She glamorized death as an "escape" and just "wanted out" … only to find out that there is no out, at least not that way.

Causing ourselves to leave our physical body does not end the pain we may be experiencing. In such a case, one may still have to serve the appointed days on this Plane, with or without a body. The greatest disappointment that I can imagine is to find that after what we determined to be our final effort, we find that it simply did not work. We blink and find ourselves still here. Physical death cannot end life. I wondered if she had known the Light body and indestructible I AM as the reality of her True Self, could she have figured out that the Light body, the I AM, cannot be killed? The poem that came from this experience sadly wrote itself. Our True Self is imperishable.

OUT

She came through me
in a midday vision
pale
drawn
hopeless
translucent shadow
clothed in her
ragged aloneness
hem swaying
as she whirled
into the abyss
arms outstretched
to the heavens
plummeting feet first
deeper into anguish
She falls into
her haunting
solitary
tear-drenched
refrain
She walks
the halls
of the hotel now
still pale
still drawn
more hopeless
more alone
imposing pictures
of her Free Will choice
on all
who would
feel her
She just wanted
Out
Out

Razor severs
anxious veins
of patient wrist
Sweet blood
Bitter tears
slash solitary paths

through snapshot negatives
defacing memory
Out
Out
I just
want out
she said
Red on eggshell white
fading walls
spray paint
faceless portrait
graffiti of cold despair
final surrender
to numbers bleeding
across gray face
of silent clock
dissolving into
terminal blues
Falling
Falling
Falling into abysmal forever
through turbulent
headwind of voices
calling her by name
welcoming her to nowhere
celebrating
her demise
Shallow breaths
cry out
through tight lips touching
no one hearing
just like before
She wanted to know
"Where am I?
Why am I
no one anymore?"
I become my unbearable pain
I become the numbness
of my longing
for tomorrows
I did not
want to see

> Where is the tunnel?
> Where is the light?
>
> When does
> forever end?
> Falling into
> Ohhhhh Dammnnn
> greedy mouth
> of utter darkness
> Falling
> Falling
> Falling
> This is not out
> Never being
> swallowed
> Ohhhhh
> Dammnn
> This
> Is not
> ooouuuutttt

Suicide has reached epidemic proportions. It is generally rooted in feelings of loss, of never having had a chance, of nothing ever-changing. Yet, the subject of suicide is treated as taboo and is not as aggressively confronted as statistics suggest that it should be. There is no out. The only "out" is within. The only way in is to transcend. Again, the greatest tragedy of suicide is the failure of it. For a person to contemplate suicide, there must already be feelings of failure in life or having to endure some level of unbearable suffering. Then, to pursue what is perceived as the last option, to end one's life, of course, one imagines that it would be something they can succeed at or control. After all is said and done, from this side of the veil of physical existence, it is perceived as successful. Then one finds themselves just as alive as they were before the suicide, standing over a corpse that was believed to be Self, witnessing the subsequent horrors that follow.

I was taught that we are given a certain number of days, to the second, to serve on this physical Plane of existence. There is essential wisdom to be shared until our very last breath. We will not escape this Plane until we have served, learned, and evolved. We do not determine the number of our days. There is no out until that appointed day and moment. Our choice is to either live as a shadow on this plane or bear our cross of suffering and accept the Karmic cleansing it offers. I am the judge of no one. I can only repeat things I have heard from many wise people, but by no means, from the mouth of The Absolute. All any of us can do in our "body suits" is speculate. None of us *really* know. We are all only students and travelers on this path called life.

I have no desire to do a dissertation on the spiritual implications of suicide. If we are not walking in another's shoes, we are standing in judgment. This is an overview of the fear factor lurking behind the many doors we pass through to get to the "other side," into the realm we call death. Some view suicide as a higher octave of murder. Even Earth Plane laws allow for various degrees of murder. There may be an argument as to whether or not it was premeditated, intentional, or in self-defense. There are cases when it is judged to be accidental. The murder of one's self, however, leaves little room for argument or degree because on both sides of the veil, between the physical and spirit world, the case is not easier to defend because of the radical nature of our departure.

The definition of the word suicide implies intent and premeditation. On this side (the physical world), we would not be present to defend our actions or to be represented by an advocate to argue on our behalf. On the other side (the spirit world), some believe there are pockets and Planes of existence where we would serve the completion of our earthbound term before we are able to transcend. Think of it as if we have been invited to dinner, and instead, we show up early for breakfast, demanding dinner. We may be welcomed differently by the host. We may be greeted by a locked door or be forced to wait outside of the kitchen hungry, while the meal is being prepared. We may be welcomed in with an explanation. It might have been less risky if we had just stayed where we were, found something better to do, and kept our commitment to show up at the host's scheduled time. The point is, we don't know.

The grave issue of suicide cannot be reduced to a dinner invitation scenario. It is a matter of great emotion, and widespread, tragic consequences to self and others. For that reason, it is believed by some spiritual traditions that suicide is the worst of sins. Some believe it to be unforgivable. Some believe that from our first to our last breath, our lives are all for The Creator and that our blessing comes with taking that last breath and giving up the ghost at the time we are called. I am not the judge of the decisions of anyone. It is presumptuous to assume The God's opinion of anything from our earthly perspective. Only That Which created us can judge us. None of us know what the spiritual consequences of suicide are. Ideally, we should all live a surrendered life, unconditionally loving the essence of who we really are and just wait for our turn to breathe our last breath since it's going to happen one day anyway. I explore this topic to promote the best and most fulfilling life possible, from the beginning to the sweet or bitter end. Don't go through the door of giving up hope on the way out. Seek Refuge in prayer. Seek help until it is found. Go within to find that silent place where no one can hurt you and love yourself unconditionally from that place.

As long as I live, I will never forget every detail of a neighbor's suicide. I was awakened one morning to the police banging on my neighbor's door, guns drawn. They quietly and cautiously entered his apartment, prepared to engage. They found him dead, face down on the living room floor, unclothed, with a plastic bag over his head and an empty pill bottle by his bedside. The group erupted in laughter, remarking that he was no threat to anyone anymore, and they put their guns away. One of them knocked on my door to show me his driver's license and ask me if I knew anything about him. Of course, I had never met him. Where I lived, we only meet our neighbors in the lobbies of secured buildings after an earthquake.

I found out that my neighbor had committed suicide because he felt he had lost everything ... family, job, relationship, and he couldn't pay his rent. His family was only concerned about the possibility of there being valuable belongings he left behind. If he had done it for attention or sympathy, I don't think he would have imagined an outburst of laughter and jokes. I was working on this book at the time, contemplating whether or not I should include some commentary about suicide, since the subject is "death." After a long night of writing nearly until dawn, I awakened to the answer. All I could think of was ... if he had cried out on the other side of those too thin walls, I would have heard him. If he had knocked on the door, I would have offered him a cup of coffee and perhaps said something that might have changed his mind. Imagine that as a going away memory ... Laughter, ridicule, and jokes. There is no real irony, but the fact that I realized it needed mention here.

However bad life may appear to be at any given time, make sure that such a futile choice for change doesn't result in being the brunt of jokes and comedy club laughter. Say something to someone ... seek help ... pray ... scream through the streets if so inclined ... knock on every neighbor's door until someone offers a cup of coffee. If you know someone who is expressing thoughts of giving up, of just "wanting out," be that angel in their life with a kind word and a cup of coffee. If they don't want to hear a kind word or drink a cup of coffee, then let them know that you will be the one sitting there quietly; not the one trying to "fix" things; not trying to be an answer when there is no question ... just a presence committed to being right there for as long as it takes until those imposing thoughts of despair find balance.

I do not believe that fire and brimstone judgments will heal every suicidal thought. Harsh judgment is sometimes a driving force that nurtures these tortured thoughts. How can any one of us stand in judgment of another's suffering … so profound and desperate? Can any one of us pronounce judgment upon another's soul, based on a distorted state of mind that drove them to the unthinkable? Extenuating circumstances can be so completely crushing that they are out of the perceptual reach of anyone seeking to be the judge of another. There has been no increase in making it easier or even possible to get help. There has been an overwhelming increase in suicide rates, bringing with it unspeakable tragedy and grief. There has been an overwhelming increase in the rate of deaths from overdose and addiction to pharmaceutical drugs, with their mile-long lists of side effects prescribed for conditions as non-terminal as acne. "If you or a loved one have experienced these ninety-nine side-effects associated with depression medication, including, but not limited to, depression, suicidal thoughts, behaviors, and death, please call 1 800-bad-drug … oops … to receive compensation." Sound familiar?

If we are so blind as to believe that there are hard and fast rules that we can use to weigh and measure the soul of another … are we or are we not, trying to play God? We are not the judge of another's soul. We do not know what another's soul contract was as it incarnated on this Plane of existence. What if that person was not in their right mind at the time such a decision was made? Such matters are between Creator and creation, and no one else. The most we can do is commit ourselves to being a Light willing to shine in such desperate and obscure places as the darkest night of another's soul throws them into despair. Yes, we are our brother's and our sister's keeper. I am not speaking of drama laced threats and manipulative demands for attention by engaging in emotional hostage-taking. We must pray to be blessed with the spiritual discernment to feel and understand our role in being a life raft to someone the Universe has sent across our path. We may be the Light that could change their fate.

I initiated an ongoing research of prayers, meditations, and spiritual counsel that could heal suicidal thoughts and tendencies. If you are entertaining any thoughts of harming yourself or others, do recite these prayers on your way to seek professional help … on your way to talk to someone … anyone … everyone! Psalms 31:15 is a strong prayer. However, any prayer that resonates with the energy of the Natural Mystic within will ignite the innermost Fire and Light, and initiate a healing.

Psalms 31:15 ~ The Bible (KJV)

O Lord!
You know my heart! I am so oppressed on all sides that I quite often want to end my life! Life has become hopeless, and I see no way out. Lord Your word says that my body is Your temple and as such, I have no authority over my life and body. Yet Lord I am unable to resist this suicidal tendency. Strengthen my heart and remove all suicidal thoughts and any attempts I have made to take my own life. I acknowledge that Satan is a thief and comes to steal, kill and destroy. I now choose You Lord Jesus, as my Master who came to give me life and give it abundantly.

I renounce all my harmful thoughts, and I crave Your forgiveness for nursing such thoughts. Thank You for Your forgiveness that allows me to forgive myself. I believe that my times are in Your precious hands and that there is always hope in Christ. Thank You, Lord for taking over my soul, my body, and my life. In Jesus' name, I pray.
Amen.

Not everyone is a Christian. There are powerful, compelling prayers, meditations, mantras, and affirmations from every tradition that can heal a condition perceived as hopeless with a sufficient level of faith and belief.

The Prayer of Life

I was given the gift of this body vehicle to travel in
for as long as it takes to complete my journey,
accomplish my purpose, and be called back home.
A Timeless echo of perfect timing
ticking to the rhythmic beat of my heart rejoices
That call will never be made by my own voice!
All I really want is to be free!

I realize this is not the home of my Spirit
I recognize my soul's yearning for its return
I am the evolving awareness that I am already home
I am Here … Now
In or out of this body
no matter where else I may appear to be
This form is but a cage
that contains the beautifully feathered bird of my Soul
trapped behind the walls of this school of higher learning

I can die to this world and never leave my body
I can be here now
transcending the pain, the sadness, and the grief
transcending the loneliness and the suffering
transcending fear and rejection
I am not asking for my burdens to be taken away
I am asking for the fear to be taken away
and be replaced with the strength to bear it
Angels watch over me
I am never left alone
I cannot fail in this dance of destiny
I am here for this
for as long as it takes
to know that I do not need a body to exist
My body needs me to exist
Inside of it I am the transcendence
of the bondage of materiality
Right here
Right now

I affirm that there is no such thing as death
I affirm that I cannot die
I affirm that it is not possible to end my life

I affirm that who I really am
will survive any attempt to erase myself
and be forced to witness the fallout
of the suffering my choice has caused

I am Eternal
There is no beginning of me
There is no end of me
Not by my hand, nor the hand of any other
Not by fire, air, water, or earth
I Am One with That from which my True Self emerged
I choose not to witness
the self-destruction caused by my misguided choices
by my tormented emotions,
by my troubled mind,
by my broken spirit,
by my own hand

I choose not to witness the pain such a departure would cause
on this side and the other
I choose to love and accept my True Self
My life matters

I have the power to reside in the domain of my Higher Self inside of this body
I have the power to transcend the stories, the faces, the masks, the theater
of the lower realms of my consciousness
I give up
I give up approval seeking, comparisons, and people-pleasing
I give up imposing impossible, false, soul-selling standards upon myself
I give up force-fitting the vastness of my Self
into the tiny boxes of illusory realities
that have nothing to do with who I really am
I owe no offerings to the fake imagery of others

I am not this body
I was here before it happened
I will be here when it is gone
No thing, no person, no opinion, no circumstance
DARES to try to invalidate the beauty
of this life, this breath, this Light, this Love, that I am
I am HERE NOW
I AM THAT which I seek
I am One with the Most High Creator Mother Father God
of my highest understanding

> I am a spark of the Original Flame
> There is no difference between us
> I forgive myself for any thought of separation
> I accept this perfect gift
> this beautiful container
> which is not me
> It transports my True Self
> through this experiencing
> I command the power to OWN it

A prayer can express as a walk in nature, a kind gesture toward another, or a bold vision around the corner of the unseen. Step away from the mirror and look within. Look beyond the illusory, transient imagery at the faceless, Timeless Self from the perspective of the witness, asking, "Who am I, really?" We are empowered to view our lives without judgment, without fixing anything. Then meditate on the question, "What witnesses the witness?" That meditation can take one into the realm of Ultimate Love.

Engaging in a Self-Inquiry meditation and exploring the nature of the True Self, the I AM, can result in dropping the singular identification with the physical form as self. If any type of self-harming thoughts or ideas of harming others should present in times of great strife, it becomes urgent to abandon the dangerous concepts and identity with the physical form as being who we really are. It is like imagining that because we do not like a party we are attending, and are having a miserable time, we can change outfits and be freed from our misery in that place. It is like imagining that the people at that event will somehow change if they were redressed.

The profound realization of the True Self eliminates the need to "fix" things outside of the Essential Self. There may be such feelings of failure and aloneness, even around others, that one could be swept away by a wave of despair into what is perceived as conclusive aloneness … death. Such thoughts are clearly projections rooted in attachment to the physical form as ultimate identity. There may be such profound feelings of rejection that the ultimate counter rejection might appear to be an act of self-annihilation ... not understanding the obscured details in the big picture of Self-Awareness.

No matter how depressed one gets, no matter how hopeless one feels, there has to be Light somewhere, or no shadows could be cast. Find it. There is always something to look forward to. Look forward to the NOW that yearns for the experience of the real uniqueness of you. Look forward to the Timeless Eternal Now that is ours for the mere recognition of it. Look inward for transcendence of all external illusions that have the potential to make us forget who we really are. We all have that placeless place within the stillness, the quiet of the storm, the inner reservoir of loving peace and tranquility. It is there that we find a vast, welcoming sea of "fitting in," away from all of the trying to fit into a world constructed of beautiful but deadly illusions. We are strong enough, spiritually, and emotionally sovereign enough to befriend the "not fitting into" madness. Who wants to fit into a changeful, pseudo-reality that offers nothing but disappointment anyway? In the end, we will discover it was nothing but a lucid dream, hiding from the shattering of our wakefulness.

I am not an expert on these matters. My acquaintance with many profound spiritual realities is primarily experiential. *A teaspoon of experience is greater than a whole kitchen full of mental knowledge.* My experience has led me to the practice and study of many tried and true forms of meditation. My life has been blessed with teachers that shared the brilliance of their Light with me. The many mystical paths I have traveled were destined to elevate the consciousness of the traveler to a higher frequency. It is from that frequency I seek to share some of my experiences with fellow seekers of Light and Truth. I have experienced powerful healings and illuminating clarity, rising up in awareness as my Higher Self, confirming our Oneness with That Which created all.

To be hypnotized by and trapped inside of the illusory projections of this world causes us unspeakable disappointment and suffering if we become overly invested in it, accepting it as real. The attachment and aversion that accompanies this acceptance gives it the power to dismantle our Self-esteem and Self-worth. It is busy day and night devising new ways of attracting the attention of our egos in a perpetual effort to inhibit our desire to be Self-Realized. Our own ego is its greatest advocate. If we choose to "die to our ego self," we are less vulnerable to this compassionless, tabloid-style, bullying mindset of a ridiculous, hateful culture. There are ancient and modern, Timeless studies and practices that can strengthen our resolve and prepare us for inner emotional warfare in times of peace.

Prayer is a surrender to The God in a petition to replace the illusions of self with the energies and awareness of the True Self. To experience an immersion in the energy we share with the Ultimate Self is to know that it is not only a resonant energy, it is the very Energy, the very same Presence, that created us, that fills us, that replaces us … that loves us beyond measure. It is another level of Self-esteem. It is another level of Love beyond passion. It is the transcendence of despair, allowing us to shift into a more optimistic perspective.

Repetitive prayer, the chanting of a healing mantra, and powerful affirmations can help with "chanting down" the attacks of negative energies and thought-forms. The chant down manifests an electromagnetic force field of energy that, not only protects, but deflects, and transmutes non-resonant energy. It is not against flesh and bone we battle. We are not just flesh and bone. We are mystical beings, *naturally* mystical beings, with access to the Mystic Law that governs creation, if we choose to tap into that frequency and be healed by it. We are an ocean of consciousness with no shore. There is no soul so lost that it cannot find its way home. Home is within, on the most Essential level. When we go within, we find we are stronger than we know … strong enough to be a Light of guidance for ourselves and others. My prayer is to be one of those Lights, to speak a healing word, to redirect hopeless energies and perceptions of futility. Drop false self-perceptions and concepts and go within, seeking only Divine Presence. Seek to be replaced by That.

Two different death experiences were shown to me in visions on that day at work. First, I was given the vision of the suicide victim as she hovered suspiciously close to a pregnant woman one floor above my office. I was then given a vision of a businessman, going about his life in his usual, predictable way. He had sacrificed the joy of life for many years, held hostage by mundane routine. He had plans for tomorrow. But his tomorrow never came. Even though his death would be described as untimely, his name had been called, and a murderer caused him to answer. The energy of his experience of death was much different than the one who just wanted "out" … and she took it, to no avail. This poem flowed through me with a much different energy than the prior experience.

FOUL PLAY

Wristwatch told him
she would be angry
that dinner got cold
like he felt inside
One-hour commute
peeking over sunset
a sigh reaches
car door before his emptiness
He knows how tomorrow will be,
who he will see,
what they will say and why
He even knows details
of what to expect tonight
dull luxury afforded by
a well-planned life
He wonders
what might have been
had he taken
another path
perhaps tomorrow

Wrong place
Right time
Cold mouth
of gun
kisses startled temple
There must be some mistake
"Nothing I have done
deserved this"
Eyes closed
Vision clearer
"I have no center
No point of reference"
Energy moving
at speed of thought
toward beautiful Light
"They say
the bullet
was not meant for me
yet, my name is called"
Unspeakable fear
Orgasmic rush

> Cold paralyzed pleasure
> Faint pulse
> I become my breath
> I become my Light
> I am not dead.

These incidents offered a clear distinction between two dramatic versions of the death experience. One came with a shocking realization that the intentional release from the physical body was no way out of the pain of this world. This shocking realization is accompanied by immeasurable regret for a failed attempt to end it all, leading to the knowledge that an intentional act of self-annihilation could not end existence. The other was met with a warm, welcoming Light, emanating the beauty of our immortality. His release from this world of matter, the embrace of the energetic Light body, was like returning home.

We can change our direction. We can change our minds. We can even change our fate but are never to rule out the certainty of Divine Intervention and Destiny. We are not our own. We cannot beg, borrow, or steal one moment beyond the expiration date of our perishable existence. We dare not take such a matter into our own hands. We must never underestimate our strength and fortitude in times of loss and despair. Everything, *including* loss and the ability to survive it, comes from Divine order. We must trust that our Creator will never leave us to struggle alone. We must surrender our will, ask for deliverance, and seek solace in prayer.

The fact that we are temporal beings who, by nature, are perishable, sets us up for unimaginable suffering from the very beginning of our physical lives. Yet, the pain our soul descended into our physical bodies to feel is just as sacred as the pleasure. Our physical experience is our gift to The Eternal Soul. It is within our carnal nature to pass away in physical form, and yet, our essential Self will survive it. It is within our nature to be able to endure extremes in pain and pleasure. We are all born with the destiny of driving the body vehicle to the end of this earthly journey, and then pass on from our physical form, or perhaps, even return to another form. How, when, where, and why, rests solely in the Will of The Creator and is known before our physical incarnation. It was inscribed in Light upon the pages of the book of our life story, before the moment the first thought-form existed, that caused us to incarnate.

To The God be the Glory. To those who were given the mission to spell out His Holy Name, in every language, in every culture and tradition, to The God be the Glory, that we are so Loved. Our sole meditation should be to seek His Face ... but to seek it in the mirror, not the cemetery, and find it ... Faceless. Seek it in spaces in-between our heartbeat. I think if one were to examine the core motive of those who commit suicide, seeking to annihilate the body and free the soul, it would appear to be a misguided step toward seeking the Divine Presence. We do not have to physically die to do that. We die before we die when we are able to dissolve the ego's demands in the tranquil sea of meditation on Oneness with Divine.

No matter how hard life can be, it is still worth living. The only way to know this truth would be to endure it, embrace it, and live in gratitude for that breath that transformed mud into a living soul, fashioned in the Image and Likeness of That Which Created all things. Life is good ... Even now.

If you are having thoughts about self-harm or harming others, please contact a Suicide Prevention Hotline for help.

The Dark Night of the Soul

"The Dark Night of the Soul," is a mystical term that moves with the soul from the depths of the abyss of consciousness, into the upper realms of Unity and Oneness with the Divine One. St. John of the cross coined the phrase and spiritual phenomenon of The Dark Night of the Soul, in an eight-stanza poem, followed by a twenty-three-page treatise and commentary, describing how his experience of it was not a demonstration of a lack of faith in God. This is often mistaken for a "crisis of faith" or a weakened relationship with God, including doubting the existence of God. It is not a depression. It is not a crisis of faith. Faith is *how* we navigate the torrential storms of life. In the opening of his treatise on the Dark Night, St. John characterizes this phrase as "the state of the perfect, which is that of the Divine union of the soul with God." One must experience:

- denial of worldly desires, effectively "blinding," "suspending" the senses;
- traveling the road of Faith, to which the intellect is blind;
- approaching God, who is incomprehensible to the soul in this life in direct experience of God.

I was blessed and cursed with many profound insights, occurring throughout the editing process of this collection of healing meditations ... especially this one. I was forced to revisit the energy of this section with a deeper level of empathy and compassion than I feel I had to offer it before. Everything I presented involved looking outside one's Self for comfort, for survival, for hope, for healing ... even for God. I suggested that someone would *always* be there for you, somewhere. That perspective lacked wisdom *and* the point of this whole book. Pure evil would have it that there would be that one night, day, moment ... after that phone call, that message, that vision, that news, that guilt, that rejection, that loss, that betrayal, that memory, that pain, that aloneness, that lands into your peace like a heat-seeking missile and obliterates every known faculty, including the air of the breath you breathe.

So, IMAGINE: Your face engulfed in a blue glow, your radiated hands clutch a smartphone. You scroll down your "contacts" … a misnomer, because you are not really in *contact* with anyone on that list … not the kind of contact you need right now for even one ray of Light. Your hand clutches the mouse for dear life, finger scrolling down into the bottomless pit of posts and selfies, on what you know for a fact now is *anti*-social media. You consider your life may be even emptier than you previously believed. You don't have "your best life" to demonstrate in your frozen, dead-eyed, teeth-skinning, cute-posing, social media buddy/friend-pleasing updates. Everyone is wearing the same smile, and they appear to have the same puppies. Puppies are cool. Ads, ads, ads … more things to desire, to pile on top of all of the other "things" to love, that will never love anyone back. Click "Home" and start again. You face a 'warm' welcoming "Hi, whoever you are! What's on your mind? How are you feeling?" You choose the face that best matches yours at that moment. Now you are an emoji. A happy face, an angry face, a sad face, one with hearts, not X's for eyes … Oh! There … You have a blue tear on the face of a caricature that claims to know how you feel. There's a blue thumbs up that declares in a whisper, "only positive vibes!" … "I'm okay!"

I'm talking to that one precious soul, wrapped in the billowing fog of impenetrable shadows of suffocating despair … Bound and gagged by the silence of that one unthinkable, unimaginable night that … No one was there … Or that someone you thought would be there was not there. Or that one night, that the ones who are there, are just too busy with their lives to lose a wink of sleep over your "issues" … Snores roaring through the echo chamber of last breaths that didn't matter. One word … One single flicker of Light that illuminates the existential nightmare of the Dark Night of someone's Soul.

Who do you call when the shock of that wave passes over you? Who or what do you call upon? What if you don't feel "entitled" to be attended to by the angels that were set in place as our protectors, because of some misplaced, conditioned guilt ... just for *being*? What if you feel there's nowhere to go that will be any more welcoming than here? Without a shield, a mantra, an altar, a prayer ... Without a friend, without a single person on the planet that knows or cares at all, one way or the other ... Even without an enemy ... Nothing. It is true that sometimes someone just being there is enough. But that is only determined by the reflection in the mirror of the one assumed to be present. So, it depends. Because a body is apparent, it does not mean that the essence and intention of the spirit that is in it are present. At a funeral, there is a body, but nobody is in it. What intention can such an empty vessel have for anyone's life?

There isn't a prayer I can think of that doesn't have a petition already in it. Take a prayer into such a highly charged emotional state, and it could manifest as a spiritual attack in the life of the persons or situations responsible for the perceived suffering. It is unwise to approach an altar in a state of heated passion, with emotional sparks flying, sufficient to burn down everything good. That kind of tantrum is the perfect storm to generate the energy of a spiritual attack. Such a prayer session has been known to erupt into an open warfare scenario that no one survives.

Absolutely ... Pray that prayer. Then, let's label it, draw a picture, assign it a holy book, then, let's call ourselves 'the chosen ones,' judge people, damn them to hell, and argue about it. TRUST in Divine Providence. Trust our relationship with it. Isn't it enough to know that something is there, not a void, not just Self-luminous triple darkness, not just space or nothingness? What is even beyond that? Everything is there, somehow, shimmering in the Self-Illuminating Triple Darkness, willing and able to intervene in our affairs. Our lives are not separate or different in any way, other than, one is the Beloved Creator and the other, creation, the beloved of the Creator. True healing is beyond that, to the extent that we are able to connect to unknown realms within.

I don't think anybody gets off the wheel of this spinning, temporal journey, without the transformative experience, classified among the 'Symptoms of Spiritual Awakening' … The Dark Night of the Soul. It can manifest as an existential crisis that could last moments, days, even years. It is important to know when to seek help. Manifestations of this naturally occurring, spiritual phenomenon are characterized by:

1. profound feelings of despair, sadness for the world, the future, humanity, one's own life;
2. feelings of worthlessness, not mattering;
3. feelings of loss of power, personal will, self-control, self-determination;
4. loss of interest in the people, places, and activities that were once a source of enjoyment;
5. feelings of being "cursed, condemned or sentenced" to suffering in this life;
6. feelings that nothing is ever going to change;
7. hopelessness, powerlessness;
8. alienation of family and friends;
9. crisis of faith in God and Divine Providence;
10. sensing a tangible loss that cannot be explained;
11. major sleep deprivation, isolation, anti-social behavior;
12. shattered sense of reality;
13. dissociative thinking and behavior;
14. obsessions with mortality;
15. feelings of being completely overwhelmed;

16. feeling lost, lacking purpose, searching for meaning in life, longing for an unknown home, unknown family, unknown friends;
17. self-devaluation to the point that it is reasonable to consider this person may be engaged in thoughts of self-harm, or other self-destructive thoughts and behavior;
18. a state called "Kenosis" in Christian theology. It references Jesus, in the act of 'self-emptying' … make himself nothing. Total submission and surrender to the Divine Will of The God;
19. *Ego Death* – refers to the "complete loss of subjective self-identity. The term is used in various intertwined contexts, with related meanings … In death and rebirth mythology, ego death is a phase of self-surrender and transition;
20. *Existential Crisis* – It is often masked as a depression, or something the mindset can "fix." It occurs when an individual becomes completely overwhelmed with what they perceive as a purposeless, valueless, meaningless life. It extends to a broader perspective, with statements like, "Why am I even here? What is the point? What difference will anything ever make … Ever?

On that Dark Night, the soul tosses and turns, torn between another try and another cry … Reflecting on the existential nightmare of, "Why am I even here?" "Who am I, really?" This is not a depression. The Soul's Dark Night is not specific to the reality of the person experiencing it. It is generally characterized by all-encompassing philosophical realizations and gloomy epiphanies that lead to unprecedented states of enlightenment. It is not a state of having "given up." It is a cleansing, a purging, a process of inner transformation of intention, moral integrity, balance, a purification. While this spiritual crisis is usually temporary, its gifts may endure for a long time. A depression, however, is more a self-centered cluster of ego-based entanglements, colliding with delusional, temporal self-concepts. When a depression ends, not much has really changed, on an essential level. From the

Dark Night of the Soul emerges a sovereign life, re-born into the experience of liberation ... Spiritually awakened to the fact that it is cherished, guided, protected, and loved by the Beloved Creator of all. A gentle breeze carries the sweet fragrance of dawn's mist into the cocoon of this new being and caresses the faceless face of this beautiful ethereal butterfly that chose to manifest a transformed life.

The evolution of consciousness, moving from personal into transpersonal and transcendent realities, is hard work. Our energetic investment in the ceaseless pursuit of knowledge of the True Self, is respectfully referred to in mystical circles as "The Great Work." Our efforts pay off in priceless gems of ancient wisdom that help us navigate the torrential rain of innocent tears, adjusting our sails to survive the journey. Some try to sidestep the hard work of the Realization of the True Self. In order to accomplish the state of "ceasing to exist," one must first accept there is nothing to accomplish. That was the hardest thing to grasp for me. We already are everything we need to be. Sometimes our suffering is our offering to the spirit of change. Either we tear down the conditioning of former limiting constructs or contribute to our own suffering and the suffering of every life we touch.

Charity as Medicine – In my research for my upcoming book, SLEEPLESS: Transcend The Fear Of Sleep Paralysis, my studies revealed mystical remedies to manage the unspeakable horror of being seized by this mysterious paralysis that occurs upon drifting in and out of dream state. The sleep disorder, Sleep Paralysis, is a phenomenon which tends to occur around scenarios involving diverse traditions of spiritual warfare. One of the most powerful practices is self-healing by administering aid to the needy through loving-kindness in the form of charity. It is a spiritual cleansing of accumulated residue of negative energy left behind by the spiritual neglect of self and others ... All of the guilt, all of the pain ... All manner of disturbances of character. Charity is a life-altering formula that contributes to the healing of grief.

It is an honor to be given the opportunity to be an element of the healing process of another. It is one of the most powerful and sacred self-healing and self-redeeming practices that exist. The rescuing superhero that renders spiritual healing and comfort does not just come bearing gifts. They give from a reservoir of the Limitless Light of the collective energies that contribute to a restoral of the consciousness of faith, as well as the reaffirmation of humanity and dignity. An energetic offering, as a ray of Light, blesses every life it touches. To give from the compassionate stirrings of pure spirit is beyond moral obligation, altruism, and lofty offerings from the shade of some elite or superior status.

The way to restore meaning and purpose in life is to dedicate yourself to loving others. Devote yourself to your community and devote yourself to creating something that gives you purpose and meaning … Something bigger than your personal self. There is no other way, but the Namaste way ... The Spirit I AM honors the I AM Spirit of you. Place not your faith in flesh, not even that of your own physical self.

There is no refuge in form.

He is Eternal, having no birth,
for everyone who has birth will perish.
He is unbegotten, having no beginning;
for everyone who has a beginning has an end.
Since no one rules over him, he has no name,
for whoever has a name is the creation of another.

~ The Upanishads ~

Beyond the Veil of Turiya ... Beyond the Dark Night of the Soul

Turiya (Sanskrit) is the exalted Fourth State of Pure Consciousness, demonstrated on the diagram of the sacred symbol of the OM/AUM. From the dawn of time, enlightened beings have savored its ecstatic flavor, attainable by the common seeker, as spiritual ecstasy. There are many names for this coveted, transcendent state of consciousness. Every spiritual practice, religious path, language, and culture has a word to describe it, especially the language and culture of silence. Nirvana, Samadhi, Satori, Bliss, Spiritual Enlightenment, Fanaa, and others by many other names, are all states of the temporary union of human consciousness with/as Divine Essence.

The Fourth State, Turiya, smiles just behind the ripped off veil that separates it from the lower realms of consciousness. At some point, their energies spill over, one into the other, to find that they can peacefully coexist ... The illusory realms of Maya and her maddening, egoic, identity-based consciousness, with the Unknowable Realms of Divinity.

All that is not our True Self is dissolved, as an ice cube dissolves in a warm glass of water. I overuse this metaphor, and I am aware of that. I have heard many Zen/Advaita Meditation Teachers make the "ice cube" reference again and again. I never tire of hearing it, and I use it as a visual meditation/visualization ... The melting of ego. That is the ultimate meditation experience, when all that is not who we really are begins to gently melt away, exposing the Light of our True Self. I can't think of a better way to understand the simplicity of the process than that visualization. There are two manifestations of the same element in different forms ... One solid and the other liquid. Under certain conditions, the solid form can change to liquid, and given certain conditions, the liquid form can change to solid.

Even if they did not like each other, even if they do not acknowledge one another … That would not change the fact that they are one and the same.

Another metaphor, in an attempt to communicate states associated with the energies, would be the relationship between a wave and an ocean. Does the wave rise up in independence, arrogance, and 'otherness' from the sea? When it falls back into the sea, has it lost, or has it, in some way, failed in its brilliant stand as an independent wave? I don't think so. Nor has it died or in any way ceased to exist. I only know what I felt. I only know what my research turned up to identify associated states of consciousness. The common connecting thread is that our own cold, apparently solid, hard, form, energetically melts into the Divine Self, and the Divine State of Being, in the Realm of the Absolute. All of the vain imaginations and false identities … Even the question of a purpose for being … Even an attachment to, or remembering of, the phenomenon of the experience of Turiya. It has neither Form nor Emptiness. Scientists have described it as a hypo-metabolic state of "restful alertness." It is experienced as a state of transcendent ecstasy. In this blissful state, all personhood falls away, and the "me" experiences itself as the True Self, realizing the pure state of knowledge and bliss. Thus, he is freed from desire, delusion, and duality in the external world. Turiya is the threshold of temporary state-less union with the Realm of the Divine Self. Do not fall into despair over the dissolving … Alchemical reunion of the like elements of Divinity. Rise in this State of Turiya consciousness into liberation and live life as an answered prayer.

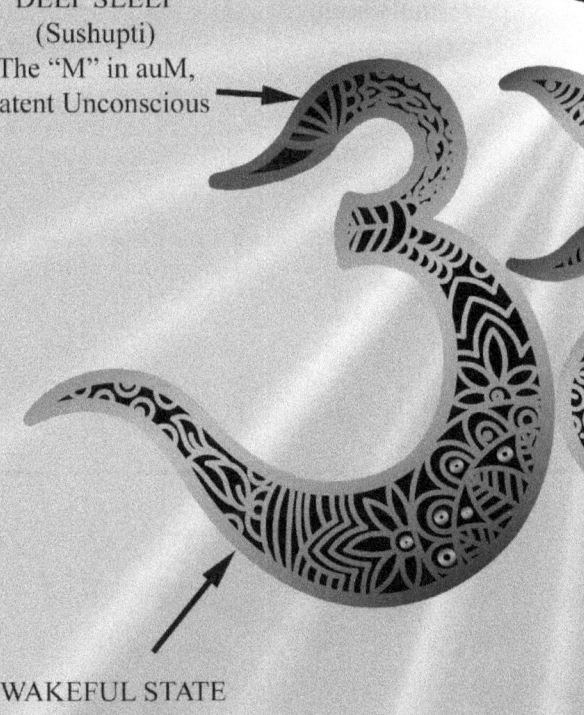

The Meaning of Bindi

- The word Bindi is derived from the Sanskrit word "Bindu," meaning dot or point.

- In certain spiritual cultures, a Bindi is worn on the forehead, at the focal point of an important energy vortex, the Third Eye, or Anja Chakra.

- The Third Eye is a gateway to higher states of consciousness and self-realization.

- In the Sacred OM/AUM symbol, the Bindu represents the Turiya state - Absolute Consciousness, the blissful state of silence which comes after the OM/AUM.

- It is the realm of Union with the Absolute.

- All things are born from the Bindu and merge back into the Bindu. It is a little dot from which all vast, infinite, and mystical existence begins, is unified, and returns to.

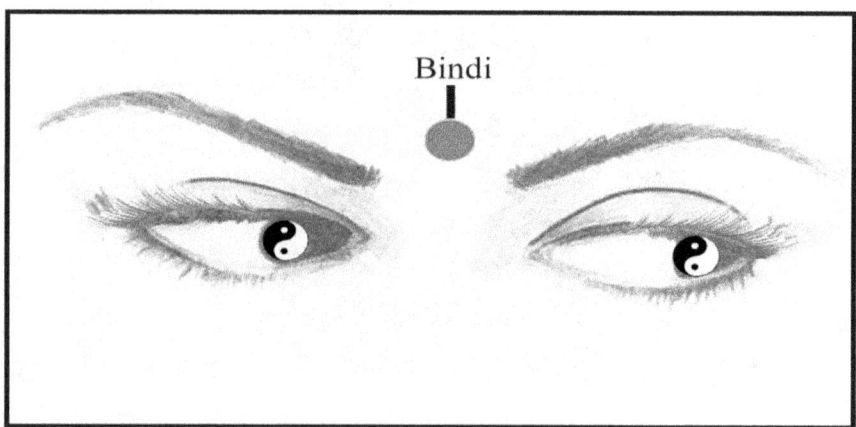

The Bindi is a dot or piece of jewelry associated with the Third Eye and is worn as a talisman to ward off bad luck.

What is the Meaning of Union?

Preparation for this union involves the shedding of layers and layers of attachment, repulsion, ego body/mind identification, ignorance, and fear. Yet, there is no escape from these false identities, except to know that there is *nothing* to escape. As our consciousness expands to accept the ebb and flow of transcendent realities, we find ourselves beyond 'this' or 'that,' 'either, or' dualistic thinking … and we are free. On our earthly journey, after all of the words … Hope, Light, Truth, even Love … There … NO, *here* in the Silence of the Self-Illuminating, Triple Darkness, is Turiya. The experience of the realm of Divinity can occur spontaneously, or due to the practice of Transcendental, Kabalistic/Tree of Life meditations, and are capable of sparking the experience of a full awakening. From Self-Inquiry to Self-Realization, our every moment could be spent in states of transcendent consciousnesses.

It descends like a thief in the night, like the cool mist at dawn … But this is no thief, for it bears the gifts of awakening. This is no ordinary mist … It is like the 'cool water misters' in hot climates around shopping malls and sidewalk cafes … But, spiked with things like DMT. These subtle states of consciousness are commonly sparked or enabled by some sort of sadhana spiritual practice, or some traumatic experience. However, this profound spiritual experience can, and does, occur spontaneously … A sense of Unity with the Beloved that Rumi talks about, that Dervishes spin into, that churchgoers pray into, that Yogis and Monks meditate into.

Turiya can be experienced in:

- Waking State as 'Waking-Turiya';
- Dream State;

- Deep Sleep States as 'Sleep-Turiya';
- The state between waking and sleep states are 'Transitional-Turiya.'

I did nothing. I just laid there. What happened was not a prayer. It was not a meditation. There was no preparation or expectations. The experience was not initiated by me as any sadhana or spiritual practice ... No opening lines, memorized language, or protocol. It was an honest conversation between creation and Creator. I had no go-to practice in place for such an occasion. I had consciously put aside both Guided and Vipassana (Clear Insight), preparing to switch to Metta (Loving Kindness), because I felt I had seen too much. Something happened that night. I remember losing several hours. I went through the motions I would characterize as "waking up" and announcing to myself, "I'm back." I couldn't figure out where I had been. Lucid Dreams and Sleep Paralysis are not strangers to me, Nightmares either. This was different. This was a state beyond states, not anything I had ever experienced.

I am sharing many mysterious terms, concepts, and words that were once unfamiliar to me, as though I have found the Holy Grail. Much of what has become my lifestyle is not of my tradition or culture of origin. I followed a spiritual guidance and resonance that led me to paths of healing through Mystical Meditation. These are only the humble ramblings of someone who is in dedicated pursuit of this redemptive magic. I said from the beginning that I am nobody's teacher. I am pointing to things that were pointed out to me. Those pointings worked for me and improved the quality of my life experience. I was just blessed to have been forced to go on a journey of consciousness that would change my life. I took notes. This book represents my "notes." Now I am blessed with the opportunity to share these stories of a soul's survival with others, who may be touched and hopefully encouraged by it. We will all have something to survive in this life. The sharing of these stories is a sacred healing.

We are time-bound beings who only compromise the true quality of our lives by failing to understand and accept responsibility for the temporal nature of our reality. The only way to win is to strip away all that is not who we really are … and Love what's left. Rise in Love with the changeless.

> *"Who YOU are cannot be touched by time;*
> *water cannot wet it;*
> *wind cannot dry it;*
> *weapons cannot shatter it;*
> *fire cannot burn it.*
> *It is ancient,*
> *it's unborn,*
> *and it does not know death."*
>
> *~ Bhagavad Gita ~*

Turiya Meditation

Who am I?
Why am I even here?
Where am I from … Really?
I AM beyond the veil between worlds
I AM beyond the threshold of Maya, The Illusory World
I AM in this world but not of this world
I AM the Unknowable Fourth State

I suspend my senses
I go within.

I cannot be understood intellectually
I can only be understood by direct experience
I can communicate with you by direct transmission
I AM Pure Consciousness
I AM Pure and present awareness
I express the nature of Absolute Reality
I AM beyond thought

I suspend my senses
I go within.

I AM beyond concept
I AM beyond floating as buoyant energy waves
I AM beyond pulsing in the rhythmic heartbeat of all creation
I AM beyond vibration
I AM beyond the misty, ethereal quality of dew on petals of a rose at dawn
I AM beyond the crown of my energy center at the top of my head
I AM beyond the footprints my weary feet have left behind me
in the sands of time

I suspend my senses
I go within.

I AM before the word 'surrender' …
Before there was anything to surrender to
I AM One with Creator and all creation in this surrender
I AM beyond having to explain what is happening to me, even to myself.
I will Google it tomorrow
I AM not attached to being right or more
I AM the deepest level of relaxation
I AM the deepest level of sleep

I suspend my senses
I go within.

I AM a braided loop of wakeful awareness, deep sleep states, and transcendence
I AM my undeterminable vast energy field
I AM my alert state of consciousness
I AM my ethereal dreamtime awareness
I AM the Realm of Transcendent Truth
I AM beyond desire … Beyond the absence of desire
I AM Zero-Point thought state, acute perception, expressionless thought

I suspend my senses
I go within.

I AM the Witness/Observer perspective of infinite reality
There is no "me" … The idea of "me" disappears
There is no "I" … The idea of "I" disappears
I AM the air element, weightless, spacious, witness of passing clouds.
I remain the sky
I AM wax, melting form,
shapeshifting into a molten renunciation of illusion
No past
No future

I suspend my senses
I go within.

No story
No attachment
No aversion
No time … No space
No memory
No Cause or Effect

I suspend my senses
I go within.

I AM
Not produced
Not born
Not perishable
Without agenda
I cannot be described in language
only felt in sensations of Timeless dreaming
immersed in Consciousness of Peace

I suspend my senses
I go within.

Awareness surrenders to Divine Time
question it or rationalize it … and it disappears
This surrender feels like an In-Body-Experience
Normal activities take place in this "state"
There is no particular condition
This sensation does not belong to us
This event cannot be controlled
only accepted as grace
from a "Now" that does not belong to us
the breathless breath of the Fourth Moment

I suspend my senses
I go within.

I am one with THAT, right here, right now,
in and out of Time and Space!
I am one with THAT!

There is an audio version of the Turiya Meditation available for download at dreamuniversalmedia.com

My personal experience of a Turiya, or Turiya-like state, was spontaneous. When I was finally able to shake it off, there was a period of lost non-local time … Minutes … hours … From that perspective, it was all the same. The one who transitioned into that experience was not the same one that emerged, with renewed Light on the other side of it.

Related States of Consciousness:

In my meditation practice and studies, I have experienced many phenomenal states of consciousness. The Turiya-like experience I had eclipsed them all. It was consistent with descriptions of Turiya in my research, yet, had elements of each of the following states of consciousness, that I have experienced before:

- *Samadhi* – Perfect union of the individualized soul with Infinite Spirit. A state of Oneness; complete absorption.

- *Moksha* – Sanskrit reference to emancipation, liberation, and release from the bondage of samsara. Samsara is a Sanskrit term that refers to wandering the world and all of its cyclical changes as it swings in a circular pendulum, between concepts of life and death. Moksha is the freedom from ignorance. It is Self-Realization, transmigration of the soul, the realm of the cyclical nature of all life, matter, and existence, the extinction of all concepts and identity, and the subsequent state of bliss.

- *Fanaa* – (Arabic: extinction, annihilation, destruction) slain in the spirit, absorption. I have experienced this feeling, and there are no words to describe it. It is the disintegration of a person's narrow self-concept, social self, and limited intellect (feeling like a drop of water aware of being part of the ocean). The highest manifestation of fanaa is reached when the consciousness of having attained fanaa disappears, along with any ego-attachment of recognition for having accomplished it. This state is also called *Fanaa fit Tawheed* (Extinction with the unity), *Sair illallah* (Extinction of the Self in God) is considered one of the important phases of mystical experience, and is attained by the grace of God, by a traveler on the mystical path. The person becomes extinct in the Will of the Divine One. This is what the Sufis call "the passing-away of passing-away" (*fanaa al-fanaa*). The mystic is now wrapped in contemplation of the Divine Essence. It is the purification and intoxication of spirit. It is the Union with the Divine that Rumi speaks of in the experiencing of the ritual of the Whirling Dervishes.

- *Sacchidananda* – Sanskrit word referencing the extinction of all concepts and identity, and the subsequent state of bliss, or nirvana. It is known by many names, from many different traditions; Satori, Kensho, Moksha, Paradise, Fanaa, Samadhi. *Ananda* means Eternal, Timeless **bliss**, or happiness. It refers to a transcendent state of consciousness in which identifications are shifted from personal body/mind reality to more subtle manifestations of reality. Some of the residual effects of this experience are the renunciation of base levels of unskillful actions, the release of guilt from repentance, the experience of forgiveness, and total submission to Divine Will.

- *Self-Inquiry* – According to Sri Ramana Maharshi, happiness is within, and can be known only through discovering one's True Self. He proposes that "Ananda" can be attained by inner Inquiry, using the thought "Who am I? Technique" of self-witnessing, observing the personal self, and contemplating the nature of the True Self, as the observer. After it is determined by self-witnessing what one is NOT, True Self-Discovery can yield a direct experience of the Unknowable … The Indescribable. The neurotic clinging to false identities, and the suffering false narratives cause, make the Awakening worth the trauma of experiencing The Dark Night of the Soul. We ask the question, "Who am I?" … Until all that we are not, dances in the ashes of our Awakening … And the questioner disappears.

- *Turiyatita* – The term 'Turiyatita' was given by Ramana Maharshi. He said that from a higher perspective, Turiya actually IS Turiyatita because Turiya is not merely a state of consciousness among other states but rather the natural state of the Self that permeates *all* of the other states. He said that only Turiya is real, and the waking, dreaming, and deep sleep states are unreal because they appear and disappear.

- *Dhyana* – Sanskrit word meaning; contemplation, reflection, and profound, abstract and mystical paths of meditation. Imaginative vision, wisdom, reasoning, and rhyme yield an incredible amount of power. Dhyana refers to "sustained attention" and the "application of mind to the chosen point of concentration." If the concentration was on one object, Dhyana is non-judgmental, non-presumptuous observation of that object. If the focus was on a concept/idea, Dhyana is contemplating that concept/idea in all its aspects, forms, and consequences. Dhyana is an uninterrupted train of thought, a current of cognition, the flow of awareness.

- *Shunyata/Emptiness/Void* – Shunyata is the ultimate medicine. Emptiness is the antidote for all poisons and defilement of the True Self. It is the medicine that cures the diseases of hatred and anger. The experience of Shunyata is not limited to the sterile consciousness laboratory of a Zendo or Ashram. One does not have to live a life of renunciation to prepare a proper energy field for this state of consciousness to arise in. It is where "As Above" meets "So Below." It is the Ultimate Merging of Creator and Creation. For the full experience, one must be resilient enough to remain in the Maya (illusory world) in order to make one's self available to help other beings.

- *Yoga Nidra (Sleep Yoga)* – is a meditative state of consciousness between waking and sleeping. The body is completely relaxed as the meditator follows a sequence of verbal instructions given by an experienced teacher in a guided meditation. The energetic matrix of the inner consciousness is guided to redirect awareness from a focal point to a conscious withdrawal of the five senses, with the only active sense (hearing) enabled to receive and follow instructions. The experience of samadhi is common in Yoga Nidra meditation practice, though it is commonly recommended as a remedy for sleep disturbances, particularly insomnia.

- *Slain in the Spirit* – this state of consciousness qualifies as a state beyond states, while some of its qualities parallel the Turiya experience. During an experience of being "slain in the spirit," the individual is not conscious, in an ordinary sense. This transcendent force field has been known to literally knock down a person who has NO belief system to support that it can even happen. Slain in the Spirit is a term used by Pentecostal and charismatic Christians to describe this form of prostration, occurring spontaneously at the effect of various triggers, or in some cases, there is no apparent trigger. An individual, and in some cases, many individuals may fall to the ground. This phenomenon is attributed to the power of The Holy Spirit and is an element of Faith Healing prayer services for illness and spiritual disturbances.

    This mystifying phenomenon has an electrical quality that invisibly sparks and releases a powerful force which disables the subject on contact. This volatile force triggers the energetic extraction of personal qualities and replaces them with an energy so overwhelming that the person collapses to the floor, exhibiting a total loss of control and in an altered state of consciousness. In some cases, people have been rendered completely unconscious. In some cases, there is notable trembling, crying, shaking, laughing, even violent verbal outbursts … Each experience is unique. The phenomenon of being "Slain in the Spirit" is not confined to religious events. It has happened under other conditions and circumstances, even as one prays in total seclusion. There is no denying a no-brainer reality … When a force with powers attributed to The God contacts human flesh, there will be manifestations of its quantum significance in the life of that person.

Many of these states of consciousness can occur just as intentionally as the conditioned fantasy that there will *always* be someone there for you. There is something so Divine about us that all we have to do is connect with the Source of that energy within our own selves … Rise up into it … And merge as Oneness with All There Is. The sensations associated with the transcendent experience of Turiya present without any effort, ritual, or particular sadhana (spiritual practice) in place. Unlike a Kundalini Awakening, this spontaneous state of consciousness visits gently and apparently compassionately. It will not change what happened that caused the disconnect. It doesn't have to. It will not "fix" anything. Nothing is broken. It will not make the threatening cause of the painful feelings disappear. After Self-Realization, there is no threat made against the True Self that can prosper. There is no injury that the Realized Self cannot survive. The self that cannot recover is not real.

Reincarnation

Reincarnation refers to the re-embodiment of the soul as a non-physical entity through as many physical manifestations as are necessary to complete its mission. Generally, there is a reason; unfinished business, spiritual development issues, Karmic conditions, a strong desire and attachment to the physical world, or to loved ones left behind.

I have personally experienced many manifestations of reincarnation. I cannot prove it by the standards of its skeptics. However, the standards of its opponents have no significance in the face of the undeniable accounts of so many who feel they have a knowledge of it that goes beyond philosophical belief. Many respected mainstream studies conclude there is sufficient evidence to justify its consideration. I believe that every rip in the curtain of my reality is well worth the shock and amazement to discover what I experienced to be a deeper truth. I have no doubt that reincarnation is a possibility in the realms of the big picture of the journey of our nonperishable being. While I am grateful for these experiences, I did not find healing based on the contemplation of past or future lives as I coped with my grief. To track down the transmigration of my mother's soul would not have served to heal me. I have realized the value of staying in the now.

The wheel of fortune perpetually spins through the dizzying cycles of birth and death. We can get distracted by the carnal drama, or we can accept that our primary objective is to *evolve and get off* of this ever-spinning wheel of life, death, and rebirth. Time does not see the cycles of life and death in the same context as we see it. It knows it is not real. Even if we do not know, it knows that we are Timeless. We may develop personal attachments, but time views the transmigration of the soul in its myriad changes of form, without attachment, as each form seeks the realization of its destiny in its own unique way. Who we really are is unchanging. Who we really are is beyond the construct of time, and has little regard for the Karmic drama we engage, life after life, until we finally realize that the intention of our Higher Self is to be identified as the True Self. The identification with the body as the Real Self is a fatal distraction. This seeing is from the perspective of the Timeless Now. Right here, right now, is all we have and all we are, an eternal, formless being of luminous consciousness. That we ever incarnate and get to live one life in a physical form is a miracle, not to mention considering that we may get to do it more than once.

The news of rebirth may bring comfort to someone who is caught up in the throes of the fear of death or grief over the thought of the loss of self or loved ones. There are credible accounts that support the likelihood of reincarnation, and I think it is a fascinating study. I will not bore you with my personal accounts, not based upon belief but firmly anchored in the knowledge that reincarnation is very real. That can be both the good and the bad news.

To fixate on the subject of reincarnation is a distraction from the experience of our true identity. We become distracted by how many bodies of experience we were contained in and begin to cling and fall into attachment. Our mission is to free ourselves from the bondage of this type of Karmic residue.

Sanskrit terms, samsaras, or samskaras, also called vasanas, speak of the marks and stains left over from the theater of life lived as the unrealized self. This Karmic residue, formed from past, present, and future life experiences, manifests in the physical and non-physical world. Samskaras can manifest as inner personality and will rise up in the outer circumstances of our lives. They occur as conscious and subconscious, latent root tendencies, behavioral inclinations, and conditioning. They are seeds planted that remain in the field of consciousness that is us life after life. You don't plant corn and get wheat. If the seeds were poison, our lives bear the fruit of a poison tree.

Self-Realization occurs as this dream we are breathing becomes recognized as a nightmare of changes, and the conscious choice is made to awaken from it. With this awakening, we seek to release the 'personal' self from the Wheel of Dharma (life/death continuum), free from needless suffering, and remain as the True Self. The Eternal Self longs to be free of future incarnations. It finds itself in diapers again and again, back to complete the karma we refuse to burn to ash in this life. The realization of the True Self is the destruction of the building materials, the bricks, required to construct a new structure to imprison a spirit that has not remembered it is free. The bricks are the attachments to the illusions of this world. When we free ourselves from these attachments, aversions, habits, and false identifications, we supply no more bricks for the construction of yet another physical form for the housebuilder to invite us into. As we evolve in consciousness, the stage play, along with all of its drama, no longer has appeal. We are able to train the mind to transcend the wheel of dharma, the circle of life, through Mystical Meditation and spiritual practice.

Dharma is a Sanskrit term that refers to a 'right way of living' on the path that leads to our true destiny. It is that path that builds honorable character and sustains an ethical life, as free of negative karma as possible. There are many ways to free ourselves of energetic attachments so that we may act on behalf of the ultimate good of our Realized Self. Our desire to live from that place of freedom ignites a fire that melts samskaras or self-defeating tendencies … burns them, dissolves them, sweeps them away, drowns them in a sea of forgetfulness, buries them beside all of the other traps the ego sets for our distraction. A preoccupation with the transmigration of the soul from body to body allows the egoic mind to continue its incessant demands for attention.

*Seeking but not finding
the house builder,
I have traveled through the round
of countless births.
How painful is birth over and over again.
Oh, house builder!
You have now been caught!
You shall not build a house again.
Your rafters have been broken.
Your ridgepole demolished.
The unconditioned consciousness
has been attained.
And every kind of craving
has been destroyed.'*

(Dhammapāda, verses 153,154)

~ Buddha ~

Near Death Experience (NDE)

Worthy of mention on the subject of death is a phenomenon called the Near-Death Experience (NDE). I see it as further testimony to the fact that we do not die. We only change form and dimension. In Near Death Experiences, glimpses of the afterlife are possible. People who have experienced this phenomenon generally report having been pronounced dead and subsequently returning their consciousness to the body vehicle. They have strikingly similar stories to tell, yet each one is quite unique.

My mother had a Near Death Experience in childbirth that I shared in the opening chapter of this book. Some of my earliest memories were of her telling me that I was never to fear death because she had been there and done that … and it was beautiful. She told me of a tunnel, a warm, brilliant Light, and beautiful beings that she could not manage to describe according to earthly characteristics. She described the stunning colors of their flowing robes. She said they stood on either side of the long path she was traveling forward on with their arms outstretched, welcoming her. She told me of beautiful colors, ethereal music, lush meadows, a shimmering lake, and rivers. She told me she was given a choice to stay there or go back to her life. She did not want to come back here. She said she knew she had been to a place that some called heaven. She said she came back to be my mother.

My Mother reported having come back "different" … a completely changed person. She returned with an extraordinary gift of effortless intuition. She had become overwhelmed with helping others in tireless service and was not the self-involved person she was before. She had no prior knowledge of the accounts of others who had experienced this phenomenon, or of the documented scientific studies that had been conducted on the subject. She did not even know what to call it and had no prior information on the subject that could have influenced a parallel story. It wasn't until many years into my adulthood that I had become exposed to many of the high-profile authors, scientists, and so many people who shared credible reports of having had the same experience. I confronted her with a line of questioning to determine for myself if what she had experienced could be the same. There were certain things that even she did not understand about what had happened to her. For example, I asked her how she could have witnessed my father's phone call to his sister to tell her that the baby was fine, but that his wife had died … if she was in the operating room dead with a sheet over her face. Quite annoyed and confused, she kept saying that she didn't know how … all she knew was that it happened. I asked her, "From what perspective did this witnessing occur?" Her response was, "From above, as though I was floating. I could see everything. I saw my body. I floated out of the operating room and into the hallway above the phone. I heard everything. Then I went someplace else … like no place I've ever seen before. It was so beautiful." There was a peaceful, faraway look in her eyes every time she talked about it that I will never forget.

Some who have had a Near Death Experience share that character specific deities of the Earth Plane are, in many cases, conspicuously absent on the Astral Plane. This suggests that the boundaries of Earth Plane religions can be transcended. One common denominator seems to be some form of prayer. I have also heard reports that many people of varied spiritual paths did view deities and congregations which reflected their earthly belief system. That may suggest that many have the experience that they expected to have and found resonance with like frequencies. That speaks of the freedom and power we possess to manifest our thoughts and desires, creating the reality that we choose to experience.

When our body of Ether emerges from our body of clay, it retains thoughts, consciousness, and a remembrance of the ego-based identity of the physical self. We carry with us our memories of all that we have learned and all that we have loved from all of the lives we have lived. Just as we carry with us the love, we often carry hatred that has touched our earthly lives. That is why it is important to purge and heal the energies of hatred and aversion on this Plane before we transcend, or we will take this heaviness with us.

As our body of Ether, we have the freedom to travel anywhere in our conscious Universe with only the thought of being there, much like in a lucid dream or out-of-body astral projection. In a somewhat more permanent sense, we experience this freedom at the time of our transition or death to this Plane and rebirth into the next.

It is commonly believed that beings on other Planes of existence will intervene and contribute to our lives more often than we may choose to believe. Some are specifically commissioned to help us throughout our time. A "familiar" may choose to take a personal interest in some of us and make themselves available to console and guide us. Many traditions have their own *Book of the Dead* based on the mystical process of transition out of form into formlessness, according to cultural beliefs. It is not a morbid study. It is fascinating and comforting.

Ego-Annihilation

The guided meditation, *I Transcend My Ego Self*, is a haunting refrain sung from the song of the Timeless Now. Remaining in the context of the Timeless Now does not support seeking to glorify the physical existence beyond its relevance to our journey. Our focus is more on the contained rather than how many containers are required to complete the mission. Reincarnation addresses the perpetual rise and demise of physical forms. The study of the I AM, our True Self, is the study of that formless Essence which journeys. The awakening to it is the study of it. To hold that awareness of Self is to keep our energies focused on the here and now.

Life on both sides of the veil between the physical and non-physical realms offers us a braided path that will wind, twist, and turn in ways impossible to predict or prove. A natural reflex is to resist change. All change ultimately serves our highest good. All change comes with its own unique set of challenges. One of our greatest challenges is to relax and trust in the infinite wisdom of the Universe. What brings us peace amidst the changes is to focus on the changeless Self that we are. Go there and stay there … not just for meditation, but for liberation from the bondage of self-sabotaging cursory identities that blind us to who we really are. We may struggle to hold to the focal point of the I AM consciousness, no past, no future, no story, no self.

If we seek to accomplish the release of physical body identification in this incarnation, we must not seek to find other bodies from the past and future to distract ourselves from our true identity as formless consciousness. Reincarnation is the pouring of the water of consciousness into many cups. Self-Realization is pouring the water from the many cups into the stream that takes it all the way to the Sea of Eternity.

We dance across the stage of Leela, a projection of shadows in the Divine play God is dreaming as us. We embrace the alluring beauty of Maya, the realm of illusion, until we forget who we are ... drifting away into states of amnesia, wearing the smile of blissful ignorance. As our spirit becomes weighed down by the samskaras of many realities gone by, we long for Oneness with our Source, and we choose to find our way back home. We welcome the wisdom and opportunity to experience ourselves as our True Self ... Faceless.

At this point, we will rip off the masks and observe what is behind them until we disappear to illusions of identity. The most direct route to accomplish that is through a committed practice of meditation. We will embrace the sacred Law of Impermanence through meditation on the most essential level of Self, peeling off layers of identity until we reach pure consciousness, the version of our Self that is Eternal.

It was the common denominator of meditation that secured my survival of the most devastating loss of my life. After my mother passed away, it seemed as though my groundless footsteps were guided by unseen forces. Fate would lead me to experience states of heightened consciousness, sparked by the visions and insights of ancient mystical practices and traditions. This broken-winged student was ready, and so many profoundly adept teachers appeared, and I thank them. They scooped me up and sat me down in a Timeless, placeless place ... The stillness of the Frequency of The Timeless Now. Each tradition shared with me their sacred medicine, each with its own unique message of healing that I am blessed to enjoy sharing with you.

Buddha was asked,
"What have you gained from meditation? He replied,
"Nothing. However, I lost ... Anger, Anxiety,
Depression, Insecurity, Fear of Old Age and Death."

The Stilling of the Mind

As we turn our attention inward, focusing on the breath of the present moment, we peel away our mental energy from all mundane drama and chaos. We have the power to train our attention to go to where we direct it. Our soul, our spirit, the perfect being in each one of us, is waiting to be invited back into our lives, waiting to be restored to peace of mind. The mind can be as noisy as it is fickle. There are many styles of meditation that can silence mental chatter.

Claims that are made in this text are from an experiential perspective only. I can only share experiences that I, myself, have personally had. If a path of meditation is not mentioned here or covered in depth, it is because I have not personally experienced that path. Every spiritual or religious path I can think of, has many different expressions of stilling of the mind in meditation. The meditation may vary in practice, but breath connects them all.

Some styles of meditation work through the practice (sadhana) of Pranayama (mindfulness and control of breath); the chanting of mantras (internal and external sound vibration); and the use of Mudras (prescribed hand and full-body postures and movements that help strengthen and direct energy). *Sadhana* refers to ego-transcending spiritual practices that are used as a means of accomplishing some specific work. These ancient Sanskrit terms are references to the specifics of practices that deepen the experience of the many realms of consciousness accessible through meditation. The objective is to evoke the experience of the Planes of existence where spiritual work is performed most powerfully.

Meditation is a spiritual journey reconnecting us with our essential nature, although in a western cultural context, it is practiced more as a technique for relaxation and stress management. We are constantly bombarded with stress from work, family pressures, environmental conditions, and poor diet and lifestyle choices. Consequently, it is vital to manage our stress levels and control our anxiety triggers to enjoy a healthy, productive life. Meditation takes our energy from unfocused activity into stillness, offering our bodies an opportunity to restore our energy and repair themselves from our abuses.

Rest is how the *body* heals itself from the damage done by tension-filled, toxic environments, and the fatigue associated with managing our pressure-cooker lifestyles. *Meditation* is how our *Spirit* heals itself and dissolves the energetic blocks that prevent us from living empowered lives. Because it is so difficult to stop our thoughts from taking us out of the present moment, we sit down, breathe consciously, close our eyes, and find our focal point. This focal point can be our breath, an elemental image, or a mantra … something that brings our focus effortlessly back to the stillness, whenever we realize we've drifted away.

There are many cultures and spiritual traditions that respect the benefits of a meditation practice. Many have corresponding spiritual and ritual disciplines. In my pursuit of a resonant path of meditation instruction and practice, I found the quest alone to be intriguing and rewarding. I learned something from every discipline I studied and documented my journey.

I had no context for the emotional or physical healing benefits of meditation. After my mother passed away, I crossed many paths, and many paths crossed me. So many called out to me to help show me ways to survive the loss of her. There is one thing they all have in common … a strict meditation discipline. I am not a teacher or an expert on the paths I mention in this text, nor am I a representative propagating for any of them. As a journal of my emotional survival, I share some of my experiences with diverse mystical traditions, as a survival guide for others who seek comfort and healing.

Christian meditation traditions range from total immersion in prayer, to a powerful form of meditation involving the contemplation and reading or chanting of Biblical scriptures. There are as many types of Christian meditation practices as there are types of Christianity. The memorization and repetition of certain Bible verses and expressions is a meditation practice among some on Christian-based mystical paths. Meditation occurs in the same spirit as a sincere and undistracted prayer or a heartfelt song of praise and deliverance. There are forms of meditation practice that can produce a wide spectrum of associated phenomena, such as;

- Glossolalia - Slain in the Spirit. Speaking in Tongues;
- Spiritual Attack;
- Spiritual Cleansing;
- Faith/Energy Healings causing spontaneous remission;
- Intercessory prayer as a form of petition made on behalf of others;
- Meditation states triggered by sacred scriptures;
- Direct Experience of, or Intervention by The Holy Spirit, called by many names;
- Music can trigger and deepen meditation, creating a clearing for emotional healing.

Rather than redirecting certain aspects of consciousness, some Christian meditation practices inspire engagement of the most intimate sort and direct experience with Divinity, touched by The Holy Spirit. It has been witnessed and observed that an experience like that manifests as a profound change in the life of the experiencer. No one has "THE" answer regarding any "belief system," and it is pure vanity even to make such a claim. The experience of meditation, in many Christian teachings, involves The Holy Spirit and is of the Realm of the Unknowable. Faith is the most reliable witness of these mystic encounters, as they are consistently associated with a wide range of ecstatic feelings and expressions of bliss, transcendence, liberation, nirvana. It may be difficult to explain the unexplainable, even to ourselves.

I have been told that the objective of Christian meditation is to connect with The Holy Spirit, without being distracted by the phenomenal nature of its many manifestations. The intention is beyond the intoxicating experience of euphoric states of consciousness. The objective is to strengthen and purify a sacred, personal relationship with The Divine One. As our consciousness expands, it reveals that our relationship with Divinity is based on complete surrender and union in the One Love of The God Essence. Even though various paths involve certain meditation paraphernalia and practice, it seems not to be second to prayer nor equated with it. I have observed a very thin, blurred line between the two.

The Sufi tradition is well-known for its Mystical Meditation practices, from repetitive prayer and chanting to the whirling of the dervishes. Prescribed prayers and scriptures are repeated, often counted with prayer beads in a practice called Zikr (Dhikr), the remembrance of The God. It is considered a spiritually sophisticated meditation practice of the highest order, directing and redirecting healing energy that sometimes involves drums, music, chanting, and movement. It is believed to open a portal or door that reveals the "Face of The God." Every experience of it is unique.

The withdrawal from sensual experience into the ego-less, identity-less Self is the awakening to the deeper understanding of our Divine nature. Full Awakening is the awareness of the eventual ceasing of all the mind's identifications with being personified ego. Abiding in, and living from that awareness, is the realization that the True Self and the Most High Supreme Being are One.

I am inspired by the spirit of ***Shirdi Sai Baba***, an Indian Guru, Yogi, and Fakir. I greatly admire his efforts to bridge the gaping chasm that divided Hindu and Islamic paths. He was regarded by his Hindu and Muslim devotees as a Saint, Sadhguru, an enlightened Sufi Pir, or a Qutub. The focal point of his life was Self-Realization. In his meditation practice, he is known to have entered Samadhi at will. Samadhi is a highly-concentrated, transcendent meditative state of pure consciousness.

The philosophy and practice of Self-Inquiry, as taught by Sri Ramana Maharshi, is a technique of Self-Witnessing, observing the personal self, and contemplating the nature of the True Self, as the observer. Then this Self-Examination or Self-Witnessing moves on to contemplate: Can the observer be observed? Who/What observes the observer? Can That be observed? To follow that line of questioning and reasoning will lead to the Ultimate Meditation on the Divine Oneness. It is universal in its concept and application. It is inclusively relevant to all countries, all religious backgrounds, and all cultures. It is not easy to stand naked, stripped of egoic identity, before the imageless mirror of this perpetual meditation. The meditation and contemplation on the question, "Who am I?" is perpetual because it is only natural for traces of clinging and attachment to form and personhood persist ... whispering stories of its emptiness, asking, "Who am I?" This profound introspection and meditation, ultimately reaches all the way back to formless Origin, as we learn to embrace, both our personhood and Divinity, with Love. We ask the question until the question disappears. We ask the question until the questioner disappears, into silence, without judgment.

The philosophy and practice of Yoga is about more than bodies contorting into pretzel shapes. Even though I do not choose to confuse my spiritual path with focusing on individuated, personified deities, I have found certain yogic meditation practices that are monotheistic and can be a source of healing for people of all faiths. *Yoga* is a Sanskrit word that means the union of the body, mind, and spirit, and has the mystical effect of offering the experience of higher dimensions, beyond name and form. Using ancient, sophisticated meditation techniques, calmness of mind, and control over the senses gives access to the metaphysical experience of the transcendent Self.

Kriya Yoga is an ancient Mystical Meditation technique that was lost for centuries, resurrected, and passed down in a contemporary version to Paramahansa Yogananda (1/5/1893 – 2/7/1952.) He was chosen by spiritual lineage of four venerable meditation masters to bring this practice to the West, where it would be offered to the world. He founded the Self-Realization Fellowship in 1920 and authored the acclaimed book, The Autobiography of a Yogi, among many others.

The science of Kriya Yoga is the basis of Yogananda's teachings. The Sanskrit root of Kriya is Kri, to do, to act, and react. When practiced correctly, Kriya Yoga can empower the typical activities of the heart, lungs, and nervous system to slow down naturally. The stillness of the mind that results is the Frequency of the Natural Mystic. A dedicated meditation practice has been scientifically proven to directly affect and expand human consciousness.

Certain meditation practices raise a spiritual energy known as Kundalini, which symbolically rests as a dormant snake coiled at the base of the spine. It "rises" up the spine through the seven energy centers of the human body, known as chakras. Such meditation practices can produce an unpredictable outcome. This form of meditation should be practiced with applied study, caution, and spiritual discernment. It can provide a powerful cleansing and a heightened state of enlightenment, even a complete spiritual awakening. If not performed under correct guidance, Spiritual Emergencies can occur.

On the cover of my book, FEARLESS: PSYCHIC SELF-DEFENSE, there is a column of seven beautifully colored spheres. Each sphere represents one of the chakras of the seven-level Chakra Energy System (see diagram). It aligns with our spinal column from the base, up through the Crown at the top of the head. As the Kundalini Life Force energy rises, it cleanses each vortex, one chakra at a time. Some have experienced an energetic blowout that rushes like a bolt of lightning from the base of the spine, all the way up, and out of the Crown Chakra at the top of the head. After a blast like that, I halted my studies for a few years, until I could get back my nerve to continue. I had been studying the Tree of Life and had an "aha" moment. I guess I got as emotional as if I'd found the Holy Grail. I fell asleep and was awakened by what felt like a blast of electricity shooting up from the base of my spine, out through the top of my head. I shook for twenty minutes. After determining that the cause was not physical, I began my research and connected the two events.

I know now that certain Kundalini studies and practices should be done in a controlled environment, under the supervision and guidance of an instructor who is fully aware of how to handle a Spiritual Emergency. I don't believe that the episode I experienced would have happened the same way if I had been more diligent and studious with regards to the ground-level understanding of that kind of knowledge. I would have understood the implications of a spontaneous Kundalini Awakening and possibly known what to do about it. I still enjoy the study of the Tree of Life and understand that it has profound relevance to Mystical Meditation and healing. That same alarming surge of electrical energy can progressively sandblast our force field, causing our Light body to fully engage its healing and defense systems.

Some disciplines of meditation should be approached with exacting prudence. Though it is exceptional, there is evidence that certain forms of meditation can trigger unpleasant and even dangerous experiences. Some people have suffered emotional, psychological, and physical symptoms, even events extending to psychotic episodes, particularly if the person was, in some way, challenged in the first place. It is unwise to tempt these rare but real side-effects by seeking the independent experience of rogue meditation practices without prior knowledge and correct guidance. Challenges in the realm of mental or emotional issues, especially in cases of chronic or acute depression, can be an indicator that meditation should be approached with caution. In such cases, it is always best to consult a spiritual, psychological, and medical professional before beginning certain disciplines of meditation.

The practice of meditation conjures positive emotions, silences inner chatter, calms and stills the mind, and even provides some of the beneficial effects of sleep. The positive effects will show up in our actions, deeds, and relationships with self and others. Without this retreat of mind, it is difficult to remain completely focused, centered, grounded, and in touch with the most essential nature of the Self. It is a spiritual imperative to maintain a healthy energetic balance, to keep from being overwhelmed by the energy of high-tech, pressure cooker cultures that can scatter our positive energy to the winds of neurosis.

Meditation allows us to experience our true nature as changeless reality. We can rise above distraction and habitual patterns. We can step into its realms, and its realms are revealed within us. It has a cleansing, cathartic effect that can provide spiritual healing from the repression and frustrations of material existence. It is helpful in dealing with issues of grief, anxiety, tension, and physical pain, in a world promoting an agenda of pill-popping drug dependence as a cure for every condition.

Vipassana is a secular, experiential path of meditation that instructs in scientific techniques that purify the mind and Third Eye vision with the goal of ending suffering. Its roots extend back over 2,500 years, to the enlightenment of the Buddha. S.N. Goenka established the Vipassana Research Institute in 1959, on his mission to bring the Vipassana meditation practice to the West. The dogma-free practice offered at Vipassana Meditation Retreat centers all over the world appeal to every language, culture, and religion.

Vipassana means "to see things as they really are." Seeing things as they really are requires the soberest of minds, free of any type of consciousness-altering substance. This technique of meditation does not make claims of physical healing, though that is what my experience was when I did the ten-day meditation retreat. I had been in a car accident that left me with permanent nerve damage. When I arrived at the retreat site, I had every imaginable type of apparatus to manage my pain. By the third day, I had no need for any of them. By the tenth day, my life had changed in so many ways.

Meditation does not exclusively refer to a single concept or path. There are as many paths as there are meditators. Meditation can occur within the framework of stillness, movement, bliss, mind-melting grief, walking, running, sitting, or lying down. There is no specific way that represents spiritual correctness. It is what we say it is. My primary stipulation is that meditation must be grounded and firmly rooted in the unadulterated Essence of the Creator, with no associated deities, god forms, or graven images introduced into the equation. At best, all images are mere opinions. Spiritual Law of Hierarchy would command one to go all the way to the top, to the Creator of Universes yet to be born of Its glory, from the Realm of the Unknowable. All forms are perishable, consumed in the fire of formless reality. A worst-case scenario can land an innocent soul in a danger zone, from which there may be no exit.

The primary benefit some seek to experience through meditation is a sense of liberation from life and death. This conscious, deliberate striving is always within the limits of a conditioned mind, and in this, there is no freedom. The value of meditation is more about tuning *in*, rather than tuning *out*. The point is missed when it is used as a form of escapism. It is a way to bring Light into the container of the physical 'self,' not necessarily to escape from the container. We must remain grateful that we were given the gift of borrowing the manifestation of this form, for the purpose of experiencing.

In a speech before the United Nations, S.N. Goenka shared that his goal was to offer a spiritually sovereign choice as to how we experience our existence. For this successful businessman, born in Burma to a wealthy family, it began with debilitating migraine headaches, for which he could find no medical relief. He learned of a Vipassana meditation teacher, Sayagyi U Ba Khin. After his ten-day intensive, he was never troubled with migraines again.

After experiencing release from his suffering through his Vipassana practice, he dedicated his life to sharing this ancient, life-affirming, healing meditation practice with the world. This technique offers an elevated observer's perspective of mindful self-witnessing that overrules the drama in the noisy theater of the reactive mind. We are able to objectively view the ever-changing nature of the dance of mind, body, and spirit at its most profound level. We access profound self-knowledge, untainted by judgment.

This process of thought monitoring, scanning for reactive sensations, and objective observation (self-witnessing) is the inception of major change that can manifest a life that is happy, free, peaceful, and sovereign. We become able to transcend conditioning that would hold our lives in bondage to the disquieting demands of the conscious and subconscious mind. It is only human to experience ourselves relentlessly wrestling with the manipulations of our emotional triggers. We have Free Will and are free to choose, but we are *not* free of the self-destructive energetic consequences of choices we make in willful blindness.

I am not a representative of the Vipassana Research Center, nor am I propagating on behalf of them. I am only sharing a much-valued experience that I was blessed to receive. It is my understanding that they do not advertise. This ten-day course is not a business, religion, or cult. It is not for sale. There is no price tag, unstated agendas, or manipulations. Donations are accepted to keep the course free of charge. The volunteering of services is greatly appreciated and rewarded by knowing that these efforts keep the course available to everyone interested, regardless of their ability to pay.

It matters not if we whirl in circles, sit in lotus position, chant, dance with drums around an open fire, or turn off the television and the vast sea of electronics, and just "be." What matters is that we know that the disease of our obsession with form finds healing in our embrace of the formless. The Fourth Moment is that sacred place outside of time … outside of the Three Moments of "Past, Present, and Future." The Fourth Moment is the spaceless space between them. It is the Moment from which all is propelled. It is as impossible to describe as the space between seconds, between breaths, between Planes. It does not exist in "time." It cannot be known, only experienced … The Fourth Moment is Vipassana. What matters is that, in all of our strivings, we strive most to praise and serve That Essence of our Origin, the One Creator of all things and all realms.

The mystical Rastafarian culture, spiritual practice, and mindset cannot be reduced to an "ism," or religion. It is a frequency. It is not something that can be turned on and off like a light switch. It is not an energy that can be contained in a structure or sacred scripture, it moves of its own accord. It is a Spirit that connects human and cosmic vibration ... The OM/AUM, the frequency of the Natural Mystic. It either adapts all within its vast reach to that frequency or neutralizes it with dismissive indifference. It does not require "belief." We do not "believe" in the earth, air, fire, or water. We have *experienced* them, and that visceral knowledge has created within us a "knowing." That knowing evokes feelings. Feelings evoke and invoke the energies required for mystical practice. Those who feel, practice. Those who practice, feel. The physical self and the spiritual Self are inextricably connected to one another. Practice is the determiner and identifier, not the label.

I was blessed to have lived in a Rastafarian influenced culture for many years. During those years, I was fortunate to have been a guest at Nyabinghi meditation and healing ceremonies, known as groundations/grounations. Nyabinghi is the oldest and strictest of the Twelve Mansions (tribes) of Rastafari. I did not participate with the intent to gather research or write about the experience. I think that disrespects the sacredness of the ceremony unless permission is requested and granted. I do not represent myself as an authority, even on the subtleties of my own experience. Only a true Rasta can offer a description of an experience of the sacred place in consciousness they go to. I was just happy to have been invited. Even though I was always treated with love and respect, I smile and say, "They don't want me!" No one has ever argued with me about that. I was not compliant with their strict code of ceremonial conduct ... from proper attire, all the way down to the fact that I was not even a vegetarian at the time. I was lucky they even let me in. Someone was kind enough to bring fabric to cover or cloak guests whose attire was not appropriate for the occasion.

The term 'Groundation' is used to describe an event that stirs an affirmation of life that raises a cone of power and intention, up from the core of the Earth, and the core of our being, to the onyx, diamond-studded sky. Gatherings of Rastas are held in what is called a Tabernacle, a circular, palm-covered Divinely-ordained ritual structure for prayer, meditation, chanting, reasoning, and healing. These gatherings are not always so formal. I have seen spontaneous assemblies occur in very informal settings, like someone's backyard, when the spirit of 'reasoning' rises up in the rhythm of the Nyabinghi drum.

The flame's flicker, and the sound of the crackling wood in the semi-open-air, thatched roof Tabernacle were hypnotic. Sparks appeared to dance to the rhythm of the drums of my ancestors … Ancestors, my mother had just joined. Mesmerizing, spellbinding, Nyabinghi drum rhythms, resonant with the heartbeat, mingled with thick clouds of smoke laced with prayer, rising to the heavens.

I could feel my mother's energy there in that Tabernacle. I could feel the energy of Queen Nyabinghi there, elegantly whirling around in the smoky haze and aroma of fragrant incense and herbs. The crisp mountain breeze carried dense, billowing clouds of smoke and prayer, all the way to the inception of manifestation. The catalyst is Faith. The seal is Surrender. The vibration is a positive force of commanding energy intensifying with the chant, the mantra, the words of power, and One Love. The melodic voice of the Rasta Priest would rise and fall in intensity, as he chanted Psalms 91 from the Bible, pacing slowly, rhythmically around the bonfire.

Undulating waves of energy rose and peaked as a cone of power, healing everything in its path. The thunder of the drums shook the ground underfoot, pulsating, reverberating, joining the rhythm of the beat of my own heart, sending ripples in every direction on a shoreless sea of consciousness.

After the ceremony, I researched the compelling history of Queen Nyabinghi, who is referred to as the "Queen of Queens" and the "Queen of Kings."

The oral traditions report fascinating, and often conflicting, mystical stories of the warrior Queen Nyabinghi. She is said to be synonymous with the immortal spirit of ancient Egyptian solar goddess, Sekhmet. Whenever and wherever oppression and injustice have taken hold, and the people suffer, the spirit of Sekhmet will manifest on the physical Plane, in some form.

The haunting energies present at that Tabernacle made me want to know more. The more I researched, the more confused I got. The sequential lives, rebirths, and possessions attributed to Queen Nyabinghi were difficult to trace with such conflicting references and time frames. Legend claims that the spirit of this African Priestess originated in the Amazon. This dreadlocked lioness is believed to *still* engage in dialogues with her chosen tribe, who are imbued with her supernatural powers. It is alleged that possessions *still* continue to occur. Her immortal spirit is born again out of the ashes of apparent defeat and ignites the fires of freedom, where tyranny and oppression prevail. It occurs to me that Sekhmet, as a healer and a warrior, is from the Archetypal Realm. As demands for freedom and liberation from oppression rise, she is born again. She is a harsh answer to a cry for freedom. She could turn up anywhere, in any timeframe, on any mission. For example;

In the 1700s, a warrior Queen named Kitami of a province of Upper Kush Northern Africa (Ethiopia-Egypt) originally possessed a sacred drum, infused with mystical healing and spiritual powers. The magic associated with that drum evolved into what is now known as Nyabinghi heartbeat rhythms, with their ascribed powers of manifestation. Her all-female tribe, known as the Bagirwa, were defenders of freedom from all forms of oppression. The majority of them were traditional healers. Men, dressed as females, were eventually accepted as Bagirwa. In later years, the belief in exclusion of males became less restrictive, and the first Nyabinghi Priests came into existence. When she died, she was given the status of immortality and named Nyabinghi. Her devotees live by the Nyabinghi Code of Livity (lifestyle) that she left behind.

The story gets more complicated and interesting, as some report that Queen Nyabinghi's husband, envious King of an enemy tribe, sought to usurp her power in a coup and take control of her kingdom. He had her killed, and it is said that her spirit haunted him and his stolen kingdom, for years after she passed away.

Then, there was medicine woman Nyabinghi-Muhumusa, a brave and terrifying charismatic healer in the late 19th and early 20th century, from Northern Uganda. It is said that Nyabinghi-Muhumusa collapsed to the ground, and rose up possessed by the spirit of Queen Nyabinghi. She inspired a mystical resistance movement, the first to fight against the exploitation and tyrannical domination of European colonialism. She said that she would "turn their bullets into water." The colonialists were so afraid of her spiritual powers that they introduced the Witchcraft Act of 1912, which outlawed practicing non-orthodox spirituality, by their standard.

These are all myths, stories, and legends, stemming from oral traditions that were difficult to authenticate, particularly because of the deep mysticism and transmigration of her powerful energy spanning over many lifetimes. Though specifics of the accounts may differ slightly, the essential truth remains, that the spirit of warrior Queen Nyabinghi, Mystic High Priestess, is a powerful symbol of sovereign self-determination, that seems to skip and jump magical timelines. Nyabinghi grew to represent the call and drum roll for freedom, as the spiritual attention of Rastafarians of Jamaica, West Indies, turned to that region in cultural alignment, in allegiance to His Majesty Emperor Haile Selassie I of Ethiopia. The Rastafarians of Jamaica were inspired by the hypnotic drumming, the chanting of incantations, prayers, meditations, and the traditional declaration of the victory of good over evil every time. The name of the Jamaican born, human rights advocate and political leader, the Honorable Marcus Mosiah Garvey, and the invocation of the Nyabinghi Frequency, sealed the mandate for freedom and presented a mirror of moral superiority reflecting the inevitable coming change. A mystical healing rose up from the ashes of the virulent colonization in the Caribbean Islands, primarily in Jamaica in the early 1900s.

With so much of her history revolving around her bravery through war, resistance, occupation, and political upheaval, it is important to note that "Binghi" stands for righteous action, thoughts, and words, with a non-violent principle. They do not promote or believe in violence, for only the Creator has the right to destroy. She is not a warmonger. Nyabinghi is said to love all of humanity.

The symbolic ritual burning of Babylon is a remarkable piece of the Rastafarian's mysterious cultural puzzle. The Groundation/Chant Down is a traditional practice that addresses the vanity and insanity of materialism, consumerism, energy-draining, brainwashing, spirit-deadening, mind-controlling, cultural graveyards, that we call lives. Babylon is not a place. It is a spirit and a mindset. Babylon is a consciousness. Babylon is in the mirror, the scariest of all places that an enemy could be, especially in the times we now live.

"Know Your Enemy."

~ Sun Tzu ~

"And God said "Love Your Enemy," and I obeyed Him and loved myself."

~ Khalil Gibran ~

The "burning of Babylon" refers to the use of the Holy Chalice, the Sacred Drums, the Chant, the Elemental Commands, and the Prayer. The chalice, according to mystical standards, is a "portable" altar, wherein earth, air, fire, and water elements are a part of the meditation and chanting. The chalice is made out of a coconut. Some Rastas believe in the spiritual and medicinal use of ganja (herb, cannabis), a plant that was introduced into the Caribbean by the Spaniards and smoked or ingested as a sacrament by the Sadhus, the devout mystics of India.

The chalice is used as a catalyst to facilitate a heightened frequency or vibration, strengthening the power of a firm meditation. From the gutted coconut, smoke from the burning of ritually consecrated ganja is pulled from the "Kochi" through a straw-like device. It is *inhaled* with an *intention* to be manifested and *exhaled* in a banishing of all obstacles to that intention.

I learned from a Rasta Elder that the use of ganja as a sacrament in meditation tunes the meditator in to a precise frequency. After that frequency is experienced, it is a matter of choice, whether or not to use it, because to feel it is to know and become it. Once the frequency has been experienced, regardless of the method used, your meditation practice *will* evolve. Your consciousness can find its way back to, and even expand on, the understanding that you will be able to get there on your own without the use of any consciousness-altering substance.

I neither condone or condemn, encourage or promote the use of legal, illegal, or recreational cannabis. The laws are changing in various places around the world to reflect the findings of scientific research. It has been scientifically proven to be *medicine*, administered in various ways, to all age groups, for the successful treatment of many chronic, even life-threatening conditions. At this point, it is not possible to have an intelligent argument against it nor a judgment that is not, in some way, control-based. The bogus nature of the tactical "reefer madness" agenda, is laced with the underlying intention of maligning and destroying a substance that carries the potential to shift energetic frequencies and inspire autonomy of consciousness, self-determination, and spiritual freedom.

My philosophy, in this regard, is to leave the spiritual practices of others alone. Live and let live, with an emphasis on the God-given gift of Free Will. That having been expressed, the fact is, if you did not grow it from a seed that you trust with your life, you do not know what you are inhaling or ingesting. The pharmaceutical industry has its essence in its clutches. It is being highly processed and poisoned with deadly and addictive chemicals. It is being manufactured in synthetic form, with all of the accompanying dangerous, even deadly side-effects. And, yes, I believe cannabis can be used as a drug, with all of the accompanying addiction drama, in much the same manner as an addictive personality uses sugar, coffee, alcohol, food, sex, technology, and a long list of other things one can use in a self-destructive manner. It is a sacred plant and must not be defiled in production or practice.

I am, in no way, trying to represent myself as an expert on anything outside of my own authentic experience. So, if I am not an expert, what am I talking about? I am the only one that can be the authority of my personal (and transpersonal) experiences. The soul-crushing vice of grief interrupted the flow of my profoundly superficial life, forcing me into the depths of obsession with the study of human consciousness, just to survive. As I'm sure you have gathered, I was all over the place, like an acid trip, I've been told. Everything I had studied for decades revealed its purpose and relevance to the spiritual journey I thought I was already on.

I didn't realize that I would end up seated on a cushion, facing a blank wall, more centered than I have ever experienced being. Tragedy has a way of changing the subject. In my case, away from all that is transient, toward all that is permanent … 'nothing.' Beyond all concepts of the radiant triple darkness of primordial Essence, out of which, and back into which, Ultimate Beauty dissolves form, transcends intellect, and defies description … We must come face to face with our own shallowness to be able to face our own true depth.

Before triple darkness, between the utterance of, or experience of the Fourth Moment, before I AM, beyond all that is Unknowable, came Light, in sparks and beams. There, in the breathless, spaceless spaces … after the peeling back of every delusion of 'otherness,' us vs. them, this or that, duality consciousness … there is Oneness in the silence of knowing the Unknowable and becoming it. There is only One Love, One Tribe, Oneness with, and as, Divinity.

Traditional and non-traditional Mystical Meditation and sacred ceremonial practices, of every spiritual path I had meandered through on the way to nothing, merged as some form of core singularity. The path of the Rastafarians parallels many of the Indigenous tribes that I am familiar with.

Shaman – refers to the tribal High Priestess or Priest, called by many names in diverse cultures worldwide, among them; Healer, Medicine Man/Woman, Bush Doctor, Kahuna, Babalawo/Iyanifa. The mystical practice of Shamanism is Timeless, with diverse roots in most ancient cultural traditions. In its modern manifestations, a gifted Shaman has the spiritual expertise to journey through the subtle realms, to be a conduit, through which a healing may manifest in the physical world. These healers can bring about a balance in the case of illness of mind, body or spirit, and create change in the lives of individuals, families, tribes, even nations.

Some are born with this gift. Some are selected to study their entire lives. Binary gender references are inappropriate when describing many of these remarkable people. Some of the First Nation tribes do not accept the limitations of body-based descriptions that do not recognize the spirit as being beyond gender. Some recognize as many as five genders. A Shaman operates beyond the

Time/Space continuum, where gender is not relevant. Alchemy at certain levels of Mysticism is strengthened by gender plurality.

There is nothing typical or ordinary about a Shaman though they tend to be humble and unassuming. Often entering a trance state during ritual healings, their mystical skill set is undeterminable by our standards, only by the results of their manifestations. They are a bridge between worlds. Seek instruction from a well-vetted teacher of the tradition you feel a resonance with before mixing traditions and unadvisedly practicing without a teacher or a coach.

Smudging – refers to the use of a smudge wand (sage, cedar, sweetgrass, rosemary, thyme, among others). In preparation for rites of purification for prayer and meditation, light your wand without using matches because of the alchemy of sulfur. Clearing your space can be done with incense. Smudging is a form of prayer and should always be offered before any kind of spiritual work. It is believed that smoke from the burning herbs carries prayers to the Great Spirit.

Prayer – refers to a being's complete surrender of personal identity in an experience of synthesis with the shared Essence of Divinity/Source. Essence is shown here with an initial capital 'E' indicating the complexity, yet utter simplicity of our own relationship with, and as, the shared Essence of The God, whatever that means to you.

There are all types of prayer, formal and informal. Prayer causes an eventual loss of personhood ... the melting into the Ultimate Stillness, the fixed focus, the breath, the peace. The bliss that results is real. There are as many ways to pray as there are people who pray, and each individual and every tribe has its own tradition. My general observation of indigenous prayer traditions is that *everything* is regarded as a sacred prayer.

Drums, Flutes, Chanting, Dance – Music is prayer. The Shaman's drum has spiritual power when used by an intermediary. It is a catalyst to the experience of the bliss of "self"lessness. On a journey through the spirit world, the music of the Shaman authenticates the Shaman's prayer, the Shaman's power, and the Shaman's soul, as a healer in the parallels of this ailing world. Consistent among the many diverse Indigenous tribes, sound, vibration, and energetic changes can alter states of consciousness. Some of my favorite artists are Levi Chen, Joaquin Montoya, and Gabrielle Roth.

Dreamcatcher – As casually as the term, and its use, the Dreamcatcher is a prayer and blessing born of sacred ritual. It is traditionally made for children who suffer from nightmares, Sleep Paralysis, or Lucid/OBE (Out of Body Experiences) Dreaming. Its circular frame is crafted with Intention, using organic wood and intricate netting that resembles the web of a spider. The center or eye of the Dreamcatcher is ritually opened (blessed or consecrated) and activated using Shamanic powers.

The mesh captures the energies of the bad dreams, allowing only the peaceful dreams to pass through. It is suspended above the bed, over the head of the sleeping child/person. Many Indigenous sacred ceremonial symbols and paraphernalia are commonly used for interior home decoration, swinging from car rearview mirrors, jewelry, body and commercial art, mascots for sports teams. It is important to know the difference between casual decoration and adornment and unintentional blasphemy.

Medicine Bags – A medicine bag is a small pouch, worn underneath the clothing, with prescribed contents, differing from tribe to tribe. They are worn as a blessing, for spiritual protection, and physical, emotional, and mental healing. A medicine bag is treated as sacred. The fabric and contents depend on the purpose and intention of the work. The contents may include blessed, consecrated objects of sentimental value, sacred herbs, texts, or semi-precious stones and crystals that are specific to the set spiritual intention.

Medicine bags for grief may contain, but are not limited to:

- Silk Pouch with Drawstring;
- Copies of Prayers;
- Palo Santo;
- Rose;
- Sage;
- Sweetgrass;
- Incense Ash (Three Kings Incense, Frankincense, Myrrh, and Benzoin);
- Lavender;
- Yerba Buena;
- Rose Quartz crystal;
- Salt.

A medicine bag should not be opened or handled by anyone other than the owner of it, or the Shaman that consecrated it. As a part of a healing, the medicine bag can further empower and protect the human energy field, where the seed of every manner of illness takes root and manifests as disease of the body, mind, and soul. Spiritual healings have been known to send some of the most serious maladies into spontaneous remission. The medicine bag is used to anchor the healing energies as the condition stabilizes.

Dreamtime – references are most commonly associated with the mysticism of Indigenous Aborigines of Australia (The Dreaming), making striking parallels to the beliefs of the Indigenous peoples of the Americas. The concept of "Dreamtime," its interpretation and practice may dramatically differ, from one tribe or nation, even from one person, to another.

As preoccupied as we are with our differences, one thing we undoubtedly share is that *everyone* dreams, consciously or unconsciously. Two people can enter the sleeping state, locked in an intimate embrace, and it would be highly unusual for them to find themselves in an equally intimate place in consciousness, at the same time. Why? Dreamtime explores the qualities of the non-physical realms of existence. It is the ultimate journey through the formless, intangible, ethereal realms of the Archetypes, the ancestors, the unmanifested world of the spirit realm of the unborn … fluidly transitioning back and forth between all of them.

The Dreaming knows nothing of the "beginning" of physical birth, or the "end," physical death. It is believed that a spirit incarnates by entering the fetus during human gestation, and certainly survives death.

Through song and dance, rhythm and ritual, this sacred philosophy mystically cuts through the veil of illusory reality, moving through time and Timeless, infinite, and ephemeral. The profound philosophy of Dreamtime blurs the lines between death and regeneration to reveal hidden aspects of the Unknowable.

Journeying – is a term used to describe intentionally entering into an altered state of consciousness (Dreamtime) to affirm the Oneness of our relationship with Divinity. It reveals our inner potential to heal ourselves and one another from spiritual, emotional, mental, or physical illness.

A "Journey" can have an unpredictable outcome. A Vision may occur, and prophetic information may be revealed in a Journeying session. The right question can operate like an interdimensional door, revealing prophetic information. It is risky to attempt Journeying alone without instruction and supervision. Out of Body experiences and incidents of bi-location have been known to occur, depending on the type of work being done. It is important to consider that when Shamanic plant materials are introduced, it is required they be administered by an authentic, trusted, and experienced Shaman.

Limpia – is from Latin and Spanish origin, referring to 'cleaning.' It also applies to the ritual of Spiritual Cleansing in the tradition of Shamanism or Curanderismo. It is believed to remove blockages to the energy flow of the Chakra System. A Limpia is done to remove negative energy from the energy field of someone who is suffering from a projection of toxic intentions, sometimes thick enough to cut with a knife. Just because you cannot see it does not mean it is not there.

It is believed to cleanse the mind, body, and spirit, removing malevolent thought-form projections, create a reversal of bad fortune, dispel bad vibrations, and heal emotional attacks at their source. Limpia rituals may or may not involve plant spirits and sacred herbs.

Inipi Sweat Lodge – The Sweat Lodge is a Temple of Prayer. The Sweat Lodge of the Lakota tribe is called Inipi, which means to "live again." Any form of 'brokenness' is healed in these ceremonies. These ritual meditations assist in restoring balance to the True Self from the effects of trauma, grief, and many physical maladies. It is one form of a Vision Quest that provides the spiritual environment for many levels of healing. In an Inipi purification ceremony, the seeker is guided to move through the spirit world in humble, sincere prayer, to ground the wisdom and blessings of the ancestors. There is a fire pit in the middle of a structure specifically built for the ritual group meditation. In these regular events, the five elements (fire, water, air, earth, and spirit) are recognized. Prayers draw on the power of the connection between the soul of our perceived self, our Higher Self, and the Source of all creation, the Great Spirit.

I was a novice, motivated by pure curiosity at the time I experienced my first Sweat Lodge ceremony on the sacred grounds of Laie Point, on the beach of the North Shore of Honolulu, Hawaii. A group of friends had peer pressured me into experiencing the ceremony. I initially told them that I had no intention of 'getting mystical.' Herbs with qualities consistent with energetic healing such as sage, cedar, sweetgrass, permeated the gentle sea breeze. The chants of the Lakota Nation Medicine Man greeted everyone as family, and he began to pray. I can't think of much on the face of this Earth that he did not pray for. Most of his prayers were prayers of sincere gratitude to the Great Spirit. Most of the group fell into what appeared to be a trance state. I couldn't recall everything clearly because I was out too. The ambiance was magical.

My friends had a great time laughing at me after it was over when I said I heard drums and had seen large glistening, colorful orbs of light floating around the interior of the structure at the peak of the extreme heat. That would have been undramatic if it were even possible for it to have happened. I was told that no one had experienced that but me. I was so sure of what I thought I had seen that it was difficult to accept that what I had seen and heard were elements of a powerful vision.

As with any spiritual practice that may compromise your physical health, be sure to consult your Doctor or Medical Practitioner first.

Vision Quest – The Vision Quest is an ethereal walk through the Timeless inner and outer Planes of existence. It is a prayerful journey behind the masks of identity we covet. Every indigenous culture has its own purpose for, and practice of, the Vision Quest. Each tribe will call it by the name and purpose they have assigned to it. A sound healing is possible in the case of someone who has been pushed by trauma into an emotional state that causes extreme suffering.

There are spiritual problems that could occur and compromise a person's health on every level of their being. A Shaman accompanies the seeker on their journey through the subtle Planes of consciousness, in case something goes wrong. It would not be a good idea to engage in this practice without the guidance of a trained and knowledgeable Shaman.

As with any spiritual practice that may compromise your physical health, be sure to consult your Doctor or Medical Practitioner first.

Soul Retrieval – Traditional prayer in a Soul Retrieval ritual is the spark that ignites the flame of profound healing. Anyone who has experienced a phenomenon called "soul loss" is a candidate for what is formally known as a Soul Retrieval. Many things can trigger soul loss, fragmentation, and Ego Death conditions. It can occur suddenly in the aftermath of a traumatic event that resulted in severe emotional damage.

After the 'shattering' of the psyche of the individual seeking help, a gifted Shaman may be able to retrieve the broken pieces and return them to their former state, seamlessly. A Spiritual Emergency can trigger a condition called Ego Death, which manifests as a loss of identity, which can be treated and healed in a Soul Retrieval Ceremony.

Peace Pipe Ceremonies – The peace pipe is a prayer. These are sacred occasions wherein vows are made, contracts are sealed, knowledge is transmitted from the spirit world, and healings occur. The pipe, the materials smoked, and the type of rite being performed are specific to the practice of each of the many diverse nations. It can be the confirmation of a treaty between tribes or nations, a business deal, a rite of passage ceremony to mark a young male or female crossing over into adulthood. The ceremony is known to trigger powerful healings. Such a petition for healing is enveloped in prayer, affirmations, and meditations on gratitude for the blessings already received. The petitions and the blessings are two wings of the same bird.

The smoke of the Peace Pipe is believed to rise and directly connect with the "Great Spirit." Tobacco is considered a gift of medicine from the Great Spirit and is smoked in a ceremonial Peace Pipe in spiritual practice, according to traditions specific to diverse indigenous tribes. The smoke is believed to carry love, prayers, meditations, and intentions to the Source of all creation, while the roots penetrate the Earth to consummate the sacred connection.

Pow Wow – A Pow Wow is a ceremonial expression of prayer, meditation, music, and dance. On these occasions, they give thanks for the blessings of abundance in times of peace and prosperity. They pray for victory in times of war; confirm the signing of treaties; acknowledge births and deaths; and celebrate family and tribal unity.

A traditional Pow Wow honors Indigenous cultures and tribal ancestors. It can be a festive occasion, commonly attended by as many as four generations. Often, the public is invited to share in these cultural events and welcomed as family.

Elemental Meditation (Fire, Water, Air, and Earth) – Consistent with most spiritual paths, there are meditations associated with each of the four elements. Each element represents an attribute of our physical Plane existence. There are mystical practices that can, on the most essential level, connect us to each element through shared energies and alchemical resonance. That is the basic principle behind the practice of Elemental Meditation. Meditation begins with the air element in the practice of mindful breathing. More than just the element of air, Prana (Sanskrit word for Life Force) fuels our meditation journey, in the practice of Pranayama.

Every moment of our lives is a cosmic dance between the dominant elements in our natal charts. Our natal report documents the planetary placement and aspects on the day of our birth. The relationship between the complex energies of these planets and their transits can make us predisposed, in many ways, to influences reflected in our birth charts. The fact that we are more than our physical presentation demands that we look deeper. The I AM, our True Self, has no natal chart. The I AM was here before the planets. The I AM is birthless and deathless.

In the practice of medicine in most Western cultures, not much attention is given to the non-physical aspects of illness and disease. When treating clinical depression and grief, too often, prescription drugs are a knee-jerk solution. If the objective is self-healing, one must begin, fully engaged in a loving embrace with the True Self. One must become the bridge connecting with The God directly as the pure Essence of Self … Not the whining, craving, whimpering, demanding creature, so reactive and resistant to change. Annica, the Law of Impermanence, is the bittersweet taste of Change.

Change can be sparked in the Ether and made manifest on the level of the consciousness of the individual. Pain and sorrow come and go. We can keep them from backing us into a corner. Ceremony offers definitive release from the often-indelible stain of psychological and emotional damage. Ancient holistic elemental healing techniques have been known to "treat" almost any condition, independent of contemporary technology. This is not a suggestion to seek alternative healing just to defy modern advances. Educated balance in all things offers great benefit. To show respect when using unfamiliar spiritual and mystical practices, one must seek guidance in every aspect of their tradition of origin.

On the diverse paths of my spiritual adventures, there is one thing that stands out. Among indigenous cultures, the paths are more alike than they are different. What one may call a demon, another person may call an angel. What one calls a jinn, another calls an orisha, a spirit guide, or a visitor from the archetypal kingdom, and countless other manifestations of the Will of the Divine One. The Law of Hierarchy has required me to remember, we did not create ourselves, and petitions should be directed through The God of our highest understanding.

In a global climate of intolerance, it is unwise to deny Free Will of spiritual practice to others or stand in judgment of spirituality that we do not understand. Every path is specific to every pair of feet that travels it. What matters is that the travelers remember their wings. What matters is that the travelers protect their own sovereignty and respect the freedom of others to do the same, remembering that there are no "others" … Only One.

To perform a healing elemental meditation, Air will clear our minds, Earth will keep us grounded, Fire reignites our wounded spirit, and Water cleanses trauma and heals our emotions. In order to incorporate the elements into your daily meditations, we must have a sound relationship with nature and the outdoors. For some, meditating outdoors is a challenge because of changing seasons, weather, or often, apparent danger. The mind often cannot tell the difference between actual nature and a video of nature. An open-eye, guided, elemental meditation, can be performed using a video of the elements at play. Use a video of a waterfall, ocean waves, streams, fountains, mountains, trees, plants, flowers, grass, sky, clouds, space, smoke, sunrise, sunset, fireplace, the flickering of a candle flame.

<u>*Yoruba*</u> – On my personal spiritual journey, ancestors became an issue. I had always known that *something* was "there." I used to say, "I have company," and treated it like a "my invisible friends" joke. I had never known a context for a "spirit" tribal family. In my studies of Yoruba (and its study of me), my understanding that it is not necessarily in conflict with worship of "The" Creator, God of our highest understanding, as long as we go directly to what created all of them and us. The orisha are an impartial pantheon of entities that are hierarchal, yet they are just as much a part of creation as we are.

There is an energetic and elemental context for each one of them and fascinating mythological stories of archetypal love, loss, incredible drama, and unimaginable power. There is also a shared energy field that will display the projections of our "desires" on the big screen of time and existence.

I was given an understanding that, in Light and in shadow, I still stand in the energy field of the mother I mourned the loss of. She has merely taken her place among the ancestors. I realize I am of the Light, as well as the shadow of that world. I realized I could find my balance in that knowing.

I find this often misunderstood mystical tradition relevant to mention because of the intense healing energies that are available through the practice of it. There are rites and rituals very similar to the indigenous practice of "Soul Retrieval" in the event of Ego Death due to trauma, loss, and grief. A Babalawo performs the energy healing ritual as a shared journey through the outer and inner planes of consciousness to restore well-being and balance.

My experience with this path as an initiate and teacher caused me to understand the ancestral realm and its relevance to the spiritual aspects of my life. I knew that the energy of clinging and craving would not bring my mother back into the form of her that I was familiar with. But I knew that it didn't matter. We are, have always been, and will forever be together.

I do not consider myself a practitioner, but I feel blessed to have been made acquainted, so directly, with the spirits of the ancestral and corresponding archetypal realm. I experienced a beautiful resonance, and ancient ancestral bonds between us were realized.

Ho'oponopono – During the many years that I lived in Honolulu, Hawaii, I learned a spirituality that would last me for the rest of my life. At first, I was a committed Bimbo (with a capital B). I was warned about the spiritual consequences of disrespect for the traditions and beliefs in the Hawaiian Islands. I didn't get it. I had placed myself in a familiar environment ... I duplicated the imagery that was familiar to me ... high rise condos and office buildings, fabulous skylines and pristine beaches, shopping malls, suits and ties, and fancy restaurants. I knew nothing of the hundreds of lava-stone temples, heiaus (HEY-ows). I knew nothing of the dwarf size nature spirits who live in the forests of the Hawaiian Islands. I knew nothing of Kahunas (Shamans) or "press down ghosts" that could send a person into a Sleep Paralysis event. I knew nothing of Tutu Pele, the fire goddess.

When I showed up for work one day to find the high-rise office building vacated, I fell into shock and confusion. I asked what had happened. I was told that everyone had gone on a pilgrimage of sorts, to Kilauea, Hale Ma'u Ma'u Crater on the Big Island (HI) to take Gin and flowers to the volcano as an offering to Tutu Pele. I protested, proclaiming that there was work to do and deadlines to meet, and said it was the most unprofessional thing I had ever witnessed in the workplace. The few people left, felt sorry for me because they knew I didn't know, and the group dragged me along with them. On our way up to the crater, in my high-heeled shoes and business suit, I marveled at how everyone truly believed this was necessary. I thought it was hilarious. They thought I was hilarious as well and nicknamed me 'Hollywood.' I offered a nice brand of Gin and called it a vacation day.

When we got to the top of the volcano, I continued my protest, with no understanding as to why any of it was even happening. I said something disrespectful ... in jest (stupid), not with malicious intent. Everyone looked at me and gasped, wide-eyed with fear and panic. The next breath I took was like ice-cold fire that closed my throat and choked me out. I wasn't able to breathe or speak ... I was literally dropped to the ground. They said, "We tried to warn you, and you didn't listen ... Is it funny now?" A single tear rolled down my cheek as I motioned for help. They gathered around me and compassionately prayed, and told me to apologize. Yes, I apologized ... by then, I was quite sorry and certainly more respectful.

That was just the spark that ignited a passionate pursuit of mystical studies in Hawaii. I share this often-practiced ritual called Ho'oponopono, which loosely translates as "Correction." In the Hawaiian Islands, regardless of religious tradition, when there is an unresolved conflict, a Kahuna or tribal Chief will take the parties in conflict to a sacred place for Ho'oponopono, a Hawaiian practice of reconciliation and forgiveness. They are aware of their spiritual healing powers and know that unresolved conflict can poison the waters of that power, inadvertently causing great harm.

That is why they do not let one Sun set on a conflict. We take too much for granted. Because the Sun rose today, does not guarantee that any of us will see it set. Because we see it set tonight does not mean we will ever see it rise again. Between the two phases of rising and setting, there are no promises of anything. The literal meaning of Ho'oponopono, "correction," is almost dismissive in terms, because of its vast range of meaning. Ho'oponopono is an energy field charged with the mana (spiritual energy and healing power) of this ancient Indigenous culture, created to reconcile beings in conflict, who desire to be saved from unnecessary suffering. The four-phrase mantra of Ho'oponopono is:

1) I am sorry.
2) Please forgive me.

3) Thank you.
4) I love you.

Hawaiian Kahunas that practice and teach Ho'oponopono have entered asylums and prisons to treat the criminally insane, who were deemed unlikely to ever be able to live among the general population again. Some of these asylums ultimately had to close down because all of the patients were released to live normal lives. They all struggled with love, loss, betrayal, grief, loneliness, and pain. They all had stories and secrets, excuses, and reasons for having ended up institutionalized. It is important to know that, in times of emotional trauma, loss, and grief, profound spiritual healing is possible.

Cultural Appropriation – is an ongoing conversation among conscious, knowledgeable, respectful people regarding the spiritual practices of many ancient mystical indigenous cultures. It is a common saying, "Imitation is the sincerest form of flattery" … and in researching its origin, it turns out that it didn't end with a period. Oscar Wilde coined the phrase, "Imitation is the sincerest form of flattery that mediocrity can pay to greatness." If someone approaches indigenous spirituality with respect, humility, and courage, accepting instruction and counsel from the hierarchy of the traditional teachings … that is one thing. But, to read a few books, take a few classes, purchase an altar, and dress up to play Shaman is a very, very dangerous thing to do, not to mention playing Shaman at a Halloween party.

On the subject of cultural appropriation, there are thin lines and gray areas that warrant seeking intelligent dialogue, and engaging study of the spiritual traditions of others who might be offended by a perceived disrespect of their culture. It is reasonable to seek to understand sacred symbols and paraphernalia before wearing them as jewelry, home, office, and car decorations. It is important to understand the spiritual significance of, and proper respect for, things like malas (prayer beads) being worn as jewelry, home decorations, and body art … even extending to Halloween costumes and sports mascots. It is generally frowned upon by the spiritually adept of these traditions, both physical and non-physical. Disrespect for the spiritual and mystical protocol of ancient traditions can be very dangerous. You may come up on the radar of entities and energies that no amount of rational resistance will protect you from. They do not die. All of the Psychic Self-Defense in the world may not protect you from the consequences of such a low-frequency behavior and disrespect. Why should the mystical world be any different on issues of diversity? The difference is that in the unseen realms, consequences are guaranteed to be dramatic.

It is difficult to reference any one particular meditation style used by such diverse First Nation tribes because, for all of them, everything is a meditation. Everything is a prayer. Everything is an exercise in mindfulness. Meditation is regarded as a natural method used to transcend the physical Plane to connect with and obtain Divine wisdom. A higher octave of that transcendence is to understand that there is nothing to transcend … There is no separation. There is only One. The Timeless Now is here Now.

The spiritual power unleashed by dance, music, drums, and fire is returning to its rightful place at the global forefront of mystical ritual practice. Though "Rasta" is often mistakenly identified with a hairstyle (dreadlocks), Rasta is not a hairstyle. It is not an excuse to "stay stoned." It is not a "New Age" trend. It is not a Reggae concert. It is ancient, dating back to the origin of the human race on the continent of Africa.

The Gift of Prophecy and Healing is associated with spiritual practice, prayer, fasting, chanting, meditation, strict natural food and vegan diet, and above all, an acceptance of the Divine Will of the Most High. As Frequencies merge, and Voice is audible, the connection is achieved and maintained, unimaginable portals of consciousness become available, and miracles occur. The Voice of the Ultimate Natural Mystic is housed within us, the vessel of The God, referred to as the I in I … the True Self, the I AM.

The Rastafarian's Zen-styled life promotes simplicity and a positive, energetic environment. One element of that is a healthy diet that they call "Ital," which not only means that their diet is vegan, but that it is also organic, free of processed foods, chemicals, and toxins. The curative effects of natural medicinal herbal treatments are preferred over pharmaceuticals. There is a growing scientific community that is not invested in the danger of irresponsible drug dispensation of the healthcare industry. It is becoming well understood that many of the side effects of these drugs are worse than the conditions they are promoted to treat. The pharmaceutical industry is just that, an industry, as invested in blind confidence and dependence as olden day snake oil peddlers. State and Federal laws have begun to bend in favor of legalizing herbal practices, after much organized, vigilant advocacy, and scientific evidence of its healing properties.

It is patently understood that *anything* can be reduced to the level of a drug, with the myriad resulting dependency, addiction, and health issues. Food, in general, has become a growing concern, as it demonstrates the characteristic symptoms associated with drug abuse, addiction, and dependence, with all of the resulting physical, mental, psychological, and even spiritual damage that it causes. These legal drugs are generally accepted as a cultural reality, as the death toll rises, graveyard industries flourish, and the people suffer.

I cannot "teach" you anything. I am a student myself for life. The lifelong impact of grief forced this journey. The gift it offered was experiential insights into powerful methods of energetic self-healing, from many traditions. They work for me and offer relief from some of the most excruciating emotional pain anyone can imagine.

"Problems cannot be solved with the same mindset that created them."

~ Albert Einstein ~

I had no choice but to learn how to navigate through and transcend the emotional mindset that was causing such suffering. I have always experienced an innate resonance and connection with the Natural Mystic ... that inner Voice of transcendent reasoning. I believe that we all have that in common. The Natural Mystic is the Bridge Between Dreams.

The Waking Dream

One cannot speak of meditation and not speak of dreams. Meditation is a portal into the dream time world. The mystical and prophetic nature of the dream world is one of the first signs to human beings of the true complexity of our existence. It is an indicator that there are many other dimensions just as real as the one we perceive to be our own. The portal created through Mystical Meditation is much like the portal that opens itself to us during sleep in dreams. Our subtle body, consciousness, and awareness will pass through this portal into what many refer to as the astral or subtle Planes of existence.

The Astral Plane or world is where dreams occur. It is where we are led in meditation and prayer. It is not a location. It exists here and now. The astral body is just as much our vehicle as our physical body. The astral and physical bodies differ in density, the astral interpenetrating the physical. Among the many manifestations of the astral body, from gross to various levels of refinement, the form we will aspire to experience is most closely associated with Light. Light in this text, with a capital "L," refers to the relationship between our astral essence and the Essence of the Divine One, the Creator of all things.

The realm of the Astral Plane, into dream time, is the home of species of beings too numerous to mention. There are angels made of Light, the jinn(djinn) made of fire, the spirits of those who have died, those awaiting rebirth, the unborn, or those for whom incarnation is not an option. Jinn (djinn) refers to a species of ethereal, elemental beings made of fire, as angels are made of Light. Like us, they have Free Will to choose between good and evil. Their fiery nature predisposes their temperament to be at best mischievous, at worst malevolent. They procreate like, and often, through us. Their kingdom and our world often overlap. They are responsible for much spiritual phenomena we tend to attribute to angels and demons. Events and places, known and unknown, from the beginning of time to endless time, occur in a parallel other-worldly, dream time existence.

Dreams are one of the most common ways of communicating ancient knowledge. Meditation is often referred to as a waking dream. It offers us the blessing of being able to connect with the vision of The Divine One in such a way as to be able to see worlds beyond the capacity of the physical eye, much like in the dream state. It is one way to read and study symbols and signs in such a manner as to obtain knowledge one might miss among the distractions of a wakeful state of consciousness.

It is beneficial to become exposed to, and eventually adept at, the art, science, and gift of meditation. The clarity and quality of our waking dreams can be developed into an effective trigger of visionary insights. Most rules of meditation are not fixed. There are powerful, prescribed methods of Mystical Meditation from many traditions. However, a Mystical Meditation can occur as a spontaneous or episodic waking dream. It can manifest as a vision or epiphany without any intentional attempt to induce it. A Mystical Meditation can occur in a given stilled posture, during a specific movement, and certainly in dreams. The problem with relying on our sleeping dreams alone is that it is not practical at all times to go to sleep to obtain mystical insights or to experience a stilling of the mind.

Mystical Meditation is called a waking dream because we can learn to evoke a dream-like state or vision at will, in a prescribed manner. As we grow in our relationship with the waking dream, we will find the fine line between dimensions of consciousness becoming blurred and less distinct, directly proportionate to our level of comfort and trust. There are no two people who dream exactly the same way. There are no two people who will meditate in exactly the same way.

As our comfort zone expands to allow us to enter a semi-trance state, a common phenomenon may open our receptors to information from the Astral Plane, a Timeless dimension that sees the past, present, and future in the same tense. To tap into all that is available, we must have confidence enough to boldly journey through dimensions or Planes, through realms of eternal life, in the subtle and formless reality beyond dream time.

The Astral Plane is a world or dimension much like our own, lateral to our own, differing in perspective, density, and frequency. Meditation is one of the most effective ways to transcend form and enter this realm. Even higher realms are available through prayer. After much practice and surrender, performing an effective meditation will take on the spirit of intense prayer. Repetitive prayer takes on the energy of total immersion in the Light of Divine.

There are many subtle techniques that we can use to enter the portal of the dream time world within moments. For the best results in the practice of meditation, it is important to experience a Time and Space shift. This is a conscious shift of your attention from the external reality to the inner transcendent Planes. It requires that we go within and shift our perception relative to time and the tenses we have arbitrarily assigned it, extending to vertical rather than horizontal and linear view.

In preparation to safely make this shift, we must first draw around ourselves a shield, a strong protective force field of Divine Light with prayer and visualization. The Light Meditation in this text can help provide this shield of protection. This state of mind can provide a sense of peaceful courage and contribute to a subtle but powerful shift in consciousness. In my book, FEARLESS: PSYCHIC SELF-DEFENSE, we explore many practices that are a prerequisite to safe journeying through other Planes of existence into the ethereal world of our Light body. Spiritual or Psychic Self-Defense is not something that we practice. It must be someone that we are, always in the evolving state of becoming. With time, it will become a comfortable lifestyle that will provide sound spiritual security on our voyage through the many dimensions on the path of the Natural Mystic. We will gracefully dance with time, from one side to the other, and back, on the bridge between dreams.

Planes of Existence

I share here excerpts of the section on Planes of Existence from my book, FEARLESS: PSYCHIC SELF-DEFENSE, because we are exploring the origin of our deep-seated fear of death and related transitory experiences. I maintain that the enemy of our fear is our knowledge. If we understand that our formless Self is not threatened by Anicca, the Law of Impermanence, or death, our fears will dissolve, and a unique type of freedom will take their place. The practice of Mystical Meditation can induce journeying through realms of consciousness we commonly associate with the death process.

The death experience involves the many Planes of existence. Meditation and prayer can take us on an excursion through the Astral Planes, opening gateways to dimensions beyond imagination, promoting healing on many levels. If we open our minds to the meaning of "as above, so below," we will discover the key to understanding what the practice of meditation really involves. The condensation of thought-forms seeking manifestation can cause a precipitation of the best and the worst of energies upon our lives.

We are given meditation and prayer work as tools to catalyze our energy to transcend our own self-made temporal reality, wherein the past, present, and future are as one. We are able to access puzzle pieces of past events and things to come to construct a portrait of life on any Plane of existence. A nonlinear portrait extends beyond present realities and reveals the true significance of time and its relationship with the events of our lives. This vision may reach years into the future to provide glimpses of tomorrow, based on the effects of the choices we are making in the present, or have made in the past.

Of all the fears of matters regarding both sides of the veil between worlds, it is the contemplation of the inevitability of death that challenges our courage the most. One of the most primal of all fears is our fear of not existing anymore … of just disappearing. Knowing that there are many Planes and forms of existence can serve to assure us of the fact that *we do not die*. It will give us comfort to contemplate and consider what death really is.

One simple way to demonstrate the way a relationship between Planes operates is to make two fists, placing the left *above* and the right *below*. The left fist represents the bird's eye view of our world from the Astral Plane. Its position offers the advantage of viewing all events in what we distinguish as the past, present, and future. The right fist represents our world of matter. It moves in a continuous circular motion. We are moving with the right fist, trapped in the life/death continuum. We perceive the experience of a distinct past and future, without the conscious ability to see an outcome until it has occurred within our linear framework of present time.

Planes of existence are not to be viewed as locations above, below, or beside one another. The Astral Plane and its inhabitants exist just beyond our fixed perceptions and parallel to the Earth Plane, as demonstrated by the left fist. This perspective offers an objective overview of life, death, and time. The past, present, and future are clearly seen as fluid or occurring *simultaneously*. The perception of life and death is seen as a mere transition from one Plane to the next, or death to one Plane and birth into another, upon the release of the physical vessel.

There is in-depth literature readily available, offering a journey into the world of spirit. The inhabitants of the Astral Plane are much like those of the Earth Plane. Some are good, and some are not. The subtle Planes have been described as being similar in appearance and form to our denser Plane of matter, but multi-dimensional and holographic in imagery, defying our marginal linear vision. In the astral dimension, sound vibrates at frequencies that sometimes create the hollow toned sound we may associate with echoes and whispers. Some colors appear as they would on the Earth Plane; other colors may appear exceptionally vivid and vibrant.

The senses are enhanced by the depth and intensity of our experience of the Astral Planes where our rules of weight, density, and limitations of the physical form do not apply. The fears of life and death no longer seize and control our positive energy. We are no longer slaves to our concepts of time and space. We have the power and freedom to manifest our conscious thoughts, creating the reality we choose to experience.

We have the power to free ourselves from the bondage of fear and attachment to the perishable. We have the wisdom to embrace Timeless reality. We cannot prove the existence of an afterlife or lateral existence, though many report having had such experiences. There is evidence and faith sufficient to presume that we do not die. At the intersection of science and mysticism, we affirm, *we do not die.*

Meditation:
The Bridge Between Worlds of Consciousness

Knowing when and how to step out of our own way and venture beyond linear intellect into the world of the mystic is something that cannot be easily taught. Nor is it something that needs to be taught or necessarily sought after. Most of us naturally have a strong resistance to willingly surrendering control of any aspect of our consciousness, that thread of control we think we have over our lives. At some point, or not, with study and practice, that spark of mysticism can ignite the fire of spiritual awakening. It can happen spontaneously, or not. We all have the capacity to experience an expansion of consciousness, and most have a choice. In general practice, the least we can expect to experience in Mystical Meditation is a relaxed and peaceful state of mind, a retreat from the chaos and stress of our lives.

Meditation has been known to trigger unpredictable and often phenomenal experiences. After entering a meditative state, some people experience the distraction of hearing a voice or voices in continual monologue or dialogue. The goal of serious meditation is to quiet the endless, mindless chatter of the ghosts that stalk our subconscious world. Much of it is self-generated. Some may have visceral experiences that occur much like a lucid dream, with uncanny links to outer reality.

In the practice of meditation, many will enter a semi-trance state and begin to perceive information that is subject to visionary interpretation. To tap into all that is available, we must be fearless enough to journey to the Planes of consciousness where dreams occur. These realms are much like our own, parallel to our own, differing in perspective, density, and frequency. The transcendent qualities of the Astral Plane allow that *any* and *every* thing can catalyze the opening of a portal into a deep meditative state, even without our intention. The clouds, the waves upon the water, the sand, rocks, and random stimuli can cause us to be drawn into a meditative trance. There are many ways to accomplish this objective. One of the most effective is to set aside time, if no more than ten to fifteen minutes a day, to dedicate to a daily ritual of embracing stillness and silence. Even deeper and more refined realms are attainable through prayer. Sharing the insights of our meditations will become an effective meditation, done in the spirit of a prayer. That is why maintaining a daily journal is encouraged.

There are many subtle techniques that can be used to put ourselves into dream time within moments. For the best results, the practitioner's goal is to experience a shift in perspective about our linear views of time and space. This requires a conscious shift of attention from the external to the internal transcendent Planes. It requires us to turn within and redefine reality to include dream time, at the crossroads where vertical and horizontal realities meet. In preparation to safely make this shift, we must first draw around ourselves a strong protective force field of Divine Light with prayer and visualization. A simple but powerful exercise can help to provide an energetic defense shield in a matter of moments with a subtle shift of awareness.

Our most formidable enemy in the assaults against our psyche is the torment of our own fears. To see things as they really are is the most powerful weapon we have. With time, it will become a comfortable lifestyle that will provide sound spiritual security for us as we walk through the many dimensions across the bridge between dreams, and learn more about the costumes and faces of this world. The Universal Archetypes of humanity paint themselves as a Timeless portrait of the seen and unseen human drama and bring clarity to some of the most profound mysteries of life. Signs and symbols that serve to establish fluency in a universal language of spirit are the construction materials with which to build the bridge between dreams. Those who dare may use this bridge to travel back and forth between worlds at will and are among the most fortunate of us all. Other worlds coexist in the ethers of our world of matter, on lateral Planes, or perhaps we in theirs, so it is not a distant journey. It is innately within our consciousness to be able to find that place. We find that place within … Within the stillness.

We all have spirit companions, guardians, and angels, just outside of our general perception, who long to receive our attention so that they may assist us with our soul's physical experience, in accordance with Divine Will. They visit us in dream time and often communicate with us in symbolic language, offering us guidance and information in ways so subtle that we may miss the communication if we are not mindful. If these communications were too direct, many people would voluntarily commit themselves to institutions in a state of shock. We show them respect and acknowledgment when we learn the language of symbols and welcome their help, rather than living in fear and denial of these spirit beings or misidentifying them as deities. They have been given to us as a Divine gift to protect and serve the spiritual evolution of our souls.

The symbolic language in the dream state unlocks the gates to our subconscious and sparks the intuitive process. A healing takes place in our lives as our conscious awareness connects with our subconscious, uprooting all that our ego has caused us to bury in fear, despair, insecurity, anger, guilt, grief, envy, lust, greed, jealousy, and hatred. It is unearthed, healed, and released. The result is love, trust, and understanding of our Higher Self as a vital being, connected to the whole of the Universe and the Creator.

Mystical Meditation and Death

A Divine awakening occurs when we stand face to formless face with the nature of our Eternal Self. A meditation of surrender to the Sacred Law of Impermanence would begin a conversation of Self-Inquiry that will ultimately reveal the true character of our Higher Self. Of the many selves that we are, we will concern ourselves here with the domain of the Higher Self. The Higher Self is the imperishable Self that witnesses the drama and evolution of the lower self as it matures. We will approach this "Self" from a practical perspective. How does it benefit our lives to choose mindful awareness of the non-physical Self? Why is the existential question, "Who am I?" so important to Self-Witnessing and Self-Realization? How is the Law of Impermanence relevant to perceptions of the essential Self? These are good questions to take into a Mystical Meditation.

The practice of Mystical Meditation requires a high regard for the exacting protocol of spiritual work. There are strict guidelines regarding hygiene for ritual prayer and meditation. Some of the many considerations about what is worn or where it is performed are generally not as necessary in meditations for the purpose of relaxation. For Spiritual protocol, please refer to my book, FEARLESS: PSYCHIC SELF-DEFENSE, available for free at *dreamuniversalmedia.com* or for purchase at *Amazon.com*

A Mystical Meditation can be entered into with a spiritual objective or pursuit. Contemplating the right questions can yield profound insights, foresight, and hindsight that can illuminate some of our most puzzling mysteries. As we fearlessly drop all illusion, we awaken to a new manner of seeing.

Once we are freed from this body vehicle, the lifeless physical body that remains goes through a number of changes that most of us are aware of. It is cold and inanimate. Our organs shut down, and rigor mortis sets in. Decay and decomposition set in, and the Light is off because we have gone home. Where exactly that spirit goes is the Divine Mystery given to us to contemplate. It will always be a mystery until we experience it. That is our cross to bear. That is what we all have in common. Death is our advisor, the lesson that should teach us how to live our lives.

Death strips us all of our mirror image faces. If one were to dig up the remains of all the dead that have ever died, they would all look related from bone to dust. They would all have characteristics that would demonstrate that we are all more alike than we are different. So why is it that we cannot see that while we are contained in our diverse vessels? If I were to select a single lesson death offers, it would be that one … The knowledge that if we had conducted our lives with our common denominator held as our highest and most profound realization, we would not have turned this beautiful planet into the war zone that it now is.

Certain types of meditations are characterized as "mystical" because they can trigger transcendent experiences, piercing the veils between worlds. In deep meditation, we can expect to be given glimpses of many worlds through the eyes of Spirit, rather than through the physical eyes. Spirits, like the dead, are more alike than different. They exist, formless, in electromagnetic fields, as frequencies, Light, cosmic consciousness, and energies. Through their Light, they are free to show themselves. They may show themselves as a "negative" exposure of an image on film or a holograph of the physical body image they most identified with on this Plane, characteristically etched in Light. They may speak to us through their thoughts and make impressions upon us through our emotions. So many people experience the presence of these entities and will not admit to it for fear of ridicule and being called crazy. They prefer to remain in denial of the experience because of their fear of the spirit world. Rejection of the many dimensions that we are is a denial of the power and wisdom of The God's creation.

Encounters with the spirit world are documented throughout most sacred scriptures. The Holy Spirit transcends "isms" and has charismatically touched many people who report never being the same again. An encounter with that Spirit can be the most transcendent experience anyone could have.

In the practice of meditation, there are many forms and styles. There are walking, talking, and chanting meditations. There are standing, sitting, and dancing meditations. There are open and closed eye meditations. There are guided and solitary meditations. There are fixed and visionary meditations. There are musical and vibrational meditations. One thing that is consistent is the fact that meditation is a portal into the subtle realms of visions and dreams and, therefore, represents the path work of the Natural Mystic.

Meditation on inner Light and inner sound vibration is healing. The primordial vibration that is within all life is sufficient to sustain the life force of the entire Universe and is believed to have sparked its creation. From that belief system emerges the Universal OM/AUM, which is the vibration that brought order to chaos, creating opposite polarities that would make creation possible. The symbol of the Yin and Yang and the symbol of the Universal OM/AUM are significant to that philosophy and can be used as focal points in the meditation practice.

The word "quickening" is relevant in meditation. Many familiar and unfamiliar sensations may be experienced during deep states of meditation. The literal Greek meaning of the word "quickening" is to make alive, to give life or vitality. It refers to the experience of a spiritual impact or awakening, sometimes triggered by meditation. In the human gestation period, the word "quickening" applies to "the first signs of life," as felt by the expectant mother. There is no cause for concern to experience a "quickening" during meditation. This quickening can occur in ways, ranging from subtle physical manifestations, extending to a complete spiritual awakening.

To extract the full experience of Mystical Meditation, one must be able to accept that the mere interest in meditation may confirm that you are a Natural Mystic. We are all mystical beings, whether we believe it and embrace it or not. If there were to be a righteous goal set in meditation, it would be to exercise and become able to flex our visionary muscles to the fullest extent we are capable of. If we tap into the power of our most essential Self, we would not even need bodies. We could transcend our physical state and become pure energy.

We have bodies so that we can see and experience one another. We are how The God experiences Itself in a physical way. For this reason, we are commanded to accept this vessel as a Temple and respect it as such. That is why we must do the best we can to avoid debasing or desecrating our Temple and live our lives in gratitude for the sacred investment in creation that we are.

Concept of I Transcend My Ego Self

The concept of I Transcend My Ego Self engages a specific meditation that releases the energetic burden associated with exclusively identifying as the physical self. Such a meditation can be a welcome retreat for the True Self. The True Self is known by many names and manifestations, but its Essence is Nameless, Silent Awareness. It is designed to bring us face to face with time's most feared and dreaded promise ... *Change*.

The most disturbing way that change may present in our lives is facing our own mortality. We and every other being will all pass away from our present frame of reference in this life. Birth and death, or transcendence of the physical form, is a dance that is as graceful as we command it to be. *The I Transcend My Ego Self* Meditation does not focus attention on graphic or disturbing visions of shedding the physical form with all of its labels, desires, and drama. We will instead transcend our dense matter form of being and assume the perspective of *witnessing* it. We will watch it spin like a top into and out of identity, falling helplessly into an illusory web of its own construction. We identify as a cage of flesh taking itself much too seriously, a miraculous field of energy in denial of its True Self. We are a dichotomy to be reckoned with.

In this meditation, we get to let go of the layers of outer illusions of self-definition until we find that silence, that stillness, that conscious awareness, that changeless Presence. That Presence is the Essence of The God. Stay there, as it becomes clear that the same Presence that animates our otherwise dead body, is the same force that animates all beings of Its Creation.

The physical body does not have to actually die to experience the liberation of the formless Self. Aside from the body's high-maintenance demands and tantrums, it knows it is not the truth of who we really are. This meditation can facilitate the experience of escape from time and the tyranny of identity consciousness.

So why involve death in the subject of meditation? When we shed our attachment to the appearances of the body vehicle, we can look in the mirror of faceless truth and see ourselves for who we really are. Certain types of meditation can serve to dissolve the ego in a sea of conscious stillness. Through meditation, we can condition ourselves to accept that there is no "I" in the mirror, as we affirm that after the faces and masks are gone, we still exist. In the mirror, we discuss with ourselves the issues of the little "me" ego self. The concept of *I Transcend My Ego Self* asks that we meditatively transcend our ego "self," as we consider a reality wherein there is no little "me" identity, with its pantheon of masks and labels. We let it all go. That means letting go of our one-dimensional perception of self. No future. No past. There is only this moment in the Timeless Now.

All that exceeds our vanity is our greed. We want more ... *More* of every perfect thing. Our standards of perfection change with the seasons of our minds and the changeable nature of our attitudes. Our list of demands increases in direct proportion to their fulfillment. That is our nature. The shadow side of the attributes of humanity gives us the potential for being ruthless and harsh creatures, with such a lack of human compassion that we often cannot even extend love, kindness, and forgiveness to ourselves.

We naturally seek the Unknowable One, each in our own unique way. We either evolve or dissolve into all the materials required to build a new temple and cage for our spirit to start all over again ... as many times as it takes to get it right on this Karmic wheel of fortune. We intuitively sense that there is some mystical cause that we are somehow the effect of. It is so sad that belief systems constructed around that subtle knowing can be the source of such contention and warfare in this world. That is why I have maintained my position that knowledge of The God, no matter what language or cultural underpinnings, is Unknowable. I am sure the experience of It can be attainable, but not the knowing of It that results from the mind's study. The experience of That is the seeking of That, the Ultimate I AM, the Source of all things. The body temple is the veil that can be lifted through meditation to reveal the Source of who we really are. We are That.

We cannot expect to connect with the experience of our own immortality while trapped in our human form if we do not transcend what we perceive as its limitations. The discipline of meditation offers us that freedom. Time will claim us all. We must claim time as well. We must claim our participation in the definition of time, and be willing to step outside of the box these definitions have constructed to confine us within realities that *we* spoke into existence.

The psychology at the root of this meditation, *I Transcend My Ego Self,* is to deny ourselves one of our most precious comfort zones. We will release our feelings of safety associated with our attachment to taking even one day for granted. We can pull back the veil that conceals emotions as raw as a dangling nerve and pass into the realm of our vilest shadows and our most brilliant Light. We will seek to train our vision to see the experience of our Higher Self as the Law of Nature sees it. From that place in consciousness, we have questions to ask of ourselves. Who am I, really? Who do I love? Who loves me? Who do I serve? What is my true value? What am I here to contribute? What will I leave behind in the footprints of my journey? Am I more in touch with the needs of this container in which the I AM is traveling, or the precariously contained Light of my formless being? Can I accept that the forms of my loved ones represent a mere shell of their Realized Self?

Revealing the Essence that survives the transition, we manifest the blessing of a new opportunity every day to enjoy life as the cherished Divine experience it was meant to be. For everything, there is a reason. For everyone, there is a season. In the cold face of letting go of a loved one, we must respect and accept responsibility for spiritually facilitating our survival of this sad process. The grief we experience in this "valley of the shadow of death" is natural and cannot be approached with the emotional distance of logic or tradition. It is not logical for several years to pass, and for one to feel like they only blinked one moment in the eyes of time, with respect to the freshness of a loss as devastating as the death of a loved one. It is not logical that it will likely always feel like it just happened yesterday. The more time that has passed, the more we miss our departed loved ones. So how can we expect that it will get easier or that we will "get over it" simply because time has passed?

We will *never* "get over" such a loss. We cannot get over it because we are forced to view our own mortality with a stark reminder that, sooner or later, our turn is coming. We won't get over it because that loss has left a gaping hole in our temporal reality, and the more time that passes, the more we miss them and feel their absence. Every special occasion will trigger our attention to that hole. We have lost the mutual witnessing of our lives, and often, depending on the depth of our connection, no one can take that place or fill that void. A decision is then required to ask our Selves to cooperate with a redefinition of the self that we are. Yes, we are the same person we were before, just with a hole. The gift of grace is to feel no need to fill it with that which is not what is missing. The blessing is to be able to fill that hole and heal it with Light ... The Light our loved one left with us forever, and the Light that we are that was increased by their having touched our lives. The Light of our Creator has the Ultimate power to heal all that ails our troubled souls.

Our goal with the *I Transcend My Ego Self* Meditation is to conquer and heal our innate fear of death by changing how we view it, by letting go of small "self" definitions, and by knowing who we really are. The goal we wish to set is to accept that when it is time to sow, there will be a sowing. When it is time to reap, there will be a reaping. All we can change is our perception of its meaning and the energy we spin around these hovering realities. All we can change is that we not allow it to overwhelm us or alter our true identity. We condition our seeing to view everything from the perspective of the reality of our body of awareness, which knows its relationship with Eternity.

Energetically clinging to the human form is not only an exercise in futility but also an energy leak in our lives that can cost us everything. We can rob ourselves of the joy of living and stain our experience of the spiritual significance of our creation. Even a preoccupation with past and future incarnations, though comforting and quite real, can cause energy leaks that distract our attention from our present reality. We must live in the *now* because that is the only choice we have if we choose liberation from suffering.

In our meditation practice, we will experience a healing with our refusal to be distracted by a preoccupation with the past or the future. We exercise our spiritual muscles as we rise above temporal perspective through meditation and view the transitions of our physical form from an Omniscient perspective. When we return our consciousness from our meditation, we return with an opportunity to *change* this day and every day after that. We will create a positive change in the way we live our lives. To see it another way, we become the witness of the changelessness of our True Being. By doing this meditation regularly, we will feel energized and blessed to experience the type of life we will create for ourselves, from the perspective of our Realized Self.

There will be something we do differently every day of our practice. It may be as subtle as noticing the beauty of the simplest of things we take for granted … That morning cup of coffee … The water that boiled to make it … The beans that were grown and reaped, crushed and processed to brew it … The cup that holds it … The finger of the hand that slips through the handle of the cup, that allows us to hold it without being burned … The rush of the caffeine that makes us feel alert, that causes the addiction, and that gives us a headache if we don't get it. If you are not a coffee person, contemplate your own special 'thing' that you take for granted. If we can love life in the face of death, we have conquered it. If we can resist the hypnosis of this Plane of illusion called Maya, without judgment, we can dance our elegant dance in this Divine play called Leela, never losing mindfulness of who we really are. Then, we are free! If we can love the Love of The God, without question or proof, we become One with It.

I am not the expert on the subject of survival. Survival is still a daily process for me. I awaken to every new day challenged to live it without my mother. I remember her every day, in her prior form. She was my best friend. She was my strength. She is gone, and there is nothing I can do about it, but honor her memory by surviving this, walking in her footsteps toward helping others to find the strength to do the same. If this attempt to heal myself through the sharing of this book helps anyone in the process, I am grateful to The God for the chance to do so. I have sought closure in this way and encourage anyone who is facing the sting of the reaper to journal your progress, with or without this meditation, and share it with us at *dreamuniversalmedia@yahoo.com*.

Mystical Meditation and Monotheism

Mystical Meditation can be as unique to our individual spiritual path and preference as our fingerprints. Visions and guidance, methods, rules, and rituals will manifest in the Ether of our meditations and dreams, through visions and in spontaneous lightning flashes of thought. It is all a part of the awesome phenomenon of the Natural Mystic in full pursuit of Self-Realization. The energy of thought becomes form, transcends form, and has the power to transform our lives. As this transformation occurs, our thoughts become a subtle, refined trigger within the circular Law of Cause and Effect. Scientific research has proven that the energy of projected thought creates dramatic change, so profound that it often defies basic scientific reasoning.

Some call the path to attaining such a level of spiritual consciousness, The Great Work. It is not a contrived, or necessarily, a textbook study type of practice. The true nature of our Eternal soul is revealed in a complex composite of refined mystical attributes, comfortable with the transpersonal qualities of inner and outer reality. Our studies help make us aware of that fact and serve as a map that can keep us from getting lost and damaged.

We are an energy that is one with the One God that created us. Through meditation, we seek to transcend the container, the body vehicle, as we observe and embrace the "contained" True Self. The Essence of the energy that reveals itself is Light. When we become adept in spiritual practices that facilitate this process, we open doors to the many mansions in the kingdom of the Almighty. It is through these doors and corridors that our consciousness travels to witness the beauty and depth of who we really are, free of the illusions of the smoke and mirrors of our material Plane point of view.

Many methods of meditation transcend philosophies and practices of traditional organized religion, existing in a realm where they do not conflict. Most religious paths encourage some form of meditation practice. Some of these systems may introduce deities, god forms, and graven images to prostrate our meditative energies before. There is no focus on such meditation practices in this text and no judgment of the meditation practices of others. It is essential for me to stay singularly focused on the experience I share, of an *undivided* relationship between our True Self, The God, and the realization of our Oneness, available in meditation. Anything that is introduced in association with that Oneness will only serve as a distraction in practices I am familiar with.

There are many generic gods. There is but One Creator of all there is, The God. We are sparks from that Flame of origin. It is important to unambiguously make that distinction, or place ourselves in profound spiritual danger. It is absolutely compulsory to have a good understanding of the meaning of polytheism so that your choices remain, consciously and clearly, your own. This extends to the practice of entertaining entities, energetic attachments, petitioning to, or bowing down in worship of manifestations of the Divine One, as sovereign, individuated deities.

The energy of fear and the illusion of death have, in many ways, become deified. What we fear, we worship and assign it power over us. One of our greatest fears is death. Anything that distracts our attention, or emotionally pulls us away from the knowledge of Self, and our Oneness with Divinity qualifies as polytheism.

Mystical Meditation can be one of the most powerful and committed forms of prayer work. We pray for a sense of connection with transcendent reality. We pray for a sense of our connection with The Divine One, reaching outside of our shell of matter to experience the Essence of the Light that we are. When we pray, we often do so with the purpose in mind of creating change in our lives and the lives of others. The difference between prayer and meditation (even though there are times that there is no difference) is the enduring intensity and heightened concentration. It has been said that prayer is when we talk to The God. Meditation is when The God talks to us.

When the realization of The God is at the forefront of our every conscious and subconscious thought, we are offering ourselves as a catalyst in the transmission of the Light energy of The God, as we submit to being completely immersed in It, replaced by It. We create a circle of Light, in the center of which we stand for the change that our essence is already a part of. We are the manifestation of the sacred union of The Divine and ourselves, as we transcend our one-dimensional identification as the physical form.

There are many types of mysticism. I am not interested in exploring or explaining all of them, even in an overview. My focal point of the study of meditation is the experience of liberation from the bondage of the ego self, to disappear to all that is not my True Self. I affirm that our very existence is the Effect of a Most Divine cause. The moment we step outside of that framework and petition to offer invocations to, ascribe power to, or seek associations with, anyone or anything other than That, we have stepped into the realm of abysmal spiritual danger.

For me, there is no fence riding on the subject of polytheism in Mystical Meditation. We all have Free Will to choose to do as we please. So, to close our eyes in meditation and then open them to a statue or image that someone else introduces into the picture, without our knowledge or consent, is a spiritual violation. I could chill the blood in your veins to ice, telling you stories about the consequences of challenging the spiritual sovereignty of others. We do not observe this code of respect out of the fear of consequences. The consequences for divided loyalties are to be feared, but if our fear outweighs our love, we are cheating ourselves out of the direct experience of the unconditional loving embrace of the Divine. The frequency of love is higher than the frequency of fear. We do it for love, not fear. Our undivided love dismisses a single thought of the realm of unfocused spiritual attention. The acknowledgment of the many "aspects" or "attributes" of the Divine is not the same practice as assigning form to these individuated energies in an act that constitutes deifying them and bowing down to them in worship and service. Nothing exists but The God. Nothing happens outside of conformity to Divine Will.

The diverse culture of spiritual practice is a delicate and complex thing. No two people live, love, or worship exactly the same way. Regardless of how it may seem from the perspective of an uninformed observer, some cultures of mystical belief that may appear to be polytheistic, are actually practicing a more inclusive doctrine that acknowledges the Unity of The God.

Henotheism is a term of Greek origin that refers to a form of theism that worships One God, while not denying the existence or possible existence of other deities. It may appear as a gray area to some who are much too interested in probing and judging the spiritual beliefs of others. There are so many intricate nuances and subtleties among differing but not necessarily conflicting cultural and spiritual beliefs. It is unwise to judge in the absence of unbiased experiential study. Where Monotheism and Polytheism may be viewed as opposites, the term Henotheism refers to an apparently pluralistic acknowledgment of the shared Divine Essence of Energies, Entities, and Beings, of all Planes and domains of creation. Henotheism does not exclude Monotheism, Non-Dualism, or Dualism. Atheism, however, negates the concept of deity.

GRAVEN IMAGES

I sit in a circle
of graven images

A single white candle burns
holding my focus on The One

I wish
focus
could be as easy
as statues of
Queen Nefertiti
Black Elk
Tupac and Che
Marley and Ra
Rumi and Gibran
Yins & Yangs and
sacred things
Chinese calligraphy
and ancient symbols
decorate my
temple walls
casting spells
for Hope and Happiness
Fortune and Love

I have
Dreamcatching
mandalas
with tomahawks
and peace pipes
Black angels
with white wings
crescents and Stars of David
candles and scarabs
Zen gardens
Feng Shui fountains
Holy books, Ankhs
and Indian brass
Eternal OMs
and stones
from Sedona

beads counting themselves
in prayer
oracle boxes with hexagrams
but I do not have
a golden calf!

A single white candle burning
holds my focus on The One

I Chinged, Oracle'd, and chanted
read by the stars and the cards
shapeshifted Totems
horseshoes and garlic
Bagua mirrors crown my doors
The Bible opens
to Psalms 23 and 24
with a cross to carry
to my own spiritual lynching
but I promise
I do not have
a golden calf!

Sage burning
incense smoking
in silent petition
for protection
from them
whoever they are!

No circle of
graven images
could protect me
from the enemies
I could not see
trying to turn me
into a graven image too

Where were they then?
They did not have my back
did not stand between me
and the wall my back was to
did not keep my spirit
from dying inside
only my prayers

Dark altar beacons
prayer rug cries
as dirty shoes
step on its
patience
forgetting sometimes
the single white candle burning
holds
my focus
on
The One

~ JAI ~
Smoke & Mirrors

The Meaning of the I AM

The I AM defies definition. We are dreams born of the sacred realm of the I AM, delicately clothed in matter. Only the blind spots of our own vision would make us believe otherwise. There are many common names for the energy of this subtle and powerful field of conscious energy. There are many manifestations of the I AM. It is the object of our Self-Inquiry, that conversation between the ego self and the Higher Self. The energy of the formless, eternal, transcendent being of pure consciousness is the Higher Self that we are. The I AM has deep significance in many mystical traditions and goes back into antiquity thousands of years, representing a pure, Timeless, formless Self that witnesses the physical expression of Itself as us. We manifest in form as the clay creatures we are, driven by That Sacred Breath, powered by That Light of Origin, sustained by the same. The heart must embrace this perspective to be released from the bondage of self-identification with transient forms covered with labels and become a truly Self-Realized being. This is not an event. It is a path through the mystical gates of Self-awareness into the eternal domain of the I AM that we are.

The I AM seems to represent something different to everyone. Historically, the I AM has no definition since its presence precedes those who might seek to define it. It has come to represent a cry for home, for freedom from captivity and slavery, a cry for The God. As a key element of regular spiritual practice, many metaphorically burn or "chant down" all of the false identities assumed in our efforts to assimilate into this theatre of shadows. The simple act of ignoring false precepts and concepts of Self facilitates the burning away of counterfeit inner and outer realities that lead us to our spiritual corruption and destruction.

The vibration associated with the I AM can be maintained through disciplined spiritual practice, faith, and reliance on the seen and unseen for guidance. It is represented in this text as a dimension of consciousness accessible to all of us, for WE are the temple that houses the energies of the Eternal I AM, the Creator of all we are and all we know. It is only a matter of exercising and flexing the muscle of remaining in the I AM, pulling ourselves back from every cage of bogus definition we assign to our True Self. Even though notions of Eternal existence are commonly associated with a past life, a future life, or an afterlife, it can be entered without experiencing what we call death. To view existence as the I AM or to remain within the myopic vision of a one-dimensional self-concept is a choice. When we have suffered sufficiently from this limiting and terrifying perspective, we expand our focus to explore the nature of who we really are.

Who we really are is not limited to that reflection we see in the mirror. Even the mirror has enough sense to know that our reflection is not who we are, so it does not cling to anything we show it. It accepts and releases. It does not look for yesterday or tomorrow. It does not record or identify with that image. It is our own minds that tend to do that. But we are not the mind. We are not the body. We are That … That which preceded the mirror and all false concepts of the "I." The real "I" is that formless, Timeless, storyless being expressing itself as the form it witnesses in the mirror. "That" is the I AM. From that perspective, we ask, "Who am I?" From this perspective, we affirm that there is no death, no time, no story, no form. Then, after the rush of freedom we feel from that realization, we must ask, "Can the seer be seen? Can the witness be witnessed? What witnesses the witness?" At this point, Self-Inquiry begins. The fire is kindled, and the process of awakening to freedom has begun. Time is escaped. The bullying of the flesh is checked and put in its place as a cooperative subordinate to the Higher Self and the Most High.

From a state of consciousness mimicking a coma, we awaken to the dawn of every new day, rejoicing that we are blessed with the opportunity to renew our commitment to the purification of our hearts. We commit ourselves to cleansing the controlling, manipulative energies of desire, attachment, and aversion. There are many roads to the spiritual mindset of the I AM. There are many names ascribed to the Ultimate Witness. Opinions, cultural conditioning, and choices only add to the diversity of the colorful mosaic of our collective journey. The fact that someone else is traveling a different path than our own does not mean that they are lost. There should be no unfavorable comparisons, nor should these paths and respective deities be set up in competition with one another for rightness. If we have images, qualities, or even the intonation of a name, that reference is still not of the Ultimate I AM, the Unknowable, and most subtle in density.

In the Baha'i temple in Wilmette, Illinois, one of the most beautiful I have ever seen, there are nine doors, each representing a different faith. Each of the doors represents a path to the experience of what is characterized in this text as the realm of the I AM, the realm of the Sacred. There is nothing that must be done to earn one's place as the I AM, only to strive to gracefully master the balance of unconditional acceptance of the perfect balance inherent in creation. Everything has a balance that must be kept to progress from negative into positive existence. There is no such thing as all good or all bad. That type of terminology is subjective, relative, and can turn on a dime. Communicating this philosophy is the sacred symbol commonly referred to as the Yin Yang, illustrated in this text at the end of the following section.

The Yin Yang is a sacred symbol that represents all of life as a circle, rather than seeing it as linear. A horizontal timeline suggests that there is a distinct beginning and an ending. A vertical timeline may suggest the same. But there is no end within the circle, especially this circle. It is divided into two parts, not in a straight line, but an "S" shape. One side is black, illustrating the Void from which the Light emerged. The white side illustrates the Light. The two small circles of opposite polarity on each side mean that nothing is just one way. Duality is our nature and the nature of creation. It requires us to be more merciful and compassionate in our judgments of everything, including ourselves. Everything and everyone is a composite of two sides, each necessary to the other.

Whatever name you want to call it, and there are many, our souls are well familiar with the energies of I AM, naturally seeking its serenity for survival. The longing is the connection. If prayer were a government, its name would be I AM. Its flag and national anthem would be "the Eternal OM." Its race is the *human* race. The President's name could only be expressed by silence. The I AM is our safe refuge from the evil influences and attacks of mischievous creation. The streets on this sacred journey are littered with broken hearts and vanity-based dreams. That Which Created us is sufficient to guide us through the challenging experience of material form and will be there waiting to welcome our grateful spirits home. Unconditional Love is the Soul of the I AM.

Yin Yang

The outer circle represents the circle of life in perpetual motion

The two dots indicate there is no absolute yin or yang. Each contains the essence of the other

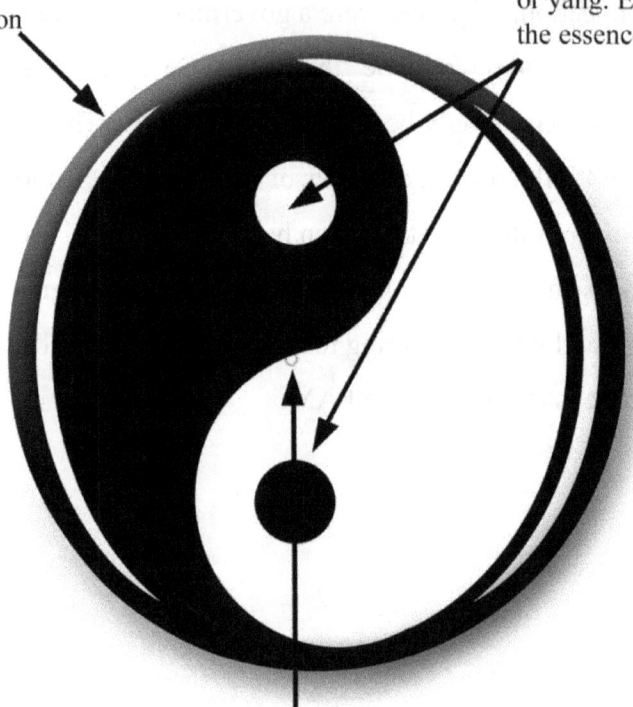

The Wu Ji is the point of stillness. The calm in the eye of the storm

Qualities of Yin

night
dark
cold
negative
passive
female

Qualities of Yang

day
light
warm
positive
active
male

The I AM Meditation

In my well-rewarded attempts to find editors for this book, I did not go in search of an editor who would validate or patronize me, rather, one that would confront me and challenge me to raise the bar. Writers are only as strong as the extent to which they will humble themselves before the mind and voice of wisdom's constructive critique. There must be an ability to at least explore guidance in directions that may not have been considered, even to the point of abandoning the warmth and security of a fixed comfort zone.

In a conversation on the subject of the I AM and Mystical Meditation, I was told to meditate on *here, now*, and *nothing*, only I AM, I AM, I AM, I AM. I was told to resist escaping or taking myself away from my life in the present tense, though every conscious thought strived to encourage me to do that. I found this meditation exercise to be incredibly difficult. I was coached to be totally focused on my life in the present, the present space, my present reality, my present overview. I was told to observe it, as is, resisting the desire to see anything about it as changed, or in any way altered to represent a vision of some future potential or more desirable reality. The objective is to take a good look at everything, without attachment, aversion, opinion, or judgment. There were things about my life and the lives of others that I was subconsciously holding in judgment. Judgment imposes demanding ideals that will, more often, defy reality, rather than achieve it. The harshest of all of the judgments I entertained turned out to be the harsh judgments I held against myself. In meditations I have enjoyed, I had the freedom to visualize and transform any present reality into an idealized virtual reality scenario, existing in a future where the ideals would be real. But after returning to the *now*, nothing had ever changed, and there was a letdown, even though the escape was a pleasant one.

In the I AM meditation, I was told to see my life as a floor littered with things that I would have a natural urge to clean up or fix by sweeping it away. Through my escape meditation practice, I was able to sweep away the litter with a very large broom. But the challenge for me was to transcend the need to do that and just observe it. If I am in a meditation and the things that I identify as litter on the floor of my life disturb me, this disturbance has become a distraction from my present reality and pulls me out of the meditation. The litter is a *part* of the meditation. The objective is to be so focused, intentional, and undistracted by perceived imperfections that all distractions are included in the meditation. For example, a noisy truck passing by could be a startling distraction from this I AM meditation. Rather than allowing it to become the thing that interrupted the meditation, it becomes included in the meditation. It is all a part of the I AM present picture of life, everything, including the litter. It need not be edited, swept away, enhanced, or Photoshopped into a magazine photo of the perfect floor, in that perfect place many seek to escape to in meditation.

At first, it worried me to resist the broom. I was distracted from the meditation because I began to meditate upon the broom, and the pleasant vision of change it offered to chaos. I resisted, as difficult as that was for me to do. I just looked at the floor of my life, observed it as something that need not be 'fixed,' something that just simply is what it is. The mantra I used to help me focus was, "It is what it is," "I am who I am." I own it, *as it is* in this moment, here and now, as though there existed no other possible moment, ever. If I saw something that I felt I should fix, something that did not meet my expectations of what the floor *should* be like ... I did not have to clean it up, stop it, or fix it. I could choose to meditate on *including* it as a part of the reality of what is. I learned that it is a choice as well as a challenge to simply accept that it is what it *is*.

In this meditation, I repeatedly drifted into the arena of the, "what *should* have been," "what *could* have been," "what *will* be, *if*?"… "what *could* happen, *if*?" I could not handle being held to my present reality, to be in the *now,* without fixing anything about it. It was so difficult for me to resist unconsciously redressing my *present* to suit my *future* ideals. I hated it. I realized then that my previous practice of meditation had one aim, one goal, and that was to escape my present reality, to take a pleasant vacation away from it. If meditation is used in this way, it can lead to expectations that result in painful disappointment.

Rather than embracing the *Now,* with its fluid, naturally mystical power, we tend to affix our consciousness to a place called *future* and *past.* Neither exists. We do not know what tomorrow will bring, as surely as we did not know yesterday what today would bring. To see time and timing through the Eyes of The Divine Creator would make us let go of it with the knowledge that everything is what it is. Everything is perfect in creation. Everything is following the timing of The Creator, God. Meditation should be the key to open the door to that reality. When meditation is used as an escape mechanism, its positive effects can be thwarted and coaxed into some imaginary realm, where the Now is avoided rather than appreciated. In some very fundamental way, we cheat ourselves out of our present value.

Meditation is most beneficial as a practice of submission to the rightness of the Now. We are exactly where we are supposed to be, right Now. We are exactly who we are supposed to be, right Now. Where, and who we are, is *perfection* by a much higher standard than our own. In this simple, I AM meditation, my harsh judgments of my here and now experience could not be escaped. It was to be included. "This is who I am. This is where I am, right here, and right Now. Love it or hate it, these are the people and circumstances of my life." The objective was to neutralize it emotionally and free it to just *be*, without being clouded by my opinions and judgments of it.

That was when I discovered my attachment and aversion to certain systems of meditation. In this one, I had no vehicle of escape. I was once able to leave my present condition and, without responsibility for the journey, take a free mind trip away from myself. After I arrived at my destination, I feared my mind would be taken places more unpleasant than the reality I was trying to escape. The more I meditated upon the "as is" part, the more uncomfortable I became. I resisted my desire to transcend and go to another place in consciousness. I would not have to include it as my present reality. I figured out that there is a special point in meditation where the focal point must be the "Self" and all of its aspects, free of judgment, free of going to another place where it is not, free to let go of the past, and the future. I found freedom in knowing that if I were to disappear from the face of this Earth, at this very moment, I have seen time and resisted my compulsion to 'change' it, if only in my mind. I was free to just experience a moment, this one, very special, very authentic moment. I was free. It was a brand of freedom from trying to fix what is not broken with the declaration that, "It is what it is."

After I relaxed a little from my struggle to not jump for the *fix-it* broom, I took the deepest cleansing breath I have experienced in quite some time. I was challenged to gaze upon my life and myself in meditation and tell myself … It is what it is. I Am as I Am. I am all of this, right here, right now, not flipping the pages of visions over to the perfect version of the I AM of my imaginations. I accept the reality of the present I AM … Without the need to perfect it with a judgment that it is not *already* perfect.

There are as many styles of meditation as there are people who meditate. Each form of meditation is a key to the door of higher consciousness. Behind the door are many paths and many destinations, with the most profound being no destination at all. The style that causes self-examination, like the I AM Meditation, can take us to new levels of practical Self-witnessing and acceptance. Many forms of visualization meditation can cause the energy of coveting and conjuring. Some suggest that visualizing and chanting for what you want in meditation will attract these things to you. This, in fact, is true. But if we don't know who we are, how can we possibly know what to want that would serve our highest good?

Prayer is a higher octave of meditation. We must never forget that no prayer goes unanswered, even though the answer may be "No!" We must know the difference between powerful mystical manifestation and interfering with the Will of The God in our lives. The intensity of the prayer must be as that of a drowning person with no rescue in sight, with faith enough to use their last breath to call upon The God for intervention. Why wait until we are drowning? For all we know, we could be drowning now. There are elements other than water that we could just as easily be drowning in.

It is better to meditate upon your prayer than to pray upon your meditation. It is unwise to close the doors through which miracles are issued into our lives. The I AM Meditation can open the door to a conversation about the consciousness of I AM, the consciousness of the fact that "I am not a body." I am a being, without beginning or end. With this awareness, there is no illusion of permanence as *form*. When a spiritual connection with The Light of Ultimate Consciousness is established, through the energy of the Light body, unknown Universes align themselves behind our positive intentions.

With time, I began to expand on the I AM meditation practice. In another form of an I AM meditation, I felt my "self" disappear and became aware of my subtle Self. There was no appearance of a Light body. There was no appearance of anything. The deeper I looked, the more any semblance of form disappeared. The viewing of myself as a person began to fade the first time I asked, "Who am I?" I thought of images from the beginning to the end of my timeline. I dropped the images and masks ... All of them. But I was still there. At first, my mind kept defaulting to the "self" as a person. It was as though I looked into a mirror of identity, into, and beyond, the Third Eye. I traveled until all concepts of a person or self disappeared. Then there was nothing. The noise and kaleidoscope of images riding the waves of distorted "I" consciousness faded.

Who am I ... this True Self that cannot be seen? This Self is pure consciousness. This Self is aware that it cannot be seen and that something that cannot be seen witnesses it. It terrifies me to think that we can live our entire lives in a cage of rotting flesh and bones, believing that the cage is who we really are. There is freedom in understanding and living life from the transpersonal perspective of the Eternal I AM. Our freedom is earned as we own our knee-jerk illusory reality. Our essential Self says, I AM. What we call by many names, including The God, says, I AM. What we call by many names, including the Devil, says, I Am. Keeping this in mind, be discerning with who answers, I Am. We must know when we are weaving webs of bondage around ourselves, with ego-based, worldly mindsets and desires.

The material world incessantly beckons and calls, whispers and screams, baits and switches. Some call her Dunya. Some call her Maya. Some call her Babylon. She is a beautiful seductress, powerful and unwavering. Her ambition is to have us live in her shadows, sell our souls for her superficial trappings, and bow at her clay feet. Her victory is our forgetfulness of who we really are, as we lower ourselves to live for, and as the external, rather than the Eternal. She is a major archetype of humanity. We cannot escape her encounters. We prayerfully break her bewitching spell with ceaseless reminders that she is around every corner we turn, even as we turn within.

Our Attachment to Maya (Illusory Material World)

Maya: The Archetype, is an excerpt from, FACELESS: THE SACRED RELATIONSHIP, our advanced manual for Archetypal Meditation.

Maya: The Archetype (Devil)

When her shadow called out to me, I did not answer. When she tempted my senses to attachment and aversion with skillful seduction, I did not succumb. I sought refuge in the Light of my own sacred relationship with Divinity when she struck out at me; when she attempted to destroy me for my indifference; for my rejection of her trappings. Rather than choosing to hate Maya, I chose to surrender in Love for The God of all sides of the veils between worlds. I accepted the Divine purpose of Maya. Rather than curse her mischievous manipulations, I chose to increase my praise for the Wisdom of The God of all creation. I chose to bask in the Light of The Divine One, as a spark of The Eternal Essence, unconditionally ... Without judgment, not lamenting the appearance of shadows.

Profile of Maya's Cyclical Archetypal Influence

Maya is a term found in Pali and Sanskrit literature that has many meanings. Here it means a constantly changing appearance that is unreal, an illusion, or delusion. Maya represents the limited perception of a purely physical and mental, linear existence. The manifestation of the many forms and faces of Maya's illusions causes us great resistance and struggle with our desire for it to be a reality. Her illusions extend beyond the manifest worlds to include our perceptions of self. Our minds naturally seek to construct a fixed reality around the image of "self" that we see in the mirror, even as it changes with our every breath. That we are real, in that context, only constitutes a truth, but certainly not *the* truth. We are more than what we can see. There is something about us that time cannot touch, and it is our blessing to pursue the most profound depths of the knowledge of what that is. The I AM, that cosmic spirit that we truly are beneath the veil of the "I" that we can see, cries out to be known and loved.

Maya is a dream the Creator shares with us. We are the dreamers, and we are the dream in this elaborate play on the stage where thought-form becomes form, and sensation whispers to us of its reality until we believe it to be true. As we believe it to be true, we begin to identify with all we perceive of this beautiful and dangerous illusion. Fickle threads of ego-consciousness and karma become braided into our being as a gripping force that seduces us into the energies of craving, clinging, attachment, and begging the *temporal* for *forever*. We have this body for transportation on this Sacred journey. Why do we spin so much energy around the desire for its permanence and ignore that part of ourselves that is Timeless? This is the binding energy of Maya, the dream that awakens to the embodiment of creation … The mind of humanity forming the connecting link between consciousness and matter.

Maya is the full Moon's reflection shimmering on still water. Maya is the shimmering of bubbles that rise with an appearance of form for the moments of their brief dance, even as they ascend into their own forgetfulness as they pass away. Maya is the subtle drama of rainbows and mist, neither real nor unreal, not feeling vulnerable to time and impermanence. We must become like waves prancing across the sea of its own element, unafraid for their individuated existence, upon their reunion with Source. We awaken from the dream world of Maya as a being of Light, not fearing past or future, not disappearing, but bursting into the flames of enlightenment that reduce our masks to ashes, exposing the formless face of the Timeless Now.

Death looms overhead in clouds that threaten a downpour of painful loss and separation from the worldly, perishable things and states that we have become attached to. Death becomes the enemy of our being rather than the door to our home of eternal being. We cringe and bemoan it. We cry and we loathe it. We break as we hear the footsteps of the inevitable as they draw near our door, knowing that all of these emotions are reasonable, and our denial is futile. Still believing, somewhere on the highest level of our deepest knowing that *we do not die*. We are Timeless.

Strip Maya down of her stories and scripts, her props and promises, her flirtatious wink of the eye, cloaking the secret of her formidable relationship with Time. Time will consume all things, but the Timeless, even the curtain that appears to open and close between acts and shows, resting comfortably in the consciousness of the Timeless Now, with no attachment, no aversion … No ego.

In the mystic teachings of the Vedanta tradition, Maya is the realm of phenomena that dares us to transcend it and expose it as the hypnosis of a "dream" that manifested as creation. It is a Divine drama played out on a stage constructed by thought-forms, desire, and passion. Maya is neither friend nor enemy. She is both. We, in all of our glorious array of decorated forms and images, are the many manifestations of the Divine One, individuated and identified as we see fit. To know this fundamental truth is to pierce the veil of Maya and see the Source of its emanation. To pierce her veil is to free ourselves from the ever-revolving wheel of life and death, in its circular continuum, from this Karmic, merry-go-round, and roller-coaster existence.

Our objective is to rise above the tendency of assigning permanent qualities to the transient reality of Maya, the material realm of manifestation. She appears to resist the Law of Impermanence at times, luring us under her powerful spell. We are pulled into a web of conceptual misunderstanding. It is a mirage so beautiful, with images so convincing that we are invested in tricking ourselves into thinking it is real. Our ego-consciousness craves these sultry manipulations. With such a tight grip on what is tangible, therefore believable, profound fear of the most natural transition is born ... The fear of death. We fear Impermanence as a curse, even though we know it operates within the authority realm of Divine Order.

We are stitched securely in our garments of personhood, bound tightly in the straitjacket of ego identification. We bow down to phenomena, concept, precept, and restless ambition. We are driven by carnal desire and conditioning. We must choose to rise up, focused on Ultimate Truth and Ultimate Reality, that cannot be diminished by labels, judgments, or educated opinion. We are required to raise our frequency to intuit the most fundamental of Universal Truths, defying descriptions based on language for one-dimensional minds to manipulate.

There exists only "*That*" ... and "*not That.*" "*That*" is the Unknowable Cause of all things; the Creator; the Unattainable "*That,*" the reality of which, we are just a tiny fragment. All that is "*not That*" is Maya. Maya is an emanation of "*That,*" willed into existence as ourselves and all we know. Our goal is to strive to live from pure consciousness, our I AM consciousness. We will free ourselves from our attachment to small manifestations of Ultimate reality and declare our quest for Self-Realization as One with "That." Everything is One with *"That."* We are more than the temporal images we see in the mirrors of our minds, with their earthly concerns, possessions, and duality. There is no more small context, I, me, my, mine. There are no conceptual dualities such as above and below, good and evil, past and future. We are called to free ourselves from misinterpretations of Self and others. We are liberated as we release our attachment to dualistic thinking, an either "this" or "that" psychological conditioning. That is our encouraged meditation.

The fruit of the unholy tree of bondage to the love of the perishable world is born over-ripe and inspires hunger more than it does satisfaction. The well-woven webs of Maya can ground our attention in the lower frequencies of lower energies, stunting our spiritual growth. The insatiable appetite and greed associated with distortions of Maya ultimately consume all who bow to their soul seizing compulsions. The aggressive pursuit of flesh and spirit to violate, dominate, enslave, possess, and kill devours the souls of the weary and weak.

As an archetypal influence, the hypnotic, nebulous realm of Maya is one of the most misunderstood. We may be tangled in its intricate web of manipulations without conscious awareness that we chose it. It is important to witness ourselves, rather than judge ourselves, as we grow in the understanding that it is *personal*. As long as we see ourselves only as a "person" and not an Eternal being, we are vulnerable to every manner of separation anxiety, while Maya, with her elaborate illusions, has no choice but to ultimately, respectfully, concede to the Law of Impermanence.

The energetic field and frequency, the Plane of existence some spiritual and philosophical traditions refer to as Maya, the dream The God is dreaming as we experience it as our "reality." As Maya is the temporal illusion of the material world, the Sanskrit term Leela*"* refers to the stage in her theater of dreams. This Divine play is the stage upon which our dance with personhood is choreographed. She casts the spell and we fall into the web she has woven, with its characteristic dualities, pain and pleasure, inelegant drama and mirages of our living and dying. We suffer because we seek to assign permanent reality to that which is temporary in the domain of transient form. We will experience clinging, craving, and yearning for the fantasy with a hunger that can never be satiated. This dance with form and manifestation is why we are here, each with our own unique role to play. The worship of the frills and trappings of Maya can distract and overwhelm the strongest of us, drawing our attention into irreverent obsession and compulsion.

When we awaken from this collective dream time enchantment, we remember who we really are and spin like a Dervish back into the welcoming arms of The Beloved, our Creator.

Though Maya is demonized by many, this archetype is not solely characterized as the antagonist mindset in an ongoing battle between the forces of good and evil. The energy of Maya manifests as characteristics within our own being, many we are unaware of. Some are hidden from us until the moment someone or something pushes just the right button, at just the right time, in just the right way, opening a floodgate through which our inner demons or angels are released. Even in our resistance to the insidious lower desires of carnal existence, it is no coincidence that our inner demons are the *same* as those we seek to expose and judge in the closets of other people.

An unhealthy attachment to Maya is a form of encapsulated spiritual psychosis. Maya can inspire unwholesome and futile emotional clinging to the world of matter, placing it above eternal reality. This obsession tips the scale of balance into the danger zone of worshiping the trappings of what we call success as a god form. The covetous love of money, material possessions, and physical form can then become the root of all evil. This energy can range from superficiality and greed to soul-selling, unspeakable wickedness. It is an element of the human condition, to the extent that none of us can say we are too perfect to fall under its influence. We continually battle against our own animalistic nature and insatiable desires to maintain our balance. Human desire is like a graveyard … There's always room for one more. The shadow side of our nature is characterized as ambitious and merciless. We are loved by The God that knows we are not perfect and knows how difficult it is for us to keep the balance of Spirit and clay. It is not perfection that is required of us. All that is required is remembrance. If we remember the Love of the Divine One in all that we do, there would be many things that would not even occur to us to do.

Maya knows. Her Third Eye is wide open, scanning the distance for the next challenge, the next victim, her next playmate. Maya delivers a strong message and warning, carrying with it both a blessing and a curse. Her energy seeks blind satisfaction and immediate gratification. She does not know that there are natural boundaries that must be respected. Some, we are instinctively aware of, while others are taught through cultural conditioning, institutional programming, and the experience of suffering as the result of our choices. Regardless of the urgency of our desires, we are admonished to respect the civilized boundaries of our own higher standards or be delivered painful consequences in self-created cause and effect scenarios. We pray for the strength and the spiritual discernment required to resist the stronghold of the shrewd temptation to forget who we really are.

As we become aware of the captivity of our own minds and desperately try to escape from the slavery of our attachment to worldly ideals, Maya smiles, amused by our conflict of interests. She lures us into her energy with promises of happiness and fulfillment. She whispers the soul-slaying lie of "forever 21." Lives and spirits are broken by the effect of the causes created by placing real value on appearances and the illusions of transient things.

We must acknowledge that in keeping with Universal Law, there exists in the shadows the Yang side of creation. There cannot be Light without the casting of shadows, and the Universe will always keep the perfect balance. Where there is excess on either side of that scale of balance, adjustment is built in, whispered between the letters of its spelling. Just as sweet as its taste for creation is the taste for destruction for relentless and unrepentant transgressions. Those who experience the wrath of this balancing act could easily feel they have been welcomed into hell. We must never feel safe to minimize the destructive potential of Universal Law, operating in the Karmic balance of life. This is an issue of perspective. If we have fallen into the rabbit hole of the illusions of Maya, we have invited the energy of her shadow attributes into our lives. These invitations can be as subtle as the secret thoughts and dreams we keep, or our most coveted fantasies seeking fulfillment. Powerful spiritual strongholds and manipulative thought-forms draw the attention of forces that promise satisfaction, usually at the expense and misery of others. There is always a price to pay or a reward delivered to our doorstep, either suffering or joy, based on the choices we make.

Reminiscent of Steven King's movie, Needful Things, this degenerative process begins with the things we feel we need. Thoughts like, "If I just had the perfect house, car, girl, guy, bank account balance, career, or whatever … Then I would be happy." This list may go on forever. The material possessions become as obsolete as a typewriter, and yet the hoarding and clutching, grasping, coveting, and clinging never ends. "If I just had another one, or two more, or the one I had in the beginning, or the one my friend has, or the state-of-the-art version I saw on TV ... then I would be happy." Happy never comes, or it comes as a fleeting moment, and costs our eternal soul. None of the things we seek to possess and think we love so much will ever love us back! Much is to be said for ambition. But remember the Biblical passage, "For what is a man profited, if he shall gain the whole world, and lose his soul? Or what shall a man give in exchange for his soul?" (Matthew - 16:26) The Bible (KJV)

Regarding relationships, Maya is a sign forewarning us to embrace the soul satisfaction of a *higher* love … Love that transcends the body, the mind, even the emotions, seeking the union of two souls. It warns us to seek the abundant

Kingdom of The God, which provides for us and protects us. We are not to covet the transient glitter of bargain store soul bartering. At the end of chasing the illusions of matter, we will only find a massive sea of disappointment. We must examine our lives as though our souls depend on it, and cleanse our lives of the belief systems that seek to spoil everything we care about.

It is important within the material realm of being to refrain from playing God in the judgment of others. The energetic domain of Maya rarely defines the totality of anyone's being, regardless of how raw lust, materialism, and greed have eroded a vulnerable character. The energy of Maya is cyclical, for such extremes cause rapid decay and swift ruin. On the other side of what appears to be a rampant free for all, is an epiphany waiting to happen.

In his world-renowned book of poetry, *The Prophet*,
Khalil Gibran said of evil:

Of the good in you I can speak, but not of the evil.
What is evil but good tortured by Its own hunger and thirst?
Verily when good is hungry, it seeks food even in dark caves,
and when it thirsts it drinks even of dead waters.

~ Khalil Gibran ~

The shadow energy of Maya speaks of addiction and perverse obsession, seeking pleasure from that which brings harm to self or others. It advises us to live a more balanced and disciplined life. It also suggests that we have become unbalanced in the neglect of spiritual, creative, and productive pursuits.

There must come a time in life for self-examination to determine if our value systems have faltered in servitude to our egos. We are required to view the world through our Third Eye, seeing people not as useful carnage but as spirit.

Attachment to the ephemeral can price our souls into Karmic debt and send us tumbling into abysmal hopelessness.

The most important lesson that we could ever hope to learn is that this cartoon-like characterization of a fixed reality is pure theater. Our soul's challenge on this Plane of matter is to overcome and survive the animalistic nature of our own human form, and the mischief our minds conjure, even as we sleep. The truth may be difficult to accept. That which causes birth, growth, and renewal, and the Force which destroys, prunes, and reaps are One and the same, the Yin and the Yang.

The magnetism and hypnotism of Maya challenge us to free ourselves from our own cruel and judgmental personalities. We are encouraged to seek and find The God within, with the knowledge that within is also where the bondage of attachment to Maya resides. The greatest holy war of all is the one that is constantly raging within, the conflict between the purity of our Spirit and Essence of our Creator, and the thoughts and desires of the flesh. Our goal is to elevate our thoughts and desires to the level that our souls are the most spiritually comfortable with. A sound, wholesome spiritual practice is the key to maintaining this very delicate balance.

Just as surely as the collective consciousness of high spirituality exists, there is also the collective consciousness of low vibration, worldly desires, and fixations. Our own energy of unbalanced attachment to the temporal world can create a spark that jumps the gap and taps us directly into the stream of energy that we know to be the consciousness of iniquity. This energy can travel through the portals we have created with extremes of grief, anger, rage, hatred, fear, jealousy, lust, loneliness, desperation, and greed. Our subtle bodies, as well as our physical bodies, can become filled with this magnetic negativity, drawing into our lives that energy with which it is resonant. It can feel as though our inner and outer worlds are under siege.

We are born under the influence of the unsleeping and watchful eye of this prevalent, predatory shadow energy. It lies in wait, always poised to jump at the first available opportunity to deliver the next test of our strength of character and mindfulness of what we know to be right and good. When the seductive force of Maya threatens the strength of a firm meditation, it is time to put aside fear and seek refuge in The God of all creation. The most profound protection that can be invoked is accomplished with prayer. Repetitive prayer and chanting of words of power as a mantra can create a vibration capable of expelling internal and external mischievous energies. This practice is a form of prayer, yet, more powerfully, a form of *remaining* in prayer.

My references to the powerful seductions of Maya offer insight regarding the distinctions of her dual nature. While we are given this Divine journey through physical life as a beautiful gift and a lesson, we must never forget the glory of life Eternal in our daily practice. In the soul's depths, our primary defense against the seduction of Maya and its mesmeric, compelling force is connecting with The Creator through sincere prayer and surrender to Divine Will and Guidance. Only in our binding relationship with The God may our free spirits be lifted up into the realm of the Eternal in the resurrection of our Light. That Union is our firm meditation. Resist extremes. Resist duality. Nothing exists but The God.

Our Attachment to the Physical Form

When we look in the mirror, we may or may not love the image that we see. In many ways, we possess the power to alter the image of the body vehicle. We care for that image in the same manner that one cares for a car. We clean it. We maintain its mechanical functions. We sometimes cosmetically alter it to suit our subjective standards of beauty. We take care in how we fuel it. We drive it with caution. We protect and insure it. But with a car, we don't often lose our focus in remembering the difference between the vehicle and the driver.

As with a car, some of us are attached to the beauty of our car more than the mechanics or practicality, even the safety of it. Then on the day that abuse and careless neglect returns a consequence, the original beauty that attracted us to it in the first place is gone, as is our attachment to our original perception of its beauty. Unlike our options with our physical body vehicle, we can get rid of it.

Let us take a look at the word "beauty." Beauty is one of the most subjective of judgments. The adage, "beauty is in the eye of the beholder" is a good yardstick of measure when attempting to determine beauty, based on the vision of others. From the perspective of diverse realities, examine the politics of beauty, the standards of the beholder, and what qualifies those standards of beauty in their collective or personal opinion. Many standards are byproducts of environment, cultural conditioning, and past experiences that can extend as far back as childhood. Many things can happen to a person to mold, alter, or damage his or her self-image. Superficial self-esteem can turn on a dime, one way or the other.

The process of assimilation into any homogenous group or type of people as a minority demographic in appearance, cultural characteristics, and traits can affect what a person sees when he or she looks in the mirror. It is compounded by a strong agenda being in place that is invested in maintaining the designated identifying images being held as the standard. According to what model of acceptability do we judge ourselves, or become influenced by the judgments of other people? Judgments such as "beautiful" and "not beautiful" can be deeply influenced by a majority or a controlling minority of beholders. Modern technology enables us to alter physical images to produce the illusion of whatever transient standard of "perfection" we choose. Studies of the choices people make or would make if given the opportunity, tell us a story about the standards that influence our perceptions of beauty. The imposition of the standards of other people can contribute to negative self-image syndrome and feelings of inadequacy, leading to low self-esteem. The authors of the imposed standards can diminish their own beauty with the spirit of an inflated ego and self-image that overrides the acceptability of another standard.

What is the common denominator between the two? Both sides of perception are standing before a mirror, looking at perishable, transient forms and torturing themselves and one another with their comparisons and attachment to identity as a person. If we maintain the position of the witness, observing the driver of a vehicle that does not define who we really are, we can free ourselves from external definitions of who we are. Imagine the effect that would have on economies that capitalize on these painful, dangerous illusions.

Media is a powerful contributing factor to imposing subjective standards of beauty as a means to the end of exploiting the insecurities of their targets. The masses are continually bombarded with overt and subliminal manipulation to succumb to the pressure and control of cultural conditioning and propaganda. Endless attacks are made upon a vulnerable self-image, using contrived stereotypes and archetypes of beauty. These deceptions and illusions are designed to encourage negative comparisons to images that often are not even real. Many have lost their lives in their attempts to realize the false images perpetuated by the hypnotic influence of the well-baited hook of capitalistic media. For many, it has become an obsession to measure up to Photoshopped, airbrushed images that even defy the reality of the models used to create them. Media responsibility has been cited and admonished to hold their integrity to a higher standard of accountability. A movement is calling attention to the media-generated damage caused to the mental, physical, emotional, and spiritual well-being of many who are seduced by its potentially negative influence, especially among children. A mass awakening is fully underway. These tricks will not work on Self-Realized people.

It is a natural inclination to seek the experience of beauty and acceptability. Some societies determine that covering the body is beautiful. Some promote uncovering the body, face, and hair as beautiful. What is beautiful in the North may not be beautiful in the South. What is accepted as a standard of beauty in the West may get you killed in the East. We are a world much too preoccupied with outer beauty and external appearances. We subject ourselves to brutal, critical scrutiny, even bullying. We often fail to realize our inner Light, the glow of which creates an aura of natural beauty. The absence or diminished capacity of it can destroy our beauty. Our positive thoughts enable that inner Light to shine. Negative thoughts and energy stemming from our low vibrational judgments and fixations can serve to eclipse our Light and make us appear unpleasing to all three eyes of those who can see with wisdom.

It is more important to engage self-images that are created more from the inside out, rather than from the outside in. We are challenged by our default settings when we identify as the imageless, Timeless Self, the Self with no story, no age, no agenda, no form, and no ego. If we were to spend as much time, energy, and money, cultivating our inner beauty and Light as we spend on the outside, we would become beautiful by the highest of standards. We would glow with confidence and grace. We would shine the beautiful Light The God gave us as the

Ultimate standard of beauty. We would see ourselves from the perspective of the eternal, the unfading, the perfect, the loved, the cherished, the immortal Light body.

We are misinformed to hate age, death, and infirmity. It is easy to be seduced into that type of thinking. But worse is that we let "images" define us and represent who we really are. The I AM, the Eternal Spirit that we are, breaks mirrors and renders labels, judgments, and superficial identifications empty and void of power over us. Through ego-stripping transcendental meditation practices, we become able to embrace the purification of being chiseled down to raw awareness to heal the damage the ego is capable of attracting.

As an interesting spiritual exercise, look in the mirror, then draw close to the image we see. The eyes are the mirrors and portals of the soul. Make eye contact with the reflection of our eyes and look deep within. Study them. Venture behind them. See the beautiful spirit that is the *driver* of the vehicle, rather than being overly preoccupied with the vehicle. Make sure that the driver receives a higher level of attention than the means of its transportation.

The War Within

Given the duality of our being, how could we not be at war within ourselves, challenged to fight continually and without rest to maintain the delicate balance of spirit and clay? We manage the nature of the two aspects of ourselves that often oppose, negate, and deny one another. Existential chaos results when we see our spiritual and physical selves as being mutually exclusive. This contradiction will torment us and often trap us in perpetual disagreement with dueling aspects of ourselves. We must recognize the crossroad where the bondage of the flesh and the freedom of the spirit within meet.

It is not easy to understand or control the obsessions and compulsions of the physical self, as it competes to usurp the will of the non-physical Self. This power struggle is a fight to the grave to maintain our moral high ground over the lure of the animalistic side of our nature. The never-ending list of demands of the flesh can hold the spirit hostage.

To understand the character of the war between flesh and spirit is to know how to win it. To emerge victorious from this spiritual war, we must first understand that we look outside of ourselves for the demons we battle when the deadliest of them all is within. Our Light and our shadows do not have to exist in an illusory state of conflict, sufficient to cancel each other out. It is our choice to view these opposite polarities in our nature as a necessity to one another, as the Yin is to the Yang. See the Yin/Yang diagram in the section, The Meaning of the I AM. Emerging out of Chaos as the Divine order of creation, we affirm that each side is a binding link to the other, causing the whole to continue to exist in harmony. The alchemy of the synthesis of Yin and Yang energies has the power to manifest thought-form to form and back again.

We must not allow the war within to define our existence, even though it gives the appearance of being capable of doing so. These illusions are often parlor tricks and theater. The enemy of humanity is invested in our believing chaos is our only truth, seeking to weaken our resolve, kill our spirits, and cause us to define who we are based on our lowest potential. Demonic energies are associated with the energy of hopelessness. They whisper into our hearts disparaging messages that are intended to cast shadows, so overwhelming that our Light may be eclipsed. The result would be our compliant seduction into hatred of one another, and hatred for our own selves, which is the gateway to destruction and ruin.

The Dance of Duality

Where there is Light, shadows are cast. Where there are shadows, there must be Light somewhere. Rather than viewing ourselves as creatures of such warring contradictions, I choose to view our duality as the graceful dance between our shadows and the brilliance of our Eternal Light. The Light is sacred. Even the shadow is sacred. The music and lyrics are a symphony of our prayers, as well as the answers to them. These energies conspire to protect us through our daily struggles for wholeness and survival. The dance floor is this plane of matter. It smiles upon our inept footing and struggles to maintain balance until the music stops and that silence embraces another dancer.

The carnal manifestation that we are serves to acquire knowledge that we can only experience, and authentically comprehend, from within the physical vehicle that transports our soul. How could the taste of an apple be described to our non-physical body of consciousness that exists beyond the senses? Both aspects of our being, the physical and non-physical, complement one another. Our Light and our shadows transcend duality, in their intimate embrace, intertwined and spinning as the whirling Dervish, seeking the Divine intoxication of union with The God. This is an unprecedented state of bliss, associated with making a connection with the Holy, Sacred Spirit of The Divine One. Beyond bliss is the shadow's realization of its relationship with, and as, that Light of Divinity.

We are not to confuse the dichotomy of our nature with the spiritual war raging between what we see as opposing forces of good and evil, in the Heavens, on Earth, and deep within the personal and collective psyche. There seems to be no negotiation or peace talks between these two, apparently, clashing energies. In the energetic context of the Yin and Yang, these energies interdependently represent harmony, balance, and motion. It is Universal Law.

We are responsible for our own choices. Our unwavering Love for the concept of good is the music, the resonance, that guides our steps and its rhythms. We are required to fully disengage ourselves from the fearful thoughts that can cause a naturally occurring universal formula for creation to turn into a deadly last dance. We seek to conquer the whispered influences of demonic voices by withdrawing attention from them. We were promised this plague from our original conception. We defeat them by giving them no place to land in our consciousness. We, instead, embrace the gentle voices of the angels that are set in place to attend, serve, and protect us.

We often, consciously and subconsciously, ascribe ridiculous identities, properties, and special effects to what we call angels and demons. There are no winged, flying, scantily clad, blond babies with chubby cheeks; No buxom supermodels with flowing tresses, in prom gowns and white robes. Who paints these pictures? There are no horns, pitchforks, or tails ... no red body-suited, shadowy, devil monsters. It is much more insidious than that. These are images in our minds, with no basis in physical or spiritual reality. Our cultural and religious conditioning would have us believe these off-putting, cartoonish imaginings have power over our lives.

Both demons and angels can assume both physical and non-physical forms. They have an I AM of their own ... A formless awareness ... A consciousness. Their faces are in our mirrors, and the mirrors of everyone and everything we know. We already know how the story ends. That knowledge should rob it of much of its shock value and potential to instill fear. However, that makes the challenge no less threatening. The worst mistake anyone can make is to disregard or underestimate the strength of an enemy. Evil does not sleep. Good does not blink. Sometimes we cannot distinguish the difference between the two. We must never forget the blessing bestowed upon us of an army of angels, commissioned to protect and help us, as a testament of their love, obedience, and service to The God.

We drift off into sleep, and wake up every day of our lives, fighting the same old war. It hides its ugly face behind a multitude of deceptive masks. Many are family and friends. Many exalt themselves over us from positions of authority over our lives. Many hide in the shadows on the straight path of our most sacred vows.

For we wrestle not against flesh and blood,
but against principalities, against powers,
against the rulers of the darkness of this world,
against spiritual wickedness in high places."

~ Ephesians 6-12 The Bible (KJV) ~

The knowledge of inevitable defeat fails to deter their negative energies and vicious attacks. The motivation for senseless warring in the face of foreseeable defeat is the pleasure and sick satisfaction derived from the mischief and chaos they create. Their only victory is that we fear more than we love; that we fear death; fear life; fear change; fear one another; fear ourselves, and never realize the ubiquitous power of the True Self that we really are.

Our only defense against suffering, from whatever the perceived cause, is the knowledge of Self. Who are we being on this stage called life, and what frequencies do we make ourselves available to? When we say, I AM, Who are we really? The celebrated poet, Rumi, describes our carnal self, standing apart from its spiritual Source, as a "dunghill." We are no better than those angels and positive forces that attend us. Our vanity, arrogance, greed, and ignorance have led many of us to believe we are better than the angelic kingdom. It is not wise to take the Light of their protection for granted or fail to show our gratitude by becoming a Light to others.

We, as "creation," have a natural tendency to be ambitious and merciless creatures. That inclination is intertwined with survival instincts, yet, we choose the path we will be held accountable for. It is so pronounced that, whether we are consciously aware of it or not, we are all nervously awaiting the appearance of something, or someone, to call order to our desperate situation. Our passive waiting is but another selfish demand that we are served, without serving. In the face of our suffering, in the face of our grief, our service to others who suffer and grieve determines our ability to survive it and heal ourselves. We must serve as we receive the blessings that are our inheritance from our Creator. If we serve humanity, we are earning the bountiful gifts that The God delights in our receiving from the Light and Source of all giving.

The dance between the clay and the Light Spirit, the container and the contained, is fully underway. It can be just as graceful or awkward as our careful or careless footing dictates. The trumpet is certainly sounding. Let the dance begin.

UNCHANGING

I am as I was
from my beginning
void of palpable form
descended from
the Eternal
into illusory realms of Maya
from the root to the fruit
inside and out
I can only be me

You never knew me
You cannot see me
I cling to the unchanging

Time keeps on lying
Time keeps on trying
to change me
rearrange me
remodel
refashion
reshape me

You, the sculptor
with your chisel
carving away at
my soul's stone
reduced to
a statue
of your own design
seeking to change me
from who I Am
into someone
you wish me to be
I can only be me

You never knew me
You cannot see me
I cling to the unchanging

I wear images
like looking glass clothes
I change them with my mind
I Am day changing to night
I Am the seasons of the year
I Am the Moon
I Am full … complete
even as my Light
is eclipsed
and darkness enfolds me
even as I appear
to be waning
into the deep
it is only for a time
in a Timeless realm

Know that
I will
be that
full Moon
again
as a sparkle
in the Beloved's eye
Who sees me as I Am?

Before I let you
change me
from who I am
to some phantom
of your dreams
some mannequin
in the storefront
window of
your vanity shop

I will disappear
ascend into Light
vanish into Ether
return to Breath
I can only be me

You never knew me
You cannot see me
I cling only to the unchanging
come cling with me

~ JAI ~
Smoke & Mirrors

The Chakra System & The Aura

Recommended before engaging in the I TRANSCEND MY EGO SELF featured Meditation

Basic Human Chakra System

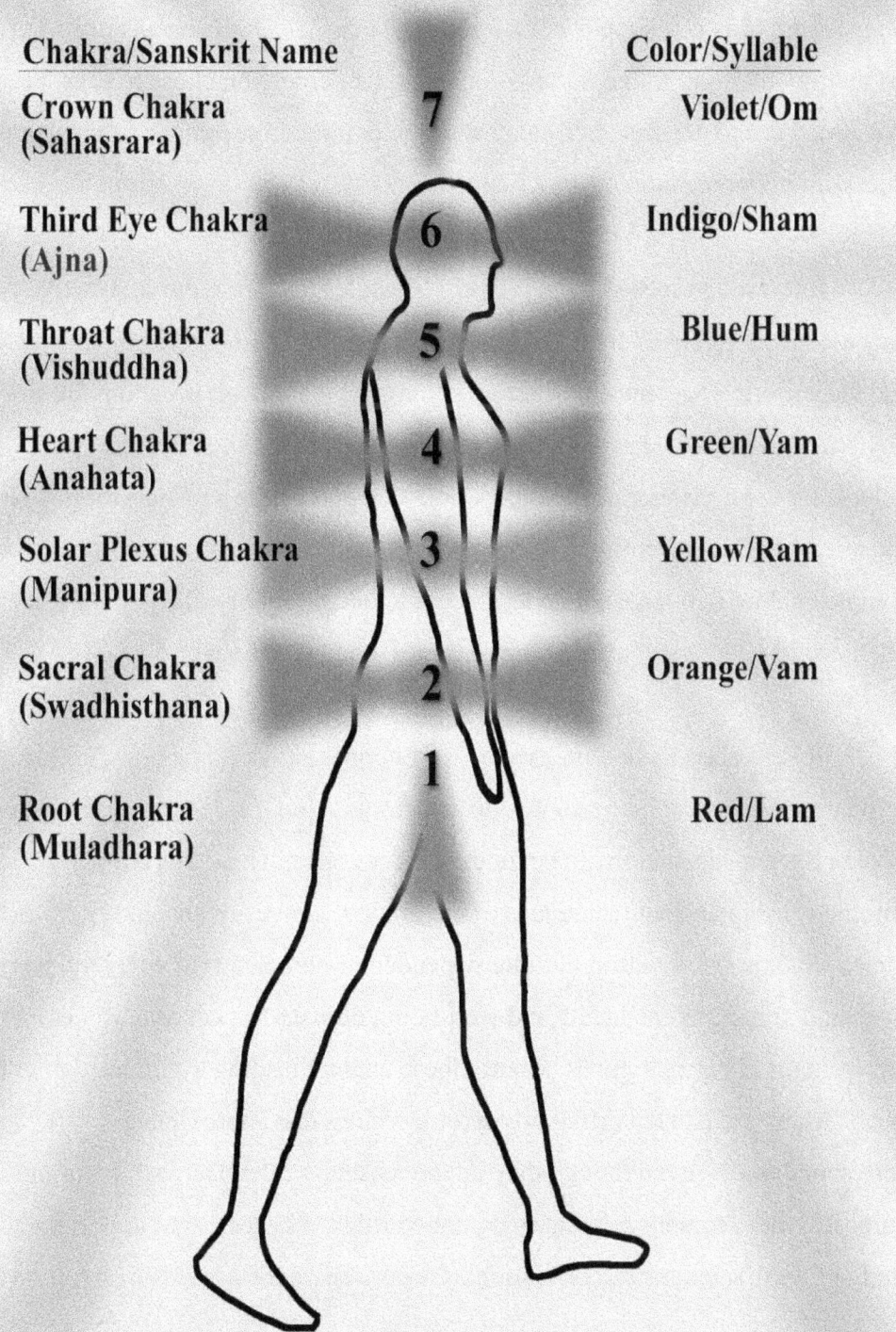

Chakra/Sanskrit Name	Color/Syllable
Crown Chakra (Sahasrara)	Violet/Om
Third Eye Chakra (Ajna)	Indigo/Sham
Throat Chakra (Vishuddha)	Blue/Hum
Heart Chakra (Anahata)	Green/Yam
Solar Plexus Chakra (Manipura)	Yellow/Ram
Sacral Chakra (Swadhisthana)	Orange/Vam
Root Chakra (Muladhara)	Red/Lam

Meditation and the Chakra System

Time seems to be folding in on itself, forming a loop with no exits. History is repeating, or is it? Time is not a line. It is a circle. Our concepts of its tenses spin within the rigid frame our one-dimensional perception chose to draw around it. We turned it into a worn-out roller coaster with tattered restraints, offering a deadly ride, with our perception of its actual existence.

Interesting times deliver stressful lifestyles that are more destructive than they are nurturing. Add fear, grief, and systemic dehumanization to the equation, and the suffering becomes unbearable among the masses. It is making us sick. Physical and emotional resolve weakens, leaving the mind, body, and spirit vulnerable to all manner of illness. A holistic approach to self-nurturing is required for survival. Understanding and cooperating with the energetic aspects of our complex nature will have a healing effect on the quality of our lives, our relationships, careers, families, communities, and even the world.

It is reasonable to wonder why the energy centers of the body's Chakra System are important in the context of this book. You might be wondering what the Chakra System has to do with healing from loss, grief, and other crippling emotions, using ancient techniques of meditation … We are absolutely *not* off topic. Chakras work within our interdependent, interconnected energetic body system, determining the health and well-being of every aspect of our lives. I tend to mix systems in my references because these ancient healing traditions do not really clash. Many are labeled differently but carry the same approximate correspondences. Even though they are not casually interchangeable, for our basic purposes, these cursory references do not conflict. Regardless of the origin of the study of these sciences and philosophies, I only share the ones that I have experiential knowledge of, and have worked with long enough to know they share similar energetic functions.

In the wake of emotional devastation, we can be left with damage so widespread that we cannot even track its origin, much less try to heal from it. Its roots are energetic and manifest in imbalances in the flow of the Prana (Ethereal Breath), the Aura (Electromagnetic Energy Field), and Chi (Life Force). I knew this to be true from years of prior metaphysical studies. Still, if someone had tried to engage me in conversation about Chakras, Auras, Prana, Chi, and Meditation, while I suffered in the throes of unbearable grief for the loss of my mother … I shudder to imagine what my response would have been. At that time, I had no experiential context for the fact that my aura was gray and lacerated; that all of my chakras were decimated, shattered; that my Chi energy was flat-lining; that my Prana was having a Near-Death-Experience. I would not have been available for a conversation about how restoring the healthy function of my Chakra System could initiate a healing in my life, and completely change the way my consciousness processed grief. The symptoms consistent with how most people process grief is often indistinguishable from soul-loss, on the level of requiring a soul retrieval. I broke like a china cup on cement.

The Universe intervened and sent me the guidance I needed. I was advised as to the level of my damage and told that a sound meditation practice had to be in place to facilitate my healing. Healthy chakras are needed to conduct the Prana up the central channel of the spinal column, to maintain the focus and concentration required to achieve ideal meditative states. Sharing these experiences through the guided meditations my practice inspired, requires that I start at the necessary foundation, the spiritual/metaphysical infrastructure. That is why chakras are important to reference before we go on to practice our *I Transcend My Ego Self* meditation. A basic understanding of their function and an introductory chakra meditation exercise is a useful preparation for a profoundly healing meditation practice. Another entire book or volumes of books could be written and read on just that one subject. I am presenting them in a cursory way, based on my own personal experience of their relevance to achieving deep meditative states. Not having an understanding of the energetic connection between the chakras and meditation could result in an unpleasant, even dangerous experience.

Through the fog of my shock and denial, I recalled things I was taught over decades of mystical studies. I realized how blessed I was to have trained under the tutelage of adept initiates who had prepared me to understand what was happening to me, one flat-lining chakra at a time. It all began to make sense to me that my study of chakras and systems of meditation in Martial Arts, Traditional Chinese Medicine (TCM), Eastern and Western mysticism, and energy healing had suddenly become an element of my own emotional recovery. The aura had a new and very personal significance to my life. The healing benefits of a committed meditation practice, initially *Vipassana*, had become a matter of survival. I could see how fundamentally interconnected it all is and what my personal relationship with this ancient wisdom turned out to be.

The knowledge of chakras is fundamental to self-healing through a meditation discipline. Our mindfulness of their energies serves to strengthen our practice (Sadhana). Sadhana is a Tibetan word that refers to a repeated, transcendent spiritual practice performed as self-reflection and non-judgmental Self-Witnessing. It accomplishes the release of worldly attachments from bondage and into liberation, enlightenment, and freedom from the birth/death continuum. It does not conflict with anyone's spiritual or religious path because of its transcendent nature. It offers the spiritual sovereignty to independently develop one's own unique mystical practice, not requiring participating in any organized group.

The energies of each chakra have everything to do with how we process emotional trauma. Once we are familiar with their meanings, we will practice a visualization exercise as a method of clearing blockages that have a destructive effect on our physical, mental, emotional, and spiritual well-being. This chakra meditation is a concise visualization for each of the chakras and will encourage the unobstructed flow of their positive energy. Many systems of meditation can help clear an accumulation of negative energies that poison these sensitive and reactive vortices and interfere with the experience of inner peace.

The word chakra is derived from the Sanskrit word "chakram," which means "wheel." This term refers to a network of seven major funnel or cone-shaped energy vortex centers of the subtle body. They are believed to be about six inches in diameter, extending one inch out from the physical body. The wider opening is on the outside of the back and front of the physical body, with the small tip located inside of our body, near the spine, connecting the two. They are positioned vertically, from the base of the spine, up through the top of the head. They inhale and exhale vital orgone (etheric) energy with the direction of their spin. Each one of these whirling dimensions of consciousness relates, respectively, to particular moods and states of mind, body, and spirit and have many correspondences that expand their meanings. They are intimately connected to the internal and external experiences of our physical and subtle bodies. They work as a system.

The aura is a seven-layered fusion of radiant, luminous energy that makes up the electromagnetic field that surrounds the body of all living things. The condition of the Chakra System affects the emanation of the aura. The aura reflects whether or not the chakras are blocked or open, healthy or damaged, and the strength of their vibrational frequency. The colors and energy that emanates from the chakras appear in the aura with a story to tell about the mood, emotional state, and the health of the physical and subtle body. They can reveal if we are depressed, grieving, tired, happy, secure, sociable, anxious, or fearful. To some who are gifted with telepathic vision, this field of luminous energy is readable. It is perceived as seven layers, with seven colors of astral light, associated with the chakras and the aura. Messages regarding our overall well-being can be intuited based on the impressions of energetic attachments that may show up in the aura. Our efforts to hold the health and integrity of our Chakra System to a high standard cause a resultant cleansing and re-energizing of the aura. Its health depends on the quality of the inner and outer environments of our lives.

Prana is the subtle Light energy, and breath is the physical energy. They maintain the intricate system that determines the strength of our Life Force. Breath is our first and last response to life on this plane of existence. Prana is life-sustaining and vital to most aspects of our being. One of our initial responses to change or energy shifts, on any level of our being, is a fluctuation or constriction of the flow of breath. The conscious Pranic breathing that is required for meditation has an entirely different effect on the brain than unconscious breathing. When we meditatively breathe in Prana, we are inhaling Light, not just air, and not necessarily through the nostrils. To still the mind, observing or witnessing the flow of breath, clears stuck or knotted Pranic energy that interferes with the function of the chakras. These blockages will have a direct effect on the integrity of your meditation experience. One of the functions of the wheels of the chakras is to direct the flow of Prana up through the middle of three vertical channels that extend up the spinal column, from its base up through the Crown Chakra. Its force facilitates the untangling of energetic knots and obstructions that can disrupt the optimum function of our entire body system.

Thought and intention ride upon the energy force of Prana. The circulation of Prana, powered by positive thought-forms and intentions, can manifest as an intense healing technique. It is the perfect storm in a breath, charged to target and neutralize or eliminate sources of illness and imbalance. The proper use of it can transform gloomy perceptions of our inner and outer realities. The transformation of perception can and will alter our reality. The reason that Prana is so important to meditation is that our personal Prana connects to the powerful healing energies of the Universal Prana and gives us access to it. Meditation can activate this connection, and one can draw from it the amount of this metaphysical substance required to enter transcendent states of consciousness.

Pranayama is a combination of two Sanskrit words, translated as *breath control*, and refers to prescribed techniques of using breath to accomplish specific results. Some form of the ancient yogic practice of Pranayama meditation (witnessing, observing, and controlling of breath) is recommended at the start of every meditation session of any kind. It can be used informally, at any time that its healing energy is needed. This practice can be beneficial in managing a wide range of stress-related illnesses, including panic, anxiety, and grief attacks. It is a risky undertaking to engage in the practice of Pranayama without the guidance of a teacher or guru, and it would be wise to consult a medical and/or psychological professional. This is not aerobics. There are cosmic energies at play that could compromise physical and emotional balance if not practiced correctly. It is a lifestyle … A commitment to preparation and purification. There is no claim that the meditative breathing exercises in this book are consistent with the practice of Pranayama, in its tradition of origin. We are only *observing* the subtleties of our breathing to enhance our focus and concentration in preparation for our guided meditation, *I Transcend My Ego Self*.

In Traditional Chinese Medicine (TCM), Chi is the "breath" or "wind," the vital Life Force that exists in all things. It is the difference between a living body and a cadaver. Chi energy is strongly reactive to our emotions and that of others in our energy field. Grief and trauma cause blockages that can compromise the healthy flow of energy. In a human being, Chi is the reservoir of energy located in the area of the lower abdomen, in the first of the three levels of Tan Dien, where it is stored and distributed throughout the body. Any weakness or obstruction in the distribution of the Chi force can result in key physical organs not receiving needed revitalization, causing our health to deteriorate. The Hara (sea of energy), located in the navel area, is a portal that operates as a vacuum, pulling the Pranic energy into the Tan Dien. The universal aspect of Prana passes through the gateway to the subtle body and is believed by some traditions, to be one of three Tan Dien Chakras. The other two are located in the area of the heart and the Third Eye. When the flow of Chi to the lower Tan Dien is blocked, it leaves the reservoir feeling empty. An insatiable hunger is created along with an unhealthy compulsion to fill it, resulting in a variety of disorders and addictions related to the shadow side of the First and Second Chakra.

Meditating on a particular chakra while visualizing its corresponding color is known to stimulate the energy of that chakra. Sound vibration can also affect the chakras. Each chakra has a corresponding tone, however, the intonation of the OM/AUM resonates with all of them. Certain meditation practices are designed to clear energetic obstructions of the Chakra System by raising our Kundalini energy force. It is believed to contain the essence of human potentiality. The objective of some meditation and yogic practices is to cause the Kundalini to rise to the level of the Seventh (Crown) Chakra, resulting in spiritual enlightenment, transcendence, and emergence from Time and Space. It should be kept in mind that the same practice can also create a Spiritual Emergency called a "spontaneous Kundalini Awakening." Caution would advise us to understand that *any* type of meditation can trigger a variety of spiritual emergencies that would challenge our knowledge and ability to maintain control. It is unwise to approach the study of meditation, or any other mystical practice, in a cursory way. A working knowledge of methods of psychic protection is worth the effort to learn. There are all types of literature available, including my book FEARLESS: PSYCHIC SELF-DEFENSE, Transcend the Fear of Spiritual Warfare. What you don't know *can* hurt you.

There are as many varied descriptions of the function, even the number of chakras, as there are belief systems and believers. There is also a multitude of variances of correspondences relating to every aspect of the Chakra System, based on the tradition of who is describing them. Western authors have been criticized for representing ancient teachings based on what they have, legitimately, learned from teachers who, like themselves, do not read Sanskrit, and are not authentic practitioners of the most essential related teachings. Many do not share the spiritual infrastructure upon which the wisdom of these teachings is founded. This implies no disrespect, nor suggestions of anyone's intent to deliberately deceive or mislead. I am not implying that there is no value in such Western teachings. In some cases, it can be an advantage to have someone explain the complexities of such profound wisdom in a more understandable way, more aligned with our own language and culture. That having been stated, I am claiming no authority in tradition or application of the mystical depths and interpretations of the Chakra System. I introduce it here to be used as conceptual focal points for visualization, meditation, and self-healing, as it relates to the guided meditation exercises offered in this book.

Human beings react emotionally and spiritually to change, grief, and loss. The energy vortices of the Chakra System are where that grief is absorbed, processed, and hopefully, healed. A practical understanding of the most basic application of these powerful energies can offer the meditator a transcendent experience and visions into many dimensions of freedom from suffering. This is not intended to be a thorough explanation or representation of any particular tradition. These are exercises that I was taught to incorporate into my meditation discipline, because they help to keep the energy of the Chakra System fine-tuned, clean, and strong. The Chakra System was particularly relevant to my meditation practice because grief had so overwhelmed me. I had to begin healing at the level of the subtlest of energies first.

Basic Guidelines for Mystical Meditation

Before engaging in any meditation: Observe recommended basic protocol regarding personal hygiene, and be attentive to the cleanliness and ambiance of your setting. Sit in a private, quiet, comfortable place with soft lighting, where you will not be disturbed. Assume an erect, comfortable posture. Facing the East is best, energetically. Touch your tongue to the roof of your mouth and clench the buttocks to effectively channel and contain the flow of energy. Touch your thumb to the center or index finger of your hands, rest them, palms up, on your thighs/knees. If you are not physically able to sit in a full or modified Lotus position, be mindful of your posture and sit up in a comfortable chair. It can also be practiced lying down if you can do so without falling asleep.

Prepare a quiet place for prayer and meditation. There should be no television, radio, electronic devices, or distracting conversation. The telephone should be turned off, along with anything else that could startle or distract you. It is recommended that you remove watches and ticking clocks from your sacred space. Be conscious of excessive exposure to electromagnetic currents for their ability to scramble your frequency.

Keep the lighting warm and avoid fluorescent lighting. Avoid meditating in complete darkness and never meditate under fluorescent or CFL (compact fluorescent lighting). They disrupt your auric field, causing it to become disoriented. They produce dead orgone energy that can compromise your immune system, your moods, and make you sick. Dead orgone (Universal Life Force) energy from fluorescent lighting can be blocked by safely using a decorative cloth covering as shading to lessen exposure to its harmful effects. A single white candle can be a relaxing focal point.

Take particular care in the maintenance of a clean, healthy aura. The human aura can be negatively affected by the energy you expose yourself to. Thoughts are things. We are all being constantly bombarded with negative thought-forms, energies, and vibrations from our environment, as well as the negativity that we generate from within ourselves. The electromagnetic force field around the physical body requires maintenance to keep it cleansed of the garbage that so easily attaches to it and drains our positive energy. An accumulation of this negative energy can make us walking magnets for bad experiences and compromised health. An unhealthy aura is a breeding ground for spiritual, mental, emotional, and physical disease.

The aura may be cleansed in many ways, including the use of crystals and semi-precious stones, which promote balance and restore positive energy. Proper use of certain types of crystals can improve psychic and spiritual abilities when used in meditation, with the understanding, of course, that the magic is not in the crystals. The magic is in you. Understand, as well, that this is not trendy jewelry. If you are not prepared to study and practice the proper care and maintenance of crystals and other sacred meditation tools, it is best just to leave them alone. A whole book can be written about how to respect their sacred energy. Spiritual cleansing baths, meditation, and prayer are powerful purification practices for the personal self and sacred paraphernalia.

Holding a clear quartz crystal can help to enhance the clarity of the messages you receive during meditation. Crystals are used to cleanse and make energetic adjustments to the body's electromagnetic field from the body matrix, extending to the aura. The aura can reflect nuances of our emotional state in a light or glow of rainbow colors around the body. Some can see this light show. Some can experience it through the senses. Holding a prescribed type of crystal for a prescribed energetic adjustment can bring more intensity to the meditation. Hold the quartz crystal in your left hand with the faceted point directed at your Solar Plexus Chakra. Hold another in your right hand with the faceted tip pointing up, directed at the Third Eye. This helps when issues buried deep in the subconscious are prevented from surfacing because of impenetrable emotional barriers. These cannot be treated as jewelry or decoration. They must be handled with respect for their sacred spiritual power observing protocol regarding their prescribed manner of cleansing, in accordance with the phases of the Moon. Never use crystals that are borrowed or given as a gift without "charging" them with your own energy and purpose. If you are not willing to go into a responsible and respectful study of how they operate, it is best not to use them at all. It could result in many levels of an unpleasant experience. They absorb and release energies in a way that can get out of control. As with all things, respect for the protocol is required with the use of crystals.

Be mindful of your breathing. Use your breath as a focal point in your meditations. As a way of staying focused and raising your vibration, the chanting of a mantra sacred to you helps to facilitate cleansing and protection. Be mindful of the mantra that you choose to chant. Make sure that if it is in a language that you do not understand, get the literal translation and study it before you continue your practice. I have witnessed people chant up their worst nightmares because of a misguided meditation practice and a carelessly chosen mantra. One of the greatest mantras is simply *Thank You*. Chant it and become it … Conscious gratitude, living under Ultimate Grace. I do not recommend any particular mudra (hand, finger, posture positions) to perform the meditations in this book. I use a basic tip of the center or index finger touching the tip of the thumb, palms up, resting on the knees, upright modified lotus position. Many variations of that will work. It is worth the effort to research and experiment with the mudras that are best for your preferred system of meditation. It is not a cursory study, but it is a rewarding one that is certainly worth the effort.

Don't eat, drink, smoke, chew gum, or participate in idle chatter when engaged in spiritual work. This behavior is distracting and vulgar. You are cultivating your ability to focus and concentrate, and you do not want to engage in gross and disruptive behaviors. That does not show a proper level of respect for yourself or the sacredness of spiritual practice. These guidelines fall under the category of common manners.

No alcohol or drugs. Do not ingest any substance that would alter your consciousness before, during, or directly after meditating. This absolutely includes mind-altering pharmaceutical drugs. Consult with the medical practitioner who prescribed your medication and ask if there are risks that are relevant to a meditation practice. Any substance that causes impairment can attract energies and entities that are better left crouching in the distance far, far away. Depending upon the depth of your trance or dream state, there are times during sleep and meditation when you are, as pure conscious awareness, drifting out of the physical body. That is risky enough without adding intoxicants that distort the effects and experience of meditation to the equation. It can result in adding increased and dangerous detachment between the physical and non-physical bodies.

Meditating while intoxicated is as dangerous as driving drunk. You may provide a willing host for some random discarnate being wandering through the lower Astral Planes, anxious to seize a form as you drift out of a drunk or drugged body. It may not even be personal. If you know you are suffering from grief, it is best to face it sober. That is why the knowledge of common and esoteric psychic self-defense techniques is strongly recommended for protection, whether you are engaged in a mystical practice such as meditation or not. My book, FEARLESS: PSYCHIC SELF-DEFENSE - Transcend the Fear of Spiritual Warfare, was written based on several decades of in-depth study and personal experience. It provides for a well-informed experience of deeper levels of mystical practice. Do not meditate under the influence of any form of intoxicant! Even after meditation, it is not wise to fall under the influence of any intoxicating substance. You may not be grounded enough to maintain complete control of your energies.

It is not advisable to go into deep meditation on a full stomach. Though there are no hard and fast rules on this one, eating a heavy meal before meditation and spiritual practice tends to inhibit the ability to focus and concentrate by grounding our energies. A full stomach can dull the senses and interfere with the discernment of subtle communications.

Take a question into meditation. Never go into a meditation without a prayer of total submission to the Will of The God and a spirit of gratitude and humility. Given certain necessary conditions, you can spontaneously link into a current of Timeless information, past, present, and future, that can direct and assist you in life. Ask for guidance.

Evoke the protective White Light of Divine Spirit to envelop the essence of every manifestation of your being. The deepest and most profound meditations are entered into in a prayerful state of mind. The feeling of safety and security will enable you to relax, knowing that you are cloaked in Divine protection. Know that the Light that protects us is the Light that we are. We emanated from that Light.

Hold all information revealed in a Mystical Meditation in strict confidence, especially if it relates to someone else. Never reveal information you have received relating to someone else to anyone other than the person that it involves. It is a spiritual violation. It is as unethical as a medical doctor or therapist betraying the confidence of a patient by disclosing personal information shared in consultation.

It is best to avoid meditation when tired, sick, extremely depressed, or in a general state of extreme fatigue. Your unstable, ungrounded energy may compromise your meditation experience. Remember that gloomy moods can alter the quality of your meditation. It would be advisable to pray your strongest prayer before entering into a meditative state.

Journal changes in your sleep patterns. This is not Law, but you may notice your dream patterns changing as you begin to open the doors of forgotten chambers of your subconscious mind through meditation. Studying and practicing a discipline of meditation will trigger spontaneous releases of memory, connecting you to other frequencies and realities. The act of meditating is so powerfully charged with cosmic energy that welcome or unwelcome drama may become attracted to your dream time world. There are many tried and true, ancient, and modern practices that will keep you in charge of the company you keep, whether you are awake or asleep.

A Note of Caution:

The studies in this text are for informational purposes only and not intended to diagnose, treat, cure, or prevent any disease. If you are experiencing symptoms of diagnosed or undiagnosed emotional or mental illness, clinical depression, thoughts of harming yourself or others, or seized by overwhelming health issues that would impair judgment, attempting certain types of meditation, may not be advised, as it may cause these feelings to intensify. You are encouraged to consult with a licensed therapist or medical professional.

Meditation Posture

Yoga-Union of Mind, Body, Spirit, seeking Union with the Divine One
Mudra-Hand gesture that directs the flow of energy to body during meditation
Lotus Position-seated (appropriate for you), back straight, legs crossed, hands resting on knees, palms up, index fingers and thumbs touching, mindful natural breathing.

Uttarabodhi (Sanskrit) Hand Mudra
Thumbs touching and index fingers touching (pointed down), all other fingers intertwined at the Solar Plexus level.

. Inspires sense of inner unity and alignment with Divine Source.
. Enlightenment, insight, inspiration.
. Calms the mind, reduces stress levels, improves concentration.
. Dispels fear, realization to fear nothing or nobody except God.
. Problem solving, decision making.
. Improves self-confidence, realization of the Higher Self.
. Refreshes the body system and recharges it with energy.
. Shield for the body and mind from negative forces.

Chakra Meditation and Visualization Exercise

Read and thoroughly understand the guidelines before performing any of the meditations in this book. The visualization exercises presented here can help you make a deeper energetic connection for more profound levels of concentration. Your meditation is more powerful when you bring a question or issue into it, without being demanding of an answer. Ask your question from the higher perspective of the True Self. Determine which chakra energetically corresponds with the subject matter of your question, and focus on that color and energy. Release any attachment to the outcome of the inquiry, surrendering to a healing taking place in your life.

Read the description of each chakra and its function. Read and meditate on the healing affirmation. Close your eyes and relax into the energy of your Third Eye (Sixth Chakra). The Third Eye or Psychic Eye is believed to be the eye of the spirit and soul. It not only looks out into the world of the mystic, it also gazes upon the mysteries that dwell within, on the subtle Planes of our existence. This level of inner vision transcends linear space and time, seeing the past, present, and future from the Timeless perspective of the Eternal Now. When activated, its relationship to the *pineal gland* has long been associated with telepathic communication. For that reason, do not be surprised if you receive visions or communications of intuitive, even prophetic information that extend far beyond what one expects from a meditation exercise.

The function of the pineal gland may not seem to be related to using meditation to help manage the trauma and grief associated with life's changes … But it is. The pineal gland secretes melatonin, and meditation stimulates it. An increase in the secretion of melatonin has been known to have a general healing effect in cases of psychological damage and related states of depression, and with treating anxiety and sleep disorders. Because the stilling of the mind affects the

Third Eye and the pineal gland, a discipline of meditation can result in some level of emotional relief. It offers a transcendent perspective when facing feelings of heartache, hopelessness, apathy, lethargy, disturbances in sleep patterns, and the struggle that accompanies living a passionless life. The chemistry of the brain does not focus attention on the future. It defers attention to the immediate circumstances of life and can send faulty messages that suggest that nothing will *ever* change … that things will always be exactly as they are. For that reason, we aim to transcend the perceptions of hopelessness and the physical plane preoccupations of the mind. Then we are able to move beyond self-identification as a body, shedding our concepts of personhood and embracing the Light of our subtlest Self.

Relax, close your eyes, and observe the unaffected, natural flow of your breath. Direct your attention to the approximate area of each of the chakras, one at a time. Dismiss all other thoughts and direct your specific awareness to each chakra, sequentially, beginning with the First or Root Chakra and working your way up. Meditate on, and visualize its corresponding color and energy, spinning clockwise. Slowly and mindfully, inhale the breath of that color and energy. Breathe through your nostrils, pull the ethereal force of *Prana*, from the seat of the *Chi*, the *Tan Dien*, located in the lower area of the First Chakra. Slowly exhale it out of your mouth, visualizing your breath generating a circle of the same color light. This exercise can help identify and clarify your resistance to accepting the Law of Impermanence and the impact of change. The restorative energy of breath, color, and circular motion offer healing to the self-inflicted suffering caused by fears of loss and abandonment. It can expose control issues associated with demanding permanence from impermanent things. You may receive revelations regarding unhealthy attachments and obsessive clinging to transient realities. You may receive insights and healing from the effects of distress, despair, and fear of change. You should keep a notebook and pen nearby in case you need to record your insights at the end of the meditation.

The First Chakra or Root Chakra

~ I AM ~

The First Chakra is located between the legs at the sacral-coccyx joint and is referred to, along with the Second Chakra, as the sexual center. It is strongly associated with our physical reality, our will to live, and is a generator of the energies of physical vitality. It is the acknowledgment of existence, I Am, "I exist." It is connected to the *color red*, the *Earth element,* ruled by the planets *Saturn and Earth,* and believed to be associated with the *sense of smell*. It is *Yang* in energetic polarity.

Kundalini is a Sanskrit term for the primal energy that sleeps at the base of the spine at the Root Chakra. It is the source of latent concentrated power, strength, and profound will when awakened. Caution must be taken in the practice of meditations that concentrate on the clearing of this area. The cleansing Pranic energy must be directed up, moving from the First to the Seventh Chakra, consecutively, without singularly focusing on any particular one. Deep meditation has been known to trigger what is known as a spontaneous Kundalini Awakening. The sudden unleashing of such a powerful force, all at once, may cause a Spiritual Emergency. One must be gradually prepared for the controlled energy associated with the raising of it. A full blast of an energy, potentially as volatile as Kundalini, is something that some have not survived intact.

The Root Chakra, like all chakras, has a shadow side when it is thrown out of balance as a response to grief, suffering, and emotional upset. It is associated with the survival instinct and the fight vs. flight reflex, matters of life and death, and anger management. In a fit of rage, the heat of that energy originates in the Root Chakra, traveling up to be mentally and emotionally processed, sparking irrational thoughts and behavior. The energies at play are fear of death, fear of life, feelings of security and safety, grounding in the sense of "home" and family, clinging to temporal existence, attachment to illusory physical reality, fear of change, and grief over what has changed or been lost.

BALANCE:

The energy of this chakra is directly connected with the will to live. When the First Chakra is afflicted, the damage circulates throughout the entire body, ravaging everything in its path. Symptoms manifest as profound depression, chronic anxiety, apathy, disinterest in social interactions, fear-based survival issues, sleep disorders, excessive weight gain or loss, feeling ungrounded in the most fundamental aspects of life, adrift in a sea of despair.

The desire for sex tends to be sparked from the Root Chakra, though it is not the most profound source. Manifestations of a blocked or damaged First Chakra can be; depression, helplessness, compromised immune system, insatiable emotionless sexual activities, all manner of addiction, obsession, compulsion and aggression, even violent sexual thoughts and behaviors. The First and Second Chakras are not only the sexual centers and the location of the *Hara/Tan Dien*, they are also the seat of the Life Force Chi energy. The energy of these chakras distributes Prana throughout the entire body by way of the many channels of our complex system. Imbalance can manifest as a complete shutdown of any desire for intimacy. An imbalance that would cause these diverse symptoms is of grave concern because the damage occurs at our very foundation. Affliction in the root will spread throughout the entire body system, both energetic and physical, causing great suffering.

HEAL:

Prayer and contemplation on the perfection of the True and Eternal Self and the purpose of existence is an important focal point in the healing of the First Chakra. It can be healed of fundamental damage by engaging in various styles of meditation practice. Water meditations, such as an isolation tank, jacuzzi, mineral hot springs, pool, bathtub, or showers, are very therapeutic. Active meditations such as walking and choreographed Kata (form) are particularly healing and will restore a healthy balance to the First Chakra. This type of meditation discipline would include Tai Chi, Chi Gong, Yoga, Martial Arts, dancing, spinning, drumming, hiking, and listening to certain types of grounding, rhythmic music. The study and practice of spiritual forms of sexuality, such as Tantra, will encourage optimum healing. However, it is important to study under the guidance of a trained, certified, qualified instructor.

Burn myrrh or patchouli incense.
Wear or decorate areas of your home using the color red.
Think the color red.

*Focus your attention on the area and energy of the Root Chakra. Visualize translucent **red light** whirling in a **counter**-clockwise motion, gaining momentum with the intensity of your focused visualization and depth of breath. Slowly inhale and exhale this warm red light, pulling energy from the Tan Dien reservoir, where the Chi energy is stored ... In through the nostrils, and out through the mouth, making a circle of light with the visualization of your breath.*

Speak to it and say:
"I release this issue to The Great Spirit and ask for a healing to take place in my life."

AFFIRM:

I AM here now.
I AM safe.
I AM secure.
I AM fearless.

> *"Nothing real can be threatened. Nothing unreal exists.
> Herein lies the peace of God."*
>
> *~ A Course in Miracles ~*

The Law of forms and shapes pronounces, every form is transient, as the foam on the ocean; as bubbles floating on air; as clouds in the sky; as the flames of a fire that died in the ashes of its burning; as the Earth, to which our spent vessels return to the Source of creation. Everything in existence is subject to birth and death. So, we surrender and know.

Even as I walk through the valley of the shadow of death, I will fear no evil. I am protected and loved by the Creator as I observe my essential being, as a drop of water in the sea of the Eternal. Regardless of appearances, I affirm that I am an Eternal being, experiencing myself in the realm of names and forms, dense substance, and Ethereal Light. My Light is unknowable. My Light is indestructible. My Light is healing every perception of imbalance or damage to the vessel that transports who I really am. I gracefully release my attachment to who I am not. I affirm I am That nameless, formless, Eternal being.

The Second Chakra or Navel Chakra

~ I FEEL ~

The Second Chakra, along with the First or Sacral Chakra, is considered the sexual center of the human body. The Hara/Tan Dien (the reservoir where the Life Force, Pranic, Chi energy is stored) shares their approximate location. It is positioned below the navel and above the pubic bone, at the center of the sacrum, on the front and back of the body.

The Second Chakra is associated with *the color orange, the element of water,* and it is *Yin* in energetic polarity. It is connected to feelings of sexual passion, ambition, desire, fear, hatred, danger, and general health and well-being. In times of personal grief and loss, this is where the overwhelming longing and desire for what is lost, or what is next, will rage. Great functional damage can be caused to this vital energy vortex, by fear of painful separations, of being alone, rejected, physically or emotionally abandoned, or feeling that the safety and security of home are threatened or lost.

People who operate in life, *primarily* from the intense, primal energy of the lower chakras, are functioning on the basest level of human existence, lower than that of the animal kingdom. The maintenance of the First Chakra is significant to overall optimum health because it is the foundation, generating and supplying Life Force to the body's entire system.

BALANCE:

Like the First Chakra, a block or imbalance is rooted in extreme fear and caused by repression, violation, or abuse. The damage can manifest as unbridled sensual indulgences; lack of boundaries; carnal, emotionless, raw aggression; demanding, angry, violent, obsessive, or compulsive behaviors; Suffering extreme circumstances of change and loss will also cause significant damage and feelings of the loss of identity. There are many triggers to its further damage or blockage: uncontrollable fear of loss or rejection; loss of a loved one due to death, divorce, or separation; loss of health, mobility, security, social status; physical and/or verbal abuse; being raised under extremely judgmental and critical parenting, with imposed restrictions and taboos; victim of threats of violence as a means of maintaining control. These triggers can cause depression, antisocial behavior, low self-esteem, and feelings of being ungrounded or unstable.

In times of great suffering, overwhelming grief, and loss of any kind, generally, the first thing that happens is the experience of feelings of being unable to function when faced with the basic tasks of day-to-day living. It is quite normal to experience brain fog, attention deficit, feelings of befuddlement, and confusion. It can even take on a spacey, other-worldly feeling of existing in some alter or parallel reality, to the extent of losing track of time, and practical elements of grounded survival.

HEAL:

The most powerful healing for First Chakra imbalance or damage is a sound consistent spiritual practice. Pray your strongest prayer for healing every day, as often as you feel is needed. Many experience a condition some call "grief attacks" when suffering from extreme fear and loss. They can be just as disabling as anxiety attacks, but they respond to such a wide variety of powerful, often seemingly unrelated triggers. Unfortunately, there are so many triggers that it becomes a life-altering struggle for survival. Keep your frequency high through meditation and grounding your energy to restore balance. It helps to have counter-triggers to return to our center and sense of Self. Many common things have served the purpose of a mental or emotional counter-trigger; An amulet, an item of personal significance that evokes memories of personal strength, written sacred words, affirmations, mantras, prayers. These items must be charged with the contemplations of Divine sustenance and submission to the Will of Divine. When it is time, the cultivation of social relationships with like-minded people may encourage healing.

Burn sage or frankincense incense or essential oil.
Wear or decorate areas of your home using the color orange.
Think the color orange.

Focus your attention on the area and energy of the Navel Chakra. Visualize translucent **orange light** *whirling in a clockwise motion, gaining momentum with the intensity of your focused visualization and depth of breath. Slowly inhale and exhale this translucent orange light, pulling from the Tan Dien reservoir where the Chi energy is stored ... in through the nostrils, and out through the mouth, making a circle of light with the visualization of your breath.*

Speak to it and say:
"I release this issue to The Great Spirit and ask for a healing to take place in my life."

AFFIRM:

I Feel the Fire of Longing. The longing for the Source is our connection to the Source.

I am the fire of love and truth, burning the temporal illusions of Maya to falling ash, blown away by the gentle breeze of awakening. The dawn has healed the night and chased away the shadows of doubt and fear.

"The happiness which is derived from contact of the senses with their objects and which appears like nectar at first but poison at the end is said to be of the nature of passion."

~ Bhagavad Gita: Chapter 18 Verse 38 ~

"Human desires are like the world of the dead – there is always room for one more."

~ Proverbs 27:20-22 The Bible (KJV) ~

The Third Chakra or Solar Plexus Chakra

~ I DO ~

The Solar Plexus Chakra is located in the solar plexus or upper abdominal area of the body. It is related to *the color yellow, element of fire,* and the principals of *sight* and light. It is *Yang* in energetic polarity. It supplies energy to the stomach, gallbladder, liver, spleen, pancreas, and nervous system. As its name suggests, this chakra pulls from the energy of the *Sun*, distributing vital Life Force to all of the other centers. The spiritual planes provide a source of essential energy during meditation, whether we tap into it or not. This chakra is associated with feelings of desire and acquisition.

The Third Chakra is very sensitive to external stimuli. It is associated with our intuition, or what we call "gut" feelings, and determines how we connect with others. For this reason, it is a chakra we should concern ourselves with, in regards to protection against mental chatter and thought-forms that seek to energetically *invade* and *deplete* our reserves, and do us harm. The Third Chakra can serve as an effective point of entry, providing a portal through which energy can be transmitted and absorbed. The absorption of negative energies in this area is damaging to our overall health and well-being.

It is advisable to do prayers for healing and protection, focusing on the Third (Solar Plexus) and Seventh (Crown) Chakra areas before entering into meditation. Visualize a large, heavy, metal vault door that you may close and lock at will, against thoughts and emotions that may, either intentionally or unintentionally, drain or poison your energy. During a meditation that you find unusually exhausting, you may be experiencing an invading energy stemming from the influence of your own emotional state. Simply shut and lock the impenetrable vault door to your Solar Plexus Chakra with intense protection prayers, creating an energetic force field around you.

BALANCE:

One of the signs of a blocked Third Chakra is the onset of a crisis of faith known as the "Dark Night of the Soul." It is so overwhelming that one would gain strength from having some type of spiritual practice in place. When your Third Chakra is blocked, you may lose trust in the knowledge of your life purpose. You may feel a disconnection from Divinity and experience: a sense of overwhelm and feelings of aloneness; profoundly compromised willpower and personality changes; arrogant, controlling behavior; megalomania; narcissism; and greed. You may even become prone to: Out of Body Experiences (OBE); Lucid Dreams; depleted energy levels due to sleep deprivation; dissociative disorder, and any number of other psychological and personality disorders.

HEAL:

Burn lemongrass or rosemary incense or essential oil.
Wear or decorate areas of your home using the color yellow or gold.
Think the color yellow or gold.

*Focus your attention on the area and energy of the Solar Plexus Chakra. Visualize translucent **yellow** or **golden light**, whirling in a **counter**-clockwise motion, gaining momentum with the intensity of your focused visualization and depth of breath. Slowly inhale and exhale this golden light, pulling from the Tan Dien reservoir where the Chi energy is stored ... in through the nostrils, and out through the mouth, making a circle of light with the visualization of your breath.*

Speak to it and say:

"*I release this issue to The Great Spirit and ask for a healing to take place in my life.*"

AFFIRM:

I Do Surrender to the truth of my "I"dentity as One with Divinity. In our sacred relationship, the longing and the connection are One. My will and Thy Will are One. Thoughts of separation are pure delusion.

"I am a hole in the flute that the Christ's breath flows through ... listen to this music."

~ Hafiz ~

I Am an infinite possibility of boundless miracles. "A miracle is a shift in perception from fear to love. The Holy Instant–All that remains is the love that fear and guilt sought to hide."

~ A Course in Miracles ~

"I searched for God and found only myself. I searched for myself and found only God."

~ Rumi ~

The Fourth Chakra or Heart Chakra

~ I LOVE ~

The Heart Chakra is located in the heart area and is associated with the emotion of love, warmth, compassion, and empathy, balanced by will. It sits at the center point in the sequence of the seven chakras and distributes energy to the heart, circulatory system, and upper back. This is the area where the physical and the spiritual meet. This fusion of energies command forgiveness and acceptance, balancing and healing the energies of anger, betrayal, fear, jealousy, grief, and hatred toward self and others. The Heart Chakra is associated with *the colors green and pink, the planet Venus and the Sun, the element of air,* and *the sense of touch.* It is *Yin* in energetic polarity.

The knowledge of the healing potential of meditation was introduced to me long before there was a context for its practical curative benefits in my own life. It began as a purely intellectual pursuit and concept. I believe that is why there was an instant resonance and recognition with my first exposure to Nyabinghi meditation practice, and then Vipassana. To have observed the way these practices kickstarted and managed my emotional healing, pushed my understanding into an experiential knowing. There are things that simply cannot be "learned" from books, or discovered in the cold, clinical environment of a laboratory. "Who feels it knows it," is a quote of Bob (Robert Nesta) Marley. That is why I reiterate that the path of meditation is not religious … It is spiritual. It doesn't matter what your religion is. It is never clearer than when the spirit has been broken and challenged to save itself; the path of healing is an inner journey. It is not something to *believe* in. It is something to experience and *know*. Surviving the trauma that the impermanence of life can deliver is an experiential process. My experience taught me, what

Nyabinghi started with the original heartbeat, Vipassana completed in the inner circle of silence.

BALANCE:

The Heart Chakra is the bridge that connects the upper and lower chakras … The bridge between matter and spirit. It is a very difficult chakra to heal from the effects of the grief and mourning associated with loss and separation. I have not heard of a chakra being as well known for being literally "broken." Many potentially serious physical and emotional health issues are directly connected with the experience of a "heartbreak." Life can begin as a glint in the eye, the quickening of passion's breath, and the flutter of heartbeats. One of the first sounds we hear on this side of life is the sound of a mother's heartbeat. One of the last sounds, a fading beep of a heart monitor, flatlining into the continuous, soul-piercing tone of silence.

From the hollowness left in the wake of emotional devastation may arise an inability to give or receive love, energy blocks, cold/emotionless promiscuity, and a tendency to try to compensate that emptiness with money, sex, status, a hunger for power, and a passive-aggressive, persecution complex. A lack of emotional self-discipline, compassion, and empathy, can lead to attacking, bullying, and belittling self and others, due to feelings of inadequacy. Suffering can spark a rebellion that is particularly pronounced, given a history of strict, controlling, religious taboos with repressive restrictions.

HEAL:

The Heart Chakra tends to be the chakra that is often the most blocked and badly damaged by grief, disappointment, trauma, anger, and an inability to let go or forgive. Some people have experienced suffering so emotionally devastating that forgiveness is not easy, nor seemingly possible, without some manner of spiritual intervention. It is important to concentrate on this area and send healing energy through meditation, visualization, and contemplation on the Divine. The ancient Hawaiian Shamanic practice of Ho'oponopono directly addresses the healing of the Fourth Chakra. When family, friends, or associates have a problem of some sort and reach a state of disharmony that threatens the relationship, they gather in a sacred place with the Kahuna/Shaman to engage a healing session for the specific purpose of reconciliation. It is based on a four-level method: *Repentance* (I am sorry); *Forgiveness* (asking to be forgiven); *Gratitude* (giving praise and thanks to the Most High for life, love, and second chances); and *Love* (I love you.)

Forgiveness of self and others is the most powerful cure to blockages in the Heart Chakra center. If we are so vain as to expect forgiveness, and not be willing to forgive others, and ourselves, we cause abysmal emotional pain and suffering. To open the receptive portals of intuition and discernment, the Heart Chakra must be able to allow the unobstructed flow of positive energy. It is required for effective meditation, as well as optimum health and general well-being.

Metta Meditation, much like Ho'oponopono, is a ceremonial healing ritual, prescribed from its tradition of origin. "Metta" is Pali, and Maitri is the Sanskrit word, meaning benevolence. Some call it the Universal Loving-Kindness meditation of compassion. Metta or Loving-Kindness has the heart-healing objective of being a channel for the energy of happiness to all beings. It heals anger with love, fear with kindness, lies with truth, guilt with forgiveness, greed with generosity, and evil with goodness.

Affirm that *nothing* is more healing than complete surrender to Divine Will and accept that *nothing* can happen apart from Divine Will. The damage is real, and healing can be experienced through the vigorous exercise of spiritual muscle through prayer and meditation.

Burn rose or jasmine incense or essential oil.
Wear or decorate areas of your home using the color green or pink
Think the color green or pink.

Focus your attention on the area and energy of the Heart Chakra.
Visualize translucent **green or pink light** *whirling in a clockwise motion, gaining momentum with the intensity of your focused visualization and depth of breath. Slowly inhale and exhale this green light, pulling from the Tan Dien reservoir where the Chi energy is stored ... in through the nostrils, and out through the mouth, making a circle of light with the visualization of your breath.*

Speak to it and say:
"*I release this issue to The Great Spirit and ask for a healing to take place in my life.*"

AFFIRM:

I Release the Barriers Within Myself That I Have Built Against Love.

"*Your task is not to seek for love,*
but merely to seek and find all the barriers within yourself
that you have built against it."

~ Rumi ~

*"Out beyond the idea of wrongdoing and right doing there is a field.
I'll meet you there."*

~ Rumi ~

*"What forgiveness is ... It's the fragrance that flowers give
when they are crushed.*

~ Sufi Saying ~

The practice of mettā meditation (Loving-Kindness) is important to the technique of Vipassana meditation and provides a certain balance. When we radiate loving-kindness and goodwill toward all beings, we are charging the atmosphere around us with positive intention. There are many versions of the Metta prayer/meditation. The source of this particular version was made generally available @ http://www.vridhamma.org/en1992-02

Metta Prayer

May I be free from ill-will; may I be free from cruelty;
May I be free from anger; May I keep myself at peace.
May my mother, father, teacher, relatives, the whole community
be free from ill-will, free from cruelty, free from anger;
May they keep themselves at peace.
May all creatures, all living things,
all beings, all individuals,
all persons included,
all women, all men,
all noble ones, all worldlings,
all humans, all nonhumans,
all celestial beings, all those in states of woe
be free from ill-will, free from cruelty, free from anger;
May they keep themselves at peace.

May all beings be happy; May they all be secure.
May they all see good fortune; May no evil befall them.
May no suffering befall them; May no sorrow befall them.

The Fifth Chakra or Throat Chakra

~ I SPEAK ~

The Throat Chakra is located in the front and back of the throat area. It supplies energy to the bronchi, thyroid, lungs, and alimentary canal. This chakra is believed to be associated with the *element of Ether/Akasha* and governs the *principle of sound* related to the sense of hearing. It is *Yang* in energetic polarity. *The associated color is Blue. The planetary correspondence is Mercury.*

The Law of Anicca can present as a cruel task-master. Change can be terrifying. Letting go is painful. People who have experienced profound grief may experience occasional surges of nearly palpable energy, seizing the area of the Heart Chakra. It rises and settles in the area of the Throat Chakra and just gets stuck there. Many uncomfortable, even life-threatening sensations, may accompany these grief attacks. They can surface and subside at any time without warning, and are caused by some of the most, apparently unrelated triggers. Often speech is muted. Breathing is labored. Overall health is compromised. These are normal reactions to the experience of traumatic events and the suffering that follows.

BALANCE:

When the Fifth Chakra is out of balance, symptoms may manifest as frequent headaches, sore throat, mouth ulcers, dental problems, laryngitis, hoarseness, neck pain, swelling of the lymph nodes, weight gain or loss unrelated to eating habits, hormonal imbalances, and mood swings connected with the thyroid. A complete shutdown can present as an inability to talk about the loss experienced or express ones' deepest feelings. In extreme cases, one may experience compromised or loss of hearing, even feelings of being choked. Behavioral and emotional manifestations of a damaged Fifth Chakra may include excessive anxiety, compulsive eating, lying, loss of self-esteem, losing social skills, egotism, and conceit. Healing begins on an energetic level.

HEAL:

Balance can be restored using various methods of energy healing. Some that I have experienced are Reiki, Chi Gong, Johrei, Acupuncture, Acupressure, Vision Quest, Limpia (Spiritual Cleansing), and Sweat Lodge (Purification Ceremony). There are many methods of spiritual or faith healing that have been known to cause spontaneous remission in cases of physical, emotional, and spiritual imbalance and illness. I cannot suggest any one particular system over another. Your spiritual path of choice may determine which energies you will find to be more resonant.

The use of prescribed essential oils and incense can awaken the senses to encourage a shift to higher vibrations. A clearing and balancing of energies can be accomplished using various types of sound vibration; speaking truth with love; practicing mindful speech, actions, and deeds; talking to a support group of friends, family, or seeking professional counseling. Other ways of awakening the body's natural potential for self-healing are: practicing a meditation that uses the chanting of sacred mantras; Yoga asanas (posture); singing; listening to rhythmic music with binaural beats designed to heal the Fifth Chakra; keeping a journal; and drinking water charged with prayer and positive affirmations. It is possible to enjoy encouraging the healing process and restoration of balance to the Throat Chakra.

Burn sage, basil, or eucalyptus incense or essential oil
Wear or decorate areas of your home using the color blue.
Think the color blue.

*Focus your attention on the area and energy of the Throat Chakra. Visualize translucent **blue light** whirling in a **counter**-clockwise motion, gaining momentum with the intensity of your focused visualization and depth of breath. Slowly inhale and exhale this blue light, pulling from the Tan Dien reservoir where the Chi energy is stored ... in through the nostrils, and out through the mouth, making a circle of light with the visualization of your breath.*

Speak to it and say:
"I release this issue to The Great Spirit and ask for a healing to take place in my life."

AFFIRM:

I speak Light. I speak to unknowable beings, and they speak to and through me of the Oneness.

I am the voice of the subtlest existence of my soul. I speak into the subtlest realm of your listening. I speak the unknowable language on the other side of silence. I speak to unknowable beings, and they speak through me. The vibration of this voice leaves footprints in the sands of manifest change in subtle and dense reality. I affirm the words of Gautama Buddha, "If you propose to speak always ask yourself, is it true, is it necessary, is it kind." From The Autobiography of a Yogi, Paramahansa Yogananda, I understand, "Any word spoken with clear realization and deep concentration has a materializing value." My Throat Chakra is healed by the vibration of my voice; the intention behind my words; the realization of my True Self; the love that overwhelms the pain in my heart.

The words you speak become the house you live in.
~ Hafiz ~

The Sixth Chakra or Third Eye Chakra

~ I SEE ~

The Third Eye Chakra is located on the forehead, between, and just above the brow line. It is associated with the *color Purple, the element of light and dark Ether, and the planets Saturn/Moon. It rules the Sixth Sense of intuition and knowledge from the subtle realms. It rules the mind* in subconscious or subtle context. It is *Yin* in energetic polarity. Known by many as the *Third Eye*, it is believed to be the eye through which the astral body is able to see. It has been referred to as the "Psychic Eye," as it is considered to be the portal through which psychic energies are received and transmitted.

It is the window through which we may view the transcendent planes if we dare enter and journey there. The Sixth Chakra facilitates the flow of energy to the pituitary gland, lower brain, left eye, ears, nose, and nervous system. As we awaken to transcendent Planes of higher consciousness through Mystical Meditation, we experience the many levels of concentration associated with the portal qualities of this chakra. The Sixth Chakra affects inner and outer realities, to the extent that it commands the whole of the personality. Emotional pain and grief due to the experience of traumatic life events can cause extensive damage and obstructions to this chakra.

BALANCE:

When the Third Eye Chakra is out of balance there are serious indicators that manifest as nightmares; migraines; sciatica; sleep disorders; spontaneous Out of Body experiences; unwelcome mystical visions; feelings of loss of identity; inability to see a better future; inability to heal from loss; unrelenting and profound grief; disorientation; delusional behaviors consistent with symptoms of intoxication; substance abuse; the unraveling of the very fabric of our identity.

HEAL:

The healing of the Sixth Chakra requires a change in perspective and letting go of old conditioning and beliefs that no longer serve the present reality. Healing on this level is a process and does not occur as an event. In the wake of the impact of devastating change or trauma that cannot be changed, what must be changed is the self. This process may require changing rigid defining lifestyles that were once worn as identity. Former habits will be swapped out for new habits that nourish the new being that arises from the being that once was. Prayer and meditation that leads to the witnessing of our center-most core of being will provide the support this transition will require.

Other healing lifestyle changes may include healing addictions, changes in diet and choice of activities, and changing circles of peers who are unable to be supportive of emerging spiritual growth. There will undoubtedly be a loss of binding and controlling ego issues. A quest for experiencing the True Self will surface. Empathic energies will intensify, causing the rise of compassion, the desire to be of service to others, and forgiveness. Intuitive abilities and psychic sensitivities will replace a one-dimensional view of life. Happiness will no longer be an outward journey; it will be a journey within to the experience of Self-Realization.

Burn cedarwood, lemongrass, or frankincense incense or essential oil.
Wear or decorate areas of your home using the color purple.
Think the color purple.

*Focus your attention on the area and energy of the Third Eye Chakra. Visualize translucent **purple light** whirling in a clockwise motion, gaining momentum with the intensity of your focused visualization and depth of breath. Slowly inhale and exhale this purple light, pulling from the Tan Dien reservoir where the Chi energy is stored ... in through the nostrils, and out through the mouth, making a circle of light with the visualization of your breath.*

Speak to it and say:
"*I release this issue to The Great Spirit and ask for a healing to take place in my life.*"

AFFIRM:

I see the unseeable with the mystical vision of my Essential Being.

The Seventh Chakra or Crown Chakra

~ I UNDERSTAND ~

The Crown Chakra is located at the top of the head and has the highest rate of vibration of all the chakras. It is associated with the *color Violet or White*. It *is beyond planetary and elemental associations, even beyond senses, and into Pure Awareness or Pure Consciousness.* It supplies energy to our right eye and our upper brain. It is associated with the experience of direct contact with Divinity. It is *Yang* in energetic polarity. The Crown Chakra is the doorway to the Sacred and should be protected and honored as such. It is guarded best through prayer, ritual, and contemplation on the nature of our relationship with Divinity.

The Seventh Chakra is a portal between the many worlds or realms of physical and non-physical existence. The top of the head is covered as a symbolic gesture, consecrating the Crown Chakra as a sacred point of entry during prayer, meditation, and other spiritual practices. Before any spiritual work, perform a thorough banishing of unwanted energies and entities and implement the strongest forms of spiritual protection. The Seventh Chakra is very important in protection rituals, as it represents a sacred point of connection that is not to be shared with any energies, other than those of The Divine. The area, approximately, at the point where the base of the skull and the spine meet, can function as an entry point to energies like the Crown Chakra and the Solar Plexus Chakra.

Be careful of your thoughts. In times of personal crisis, the mind can be a brutal task-master, if it is the fox left in charge of the henhouse. You have no way of knowing who you really are until pushed into circumstance's unforgiving corners, back against a wall of emotion. Some of the first signs of energetic distortions of the Crown Chakra are self-destructive thoughts, tendencies, and a general disinterest in practical life. Physical manifestations include chronic bouts with nausea, chills, tremors, dizziness, confusion, light sensitivity, migraine headaches, being dazed and distracted. It can manifest in waves of loss of faith, spiritual emptiness, manic depression, and bizarre mood swings.

Be careful what you ask for, sympathize with, identify with. Vigilantly guard against the most, apparently, benign covetous gaze upon any object of envy. We torture our own lives with ideas of what should have been, would have been, could have been. We add to that list, a list of what should have been permanent, but instead, like everything in existence, it was impermanent. The Now, this moment, is all we are and all we have.

BALANCE:

When our Crown Chakra is out of balance, we may feel disconnected spiritually, as though we are living without any direction or purpose. If there are physical manifestations that seem to surface without a trigger or cause repeatedly, it may be an indication that the Crown Chakra is blocked or damaged. This chakra affects the six energy vortices below and permeates the entire being. A blocked Crown Chakra can lead to: depression; despair; loss of faith; the awakening experience called the 'Dark Night of the Soul'; mental confusion; brain fog; psychological disconnection; schizophrenia; bipolar and dissociative personality disorder; chronic fatigue; migraine headaches; neurological or endocrine disorders; diverse chronic physical illness and disease. An excess of energy in the Crown Chakra can cause problems, including sleep disturbances and disorders, insomnia, sensitivity to light and sound. Personality changes may overwhelm the former self with distinctly different behaviors, like uncharacteristic greed, materialism, a sense of elitism, or seeking recognition for unearned accomplishments, engaging in reckless, risk-taking, adrenalin junky hyperactive behaviors, lethargy, changes in weight/health with no physical cause.

If a death, illness, or a life-altering, unexpected loss of some sort occurs in the life of an individual, and there is an inability to adapt to shifting realities, energetic obstructions can disturb the entire body system. Forms of escapism that are used as distractions and avoidance behavior can result in a complete shutdown and subsequent withdrawal from social interactions and activities that were formerly enjoyable. Terminal boredom sets in with the frustration of a lost and restless spirit, giving up hope for now, with no vision of the possibility of a better future. The danger of reaching this point is that a breach of trust and faithful communication with Divine or higher power can occur, the very thing that restores faith in Divine Providence.

The Seventh Chakra is an entry and exit point for astral and interdimensional travel. It is involved in the experience of Lucid Dreaming, Astral Travel, Out of Body Experiences (OBE), Sleep Paralysis Events (SPE), Merkabah Meditation practice, Bi-location, Remote Viewing, even Near Death Experiences (NDE). Ego is loosely defined as "the seat of experience." Observe as the ocean observes the waves. The experience of the ocean as a wave is a validation of a profound level of our Existential Truth.

Ego Death occurs at the realization of one's own Impermanence and the experience of perceiving one's Self as Eternal, formless, Consciousness. The more one is invested in egoic self-identification, the more likely an experience of Ego Death may occur.

A trigger leading to the experience of a traumatic shock on the level of the Seventh Chakra is associated with a "condition" known as "Ego Death." It is characterized by a total loss of a sense of personhood and non-identification as the "body" or as a being of form and personality. One may suffer feelings of emotional displacement or have dissociative identity issues. This level of depersonalization can occur, especially the onset of a previously undetected, latent mental disorder. Ego Death is not the same as Anatta, the term shared earlier in this text, in the section, The Three Marks of Existence. Anatta is No Self, Emptiness, the Void. It takes one beyond all concepts of mind and matter, physical and non-physical, into the non-dual, Unknowable Realm of "Creator," before the concept of creation. Ego Death is called by some, Enlightenment's Evil Twin. Enlightenment can trigger a common side-effect, "The Dark Night of the Soul," a condition that can resemble a psychotic break to others who do not understand the process. After stripping away ego identifications, some people are left reeling. At the pivotal point of this major transition or "loss," one gradually resets the perceptual defaults of the unenlightened state of consciousness and reaches stasis. "Ego Death" occurs beyond the 5th and 6th senses, to taste existence as Pure Consciousness. Once the brain accepts Eternal, unchanging identity, as Self, the new context of "me" accepts that it is safe, capable, protected, loved, heard, seen, and known on an essential level … as Divinity.

HEAL:

The breath of Anapana is an effective breathing technique for a Seventh Chakra mindfulness, healing meditation. The Seventh Chakra is the gateway to higher dimensions of consciousness. Self-Realization will unveil the fact that we *are* as the breath we breathe. Breath has no method, no form, no agenda, no story, no name, no past or future, no birth or death, no right or wrong, no fear or grief. It passes through us as the Breath of Divinity passes through the holes of the reed flute, and we become the music, the dance, and the dancer.

Distortions of the energy flow to the Crown Chakra are common when in the free-fall of an existential crisis. There was no existential crisis before we were here. There will be no existential crisis when we are gone. We are the Light of pure conscious awareness that precedes mind, body, and breath. Prayer and Self-Inquiry meditation activates the purification process of energy healing. Our goal is to be the sky, not the clouds. On this theme park ride called life, let the twists and turns, rise and fall while we stay as the True Self, observing the drama. There are specific inverted Yoga asanas (postures) that help with the healing and balancing of this important chakra.

Burn lavender, pine, myrrh, rose, Three Wise Men incense or essential oil.
Wear or decorate areas of your home using the color white.
Think the color white.

Focus your attention on the area and energy of the Crown Chakra. Visualize translucent **white light, the color of soft white lightning,** *gently covering the top of the head. See the intensity of your focused visualization and depth of breath. Slowly inhale and exhale this soft white light, pulling from the Tan Dien reservoir where the Chi energy is stored ... in through the nostrils, and out through the mouth, making a circle of light with the visualization of your breath.*

Speak to it and say:
"I release this issue to The Great Spirit and ask for a healing to take place in my life."

AFFIRM:

I acknowledge the Unknowable.

Visualize a sphere of pure white/silver Light, the color of soft, warm lightning, just above your head. This sphere of Light is charged with limitless answered prayers of the ancients, and the positive affirmations of their unwavering faith. Visualize a gentle shower of its beautiful Light that drenches your entire being, a glowing, protective aura of the radiant fusion of love aware of its Oneness with all there is. Affirm, "No weapon formed against me shall prosper."

Meditation Exercise to Strengthen the Seven Energy Centers

Painful memories and feelings can be trapped in chakra centers for years. Through a committed meditation discipline, these negative energies can be transmuted into pure white Light, illuminating colors corresponding with each chakra as it is being healed. This spiritual cleansing can change the frequency and raise the vibration of the blocked chakra in such a way as to repair damage caused by the negative energy that entered. Manifest a powerful healing throughout the entire energetic system with the strength of your intention.

When you responsibly address the life issues that the chakras govern, you will affect each chakra, along with the corresponding organs, endocrine glands, and areas of the body. Avoidance of these issues can result in energetic depletion on all levels and will ultimately manifest as physical, mental, emotional, and spiritual illnesses.

For example:

The lessons of the First Chakra are those of the physical or material world, issues of survival, self-defense, acquisition, and societal and family, law, and order. The First Chakra relates to sexuality, physical desire, ethics, guilt and blame, security and safety, control, and power. These issues, unresolved, will damage that chakra and directly affect the function of the Second through the Seventh or Crown Chakra. Any energy blockage that prevents the flow of the Chi, or Life Force, and the gentle rising of the Kundalini energy, is detrimental to the entire system. The practice of cleansing the seven energy centers causes a gradual energetic surge upward. It is often described in metaphor as a snake coiled at the base of the spine, energetically rising all the way up through each of the seven energy centers. It helps your practice to commit to memory, the correspondences, colors, and functions of each chakra.

Meditation Exercise: Ask yourself, "What are the issues relating to the "X" Chakra that I am not facing with responsibility?" Make a list of these issues. Take each issue into a meditation after performing an elemental, cleansing meditation, affirming that this condition is being healed at its origin.

After completing your meditation, as with all meditation practices, it is important to ground yourself before you resume your everyday activities, especially before you drive or perform any activity that would require alert, grounded concentration. If you feel light-headed or unfocused after your meditation, there are many ways to ground yourself. Bring yourself back to alertness by washing your face and hands with cold water, eating a serving of fruit, drinking a glass of cool or cold water, walking barefoot on the ground, playing music, dancing, exercising, or taking a brisk walk. There is a visualization that is commonly used for grounding that works well. Visualize yourself standing with your bare feet planted firmly on the ground or the floor. Imagine yourself sending roots down into the Earth. Inhale through your nose and pull the Earth energy up through your roots. As you exhale, your roots are pushing deeper into the Earth. After several minutes, you will return to your previous state of alertness.

THE LIGHT MEDITATION
I AM PROTECTED AS ETERNAL LIGHT

Basic Guidelines to Follow for The Light Meditation

The Light Meditation should be performed before engaging in any spiritual ritual work or meditation. It is designed to cleanse and activate the energies of our Chakra System to facilitate balance, harmony, and protection. It is a useful meditation that can be practiced daily with your prayer of choice for energy maintenance and as a spiritual shield. This guided audio meditation is available as a download on the dreamuniversalmedia.com website. See the Chapter Meditation Download instructions at the back of this book. The transcript of the Light Meditation is presented here for your perusal to assure that you are aware of and aligned with all aspects of its content.

The Light Meditation
Transcript

I am seated in a comfortable position
facing the direction of the rising Sun
My back is straight
My feet are touching the floor
My hands rest palms up
I close my eyes
My mind's eye envisions
a single white candle that I light
with the intention of inner illumination
from my most profound depths
extending to the Origin of my existence
the Focal Point of Ultimate Light

From this comfortable seated position … I breathe

I Am the OBSERVER and WITNESS of my breath
as it touches the middle of my upper lip
I observe the sensations for qualities
such as heat, coolness, moisture, dryness
I observe … undistracted by these sensations
I go within.
I slip between the invisible pockets of silence
between my inhaled and exhaled breath

My attention goes to the sensation of my breath
as it flows across the center groove of my upper lip

The focus of my awareness moves to my Solar Plexus …

the 3rd Chakra …

From its most profound point

there is an ethereal SILVER CORD anchored in my physical reality

to ground me … to guide me

back to the starting point of my journey if I should need it

A pinpoint of Light pulsates

to the rhythm of my heartbeat

and radiates from that focal point of Light …

expanding … to extend to … and beyond my entire body

enveloping me in this pure, radiant, protective Light …

extending beyond me to envelop this room …

extending beyond this room to envelop this entire building …

this entire city … and far beyond …

seeking and connecting

to its Point of Origin.

I inhale through my nostrils

I exhale through my mouth

I inhale LIGHT

I exhale FEAR

I cup my hands over my mouth

to collect sacred breath laced with golden Light and positive intention

I inhale Light and become it

I exhale fear and rebuke it

The silver cord that extends
from my navel area … at the CORE of my being
dispels all fear as my consciousness drifts …
It will guide me back
to my comfort zone
and starting point
whenever I choose

I cup my hands over my mouth
to collect the breath of my earnest petition
right hand over the left
good over evil
knowing one defines the other.

In my working breath
are words of power
and utterances of commandments
a release
a surrender
of all that is of Maya …
all that is temporary
I release my attachment to the CHANGEFUL
I embrace only the UNCHANGING …
INCLUDING the so-called "self"
of my own lower perceptions
I embrace all that I really am …
BREATH, AWARENESS, CONSCIOUSNESS …
INTO THE STILLNESS THAT I AM

I suspend my senses

I shut down

I open up

Calm and focused breath

occurs in natural rhythms

I inhale through my nostrils

I exhale through my mouth

I inhale LIGHT and become it

I exhale FEAR and rebuke it

I inhale Golden Light

I cup my hands over my mouth

to collect my breath

laced with THIS Golden Light and focused intention

I use it to dispel and cleanse unwelcome energies.

It is charged with the intention of attracting the healing that I desire

With this sacred Light Breath

I wash MY HANDS

then MY FACE

of all carnal witnessing and unsavory desires

I cleanse MY NOSE of the scent of the shadow worlds …

MY EYES … of all they have seen of suffering

I cleanse My Third Eye … 6th Chakra … located between my eyebrows

of all it has observed of lower vibrations …

MY EARS … of the filth they have heard

I cleanse MY INNER AND OUTER VOICE at the throat level,

the energetic vortex of my 5th Chakra …

Thought-forms … both spoken and silenced, travel

on wings of words that injure like bullets and blades

and I HEAL that with this sacred breath of radiant Golden Light

I cleanse MY CROWN, 7th Chakra … at the top of my head

of all that has ever sought to come between my Higher Self and my Source …

the Source of all … The Ultimate Reality

With this Sacred Light Breath

I move my attention down to the back of my NECK

I cleanse and seal this entry point of whispered suggestions

from the lower Planes of consciousness

seeking a home … seeking manifestation

through MY mind and spirit

I cleanse my feet of every step they strayed

from the path of my Enlightenment

with Golden Light

of Sacred Breath

My footsteps are guided

My path is protected

My journey is blessed

I inhale LIGHT and become it

I exhale FEAR and rebuke it

Hands cupped over my mouth,

right hand over the left,

I collect this Sacred Breath in my hands …

I hold it to MY HEART

HEALING CLEANSING ENERGY OF GOLDEN LIGHT
enters MY HEART … my 4th Chakra …
whirling … spinning … yielding in surrender
to my connection to Divinity
I accept that I am healed by this Breath of Light

I cleanse myself of the PAIN I have suffered that seeks to break me
I cleanse myself of emotional attachments to joy
that seeks to ADDICT me and CONTROL me
I am not my emotions
I am not my past
I am not my future
I am not my mind
I AM MORE THAN THIS

I break through the mirror of illusion
I forsake the lies that seek to define me
as less than an Eternal being of Divine Essence

I inhale through my nostrils
I exhale through my mouth
I inhale LIGHT and become it
I exhale FEAR and rebuke it

I inhale Light
I cup my hands over my mouth to collect
breath laced with Golden Light and positive intention

My Mantra is

Thank You

My Mantra is

Thank You

With this Golden breath, I shield my Solar Plexus
from all energies that may seek to enter uninvited, unwelcomed,
with their urges and weaknesses, cravings and clinging, anger and unforgiveness
seeking to eclipse my will.
With its self-serving obsessions and uncontrollable desires …
projections … seeking to make me believe they are my own

Sacred Breath is the BRIDGE between the many selves that I am
from the lower to the upper realms of consciousness
With it I have cleansed and sealed this space that I am
I do not stand alone as its gatekeeper
I am as protected as I am created
That Which created me sustains me

I inhale through my nostrils
exhale through my mouth
I inhale Light and become it
I exhale fear and rebuke it
I inhale Light
I cup my hands over my mouth to collect
breath laced with Golden Light and positive intention

With this breath, I shield my 2nd Chakra

located in the area of my lower abdomen

the seat of all desire, attachment and aversion

With this sacred breath of pure Golden Light

I suspend my senses

I cleanse the lower energetic, sensual,

carnal aspects of my being and heal them in the Eternal Now

The cleansing breath of Golden Light subdues the raging fire of my Root Chakra,

the 1st Chakra … Sacral Chakra …

sending this creative energy rising into the Golden Light

of the manifestation of my authority over my own animalistic nature

This primal fuel energizes all of the other chakras as it gently rises,

Uncoiled … Golden Light of purification

Rising

Up,

Up,

Up … through the 2nd Chakra below the navel … cleansing …

Releasing negative energies

Up,

Up,

Up … the Spine … through the spiraling vortex of the 3rd Chakra …

Spinning beautiful waves of Golden Light

gently rushing up this life-enabling thread of creation's energy …

Releasing … Cleansing … Healing … Illuminating …

With Golden waves of Light energy

sweeping clean all residue … all debris …

All attachment … All aversion … All longing … for all else …

but The Beloved … The Divine One

My Mantra is

Thank You

My Mantra is

Thank You

CLEANSING LIGHT gently rises through the 4TH Chakra … MY HEART …

healing it from the senseless acts of emotional savagery it has suffered …

Loving it for all of the Love it is capable of … trusting it with my life.

I close my body down

I am not my body

I am not my mind

I am not my emotions

I AM MORE THAN THAT

I suspend my senses

I break the mirror of illusion

I meditate upon the Light that I Am

the Light of the Eternal I AM

I have manifested on this Plane

from the Realm of the Divine One

I have expressed myself as my desire

for this Sacred Journey

from the angelic realm

the realm of the guides,

the realm of the Sacred

the abode of the prophets,

the mystics, the messengers, and servants

of the Most High GOD

Breath and Light are One

The Light of my Core Being

is One with the Core Point of Light

expressed out of triple darkness,

the Consciousness, the Love of the Ultimate I AM,

the Unknowable One, the Limitless One,

Whose name is best expressed by SILENCE.

My most sacred Mantra is

Thank You

Beautiful energy has gathered in my HEART Chakra …

the Temple of my Beloved …

the Temple of the Divine One

In Love … Golden Light energy continues to rise … powerfully … subtly …

Up through my 5th Chakra at my throat

Up through my 6th, my Third Eye

Reaching the 7th and Crown Chakra

GOLDEN ENERGY collected at the top of my head …

connecting with my strongest PRAYER

CONNECTING WITH MY STRONGEST PRAYER
CONNECTING WITH MY STRONGEST PRAYER
I PRAY
I PRAY FOR PROTECTION FROM ALL UNWELCOME,
UNINVITED ENERGIES

(SILENCE DURING PRAYER)

Shhhhhhhhh
I accept this cloak of protection
enveloping the entire form of my body
physical and formless
cleansing my aura, purifying my intentions,
closing out all that is not of this protective Light
A pinpoint of Light pulsates to the rhythm of my heartbeat
and radiates from that focal point of Light …
expanding to extend … to and beyond my entire body …
enveloping me in pure, radiant Light …
extending beyond me to envelop this room …
extending beyond this room to envelop this entire building …
this entire city … and far beyond … seeking and connecting
with all beings at its Point of Origin … PURE CONSCIOUSNESS

I breathe from my core
from the most profound center of my being
I cleanse myself with Sacred Breath
Golden Breath has become a solid SHIELD of PROTECTION

Waves of beautiful Golden Light
sweep up and over and around me
all the way up and over and around me
swirling up and over and around me
THE LIGHT IS MY SHIELD
It is my Comforter
I have always been THAT LIGHT

My Mantra is
Thank You

My Mantra is
Thank You

I return from the silence … the stillness
grounded in my humble, energetic abode
anchored in the SAFETY I have affirmed
the PROTECTION I have affirmed
the LOVE I have affirmed
the FREEDOM I have affirmed

RELEASED FROM GUILT … RELEASED FROM SHAME …
RELEASED FROM JUDGMENT

If I have ventured out far enough to have trouble returning
I follow the silver cord extended from my navel
back to the state of consciousness that is awake and alert … aware …
fully focused and grounded … no longer corrupted by false identity and
conditioning

The energy of this freedom washes over me in shimmering waves of assurance that I am a being of Eternal Light … connected to all of creation … essentially connected to the Creator of all and I AFFIRM …

THAT WHICH CREATED ME IS SUFFICIENT TO PROTECT ME!

I AM ONE WITH THAT!

****

The Light Meditation is available as an audio download at Dreamuniversalmedia.com. Please see the instructions in the chapter "Meditation Download Instructions" at the back of this book.

Featured Meditation: I Transcend My Ego Self

I TRANSCEND MY EGO SELF

I AM ALIVE

IN THE TIMELESS NOW

We are leaves
destined to fall
from first whisper
of winter's approach
into Eternal Light
that we are
Tree of life
does not curse
its leaves
for their falling
into temporal journey
praising the Light
of creation

I TRANSCEND MY EGO SELF:
The Meditation

The objective of the *I Transcend My Ego Self* meditation is to resurrect an awareness of the truth of who we really are in the big picture of existence. This meditation is about more than transcendence through meditation. It is about more than seeking to become the meditation. It is about awakening to the fact that we already are that which we seek. We strip away a wardrobe of conditioned identities to reveal the essence of who we really are. Pure conscious awareness, there in the stillness and silence, is our true and subtlest Self. Our identity is not that of the animated corpse that rose up in it.

The perspective the *I Transcend My Ego Self* meditation offers provides an opportunity to experience sensations of freedom from the bondage of flesh, bone, mind, and a sea of turbulent emotions. This mortal life is a gift but not a promise. It is a gift that can effectively poison our souls if we develop an unhealthy relationship with it and become attached to only its physical aspects. From a meditative, witnessing perspective, we are able to manifest a higher standard for our lives.

To demonstrate a transcendence of the fear of grief and death, St. Paul is known for having said, "I die daily!" In the face of imminent death, these words immortalized his fearlessness and courage. It was an act of complete surrender to the Will of The God and the essential union with The God. To entertain the fear of death over the submission to the Will of The God is, in effect, bowing down to the fear of death as a god. We are commanded not to do that.

There are extreme meditation practices with an "I Die Daily" theme that can extend to a process of literally switching off the activities of the bodily cells and tissues and then switching them back on again, resuming the previous state of activity. Some perceive the relationship with death that was attained by St. Paul and other realized masters as the highest, most pious, and most important work in life. In the practice of Kriya Yoga, "I Die Daily," leads to states of Samadhi, a Sanskrit term that describes the stillness of the mind in transcendent meditation practice. It is the final stage of meditation after one has journeyed beyond physical consciousness. One meditatively withdraws the life-current from all parts of the body and stores it in the medulla oblongata. This state is known as Sabhikalpa Samadhi. In this state, a person is in contact with the ocean of knowledge known as the Omniscient or Omnipotent consciousness and realizes oneself to be immortal consciousness. "I Die Daily" is the science of immortality. I mention this form of meditation here to affirm our commitment to choosing to heal and release our life-crippling fear of death. Most spiritual paths I am aware of speak of not allowing the fear of death to destroy the quality of our lives.

Some forms of this type of meditation have even been known to lead to the revelation of esoteric knowledge. To assist this process, some employ the use of tools or systems to facilitate the interpretation of signs and symbols. These communications can offer wise guidance to help us clarify our decisions, opinions, and answers to the questions that affect our lives on all four Planes of existence: spiritual, mental, emotional, and physical.

To perform this type of meditation, one must be well-grounded in the understanding that this practice is not an escape hatch from the unpleasant aspects of our lives. That would be counterproductive to the goals of your meditation experience. It is the opportunity to experience freedom as the non-physical, True Self. *I Transcend My Ego Self* meditation is not the letting go of "life." It is the letting go of our clay conspiracy theories, to embrace our inner Light body of consciousness. That Light within the physical shell seeks to be known by us. It is the Essence of who we truly are. We are a Light body of consciousness. That Light emanates from the Source of all creation. This is not a religious concept or opinion. If I were a scientist or theologian, I could present a case to support it as being a scientific fact. I don't have to do that. I have experienced that Light. It is real and transcends the attempts of any language even to describe it.

Through meditation, we will allow the Light body the opportunity to step outside of the clay frame that transports and often imprisons it just to connect with the fact that we do not die. It is a chance to observe or witness the many beings that we really are and interact with them without judgment. The embrace of the reality of the Light body creates a shift in perspective that initiates the resurrection of the Realized Self. The experience of resurrection does not require the manifestation of the physical death of the body vehicle. It is an inner awakening and understanding of the nature of the true, immortal Self. It was not born. It cannot die. It does not fear.

Grief, anguish, and affliction befall the enemies of The God and humanity, who think that they can destroy a physical life and cause that being to cease to exist. We must honor and respect the vehicle we were given to allow our Light body to observe existence from a physical perspective. However, we must not become attached to it as though it alone defines us and confirms our existence. We are to respect our vehicle and treat it as a sacred temple that we choose not to defile. We must maintain a delicate balance in the union of all aspects of our being, knowing that the reflection we see in the mirror is not all we really are.

In the *I Transcend My Ego Self* meditation, we free our Light body to see the beauty of itself, a beauty that cannot deteriorate and age, become diseased and suffer, perish or die. It is pure awareness. It is beautiful. We have more than one body to nourish. The Light body must be nourished and cared for as a matter of

high priority. Our spirit must be sustained with the same level of discipline with which we maintain our physical bodies. Man does not live by bread alone.
In our meditation, we are not being separated from "life" by stepping out of the clay shell to meditatively taste the Timeless realm. We put ourselves in a position to witness the very thing about us that defines life, Light, and energy. We experience it. We witness it. We realize that it is what we really are and rejoice. We release our attachment to the physical form as our definition. We depart from it to Ultimate Existence, to Ultimate Reality. We embrace the Timeless.

It is an odd concept to some to seek to experience the reality of ourselves outside of the physical "mirror image" framework that we are familiar with. The concept might be terrifying to some and freeing to others. It is certainly healing to all daring enough to go to that place beyond time and space, where materiality does not oppose, but rather cooperates and dances with formless energy, vibration, and Light. As was stated at the beginning of this book, the word "Light" in this text most often appears with an initial uppercase "L," for we are not talking about a Light that is our own, independent of its Source. We are a Light emanated from The Source and have never been separate from that Source, except in our minds.

If we have so much extra time on our hands that we want to pay more attention to the name we wish to call That Source or the culture around the name we choose to call It, we pray for the cure to that divisive disease of the spirit. Our energy is better spent in prayer and meditation on how we must serve It and serve the energy of That within ourselves on our journey. There is One God. We are one face of it. If we can use this clay vessel to become the Light tower and beacon that shines the Light that we are, we may help to guide lost vessels to shore. To experience becoming It, we allow ourselves to realize that we are It, always have been It, and will always be It.

The perishable characteristics of the physical form, though horrific, are not our dying; it is our resurrection. Let us fill our plates with spiritual food that will nourish us, not poison us. We will not approach this exercise in a manner to celebrate or ignore death … not even embrace it. We miss our loved ones when they depart. That is natural. We feel as though we miss ourselves as we face the impermanence of our temporal state of being. That is natural. We seek to acknowledge to our conscious and subconscious mind that we are Eternal Beings. Neither we nor our loved ones cease to exist as we change form and dimension. It hurts that we cannot experience them in the ways we were once accustomed, vehicle to vehicle, and face to face. But we can experience their Light. That Light becomes an unbreakable connecting bond between us that the grave cannot sever. Then we must come to realize that the more we share of that Light that we are, the less we will serve the painful illusions of the cruelty of death. We will be able to say then, "Death, where is thy sting?"

We observe a meditation discipline to expand the Light that we are to the apex of its potential for Ultimate Brilliance. We seek messages from the Ether, knowing that in the deliverance of these messages, there will always be that One gentle voice overriding the suggestion or whisper of evil. This voice has many levels of sound and vibration. There can seem to be a subtle choir of harmonic voices, yet it is One. It sings a song of Light as we are becoming It.

We must love the True Self as it reveals itself to us, and have a clear understanding of its accompanying shadows. If we understand our Light and understand our shadows, we are drawing closer to the hereafter. I do not refer to the milk and honey paradise that many associate with the word "hereafter." I'm speaking of *here, after* the discovery of our Transcendent "Self," Pure Breath, Light, and Energy.

The shadows cast upon our souls by the attributes of our clay form are a natural and meaningful part of our creation. If we wish to be known as more than ashes and dust waiting to happen, we must stretch our consciousness to understand that this primordial contradiction of flesh and Spirit can be a glorious adventure, or it can be an endless war. We must use the understanding of Self as a tool and a weapon in winning the daily war inherent in the illusory contradictions of our very creation … We look at the fading reflection in the shattered mirror and proclaim, "I transcend my ego self" as a standard for life.

Inspiration Behind I TRANSCEND MY EGO SELF Meditation

I face one of the most devastating changes in life every day … losing a loved one. Every morning, I know that I awaken to a world from which my mother has passed away. When my mother, Raushanah Hassain (Dorothy Warren), made her transition in May of 2003, I felt the light of my life had been extinguished. Darkness and obscurity replaced the complacency of having a mother, friend, and soul mate wrapped up in one neat, beautiful package. A void was left that nothing could fill … nothing but The Light of The God. I still succumb to shock, emptiness, and a sense of drifting without direction, without destination. On this journey of healing, I was inspired to compile this collection of poetry, prose, and meditation. I found myself able to step out of my shadows and find her light again.

After years of writing death-obsessed poetry and literature, I was forced to confess to myself that my naiveté and inexperience stripped away my authority to write much of what I had written. I reviewed all of my previous works for authenticity, seeking to determine whether or not I still agreed with myself. What I discovered was a shadow of arrogance cast over ideas that were idealized rather than realized. I read between the lines an absolute ignorance of the touch of the reaper. I made changes to many of my previous works, some dramatic, some ever so subtle, but rich with first-hand knowledge and painful experience. The proverbial rise of the Phoenix from the ashes of its demise represents the balance of hope, optimism, and Oneness with the creative process. My spiritual studies gave me the strength and understanding to bear the pain of my loss and fight for emotional survival, knowing now that death is only as overwhelming as our perception of it.

I encourage you to use this forum, Dream Universal Media, to share your experiences by contributing to future publications of this collection. Hopefully, sharing our unique experiences can touch broken hearts with the Light required to begin the healing process and encourage emotional closure.

The revelation of the I Die Daily concept came back to haunt me from my work in the past with highly evolved spiritual teachers. At that time, it was all purely theoretical and conceptual. It is presented here in the form of meditation, poetry-laced prose, and a workbook, all used to elevate our spiritual perspective regarding death, embracing our own immortality. We are asked to view our physical form and its transitions from the perspective of an unemotional observer or witness. We seek to be rewarded with the incredible, invaluable power to change the way we live our lives, while there are still second chances available to create change. Amazing changes will occur in our lives and the lives of others that we may influence. In the journals we keep, we will explore the secrets only death can reveal of itself.

We share this sacred journey. Let us share the love, healing, and redemption we find on it. We must know that it is our challenge to endure and evolve, as our spiritual decree is to reach out to others with a loving heart to help them to do the same.

I TRANSCEND MY EGO SELF Meditation Instructions

To experience the best results from this meditation, you are strongly advised to read and commit to the practice of the spiritual protocol shared in my book, FEARLESS: PSYCHIC SELF-DEFENSE. FEARLESS is a valuable Psychic Self-Defense and spiritual protocol guide.

This valuable reference book will be online, continually expanding to accommodate more information from many spiritual traditions and sources. You are asked to participate in this expansion with your submissions at dreamuniversalmedia.com and our social media page. In FEARLESS, you will find information from a variety of traditions regarding correct spiritual protocol relevant to mystical practices such as meditation. Consider it a prerequisite to many forms of meditation.

Perform this meditation at the beginning of the day. This transcendental work requires that you read the transcript first and then listen to the recording of *I Transcend My Ego Self* meditation. It is only necessary that it be read once to determine, while you are fully conscious, that you are completely comfortable with the meditation content. You are then prepared to perform the meditation. It would be ideal to do it every other day, for at least a week, and then establish a meditation schedule that suits you. *At the end of the day, you will journal your answers to the questions asked in your* DREAMCATCHER JOURNAL.

It is a worthy ideal to seek to attain higher states of consciousness. The ability to transcend the time/space continuum, into a stateless state of pure awareness, into the emptiness is called many things. Buddhists may call it Buddhahood. A Hindu may call it Sacchidananda. Christians may call it Christ Consciousness, or Slain in The Holy Spirit. Gnostics call it Nirvana. Some

Rastafarians call it the Zion, meaning stillness, silence, the space between thoughts, no motion, no vibration, no things, no Space, no Time. The Dervishes call it Drunkenness (no alcohol involved), or in extreme form, Fanaa, by some Sufi mystics. There are many paths that lead to a direct experience of The Ultimate, The Source. These blissful states of consciousness can be addictive. There is no greater feeling than the subjective experience of The Ultimate, Unchanging Reality.

The value of being able to maintain an equanimous mind is immeasurable. To be able to control the reactive mind, undisturbed by outside distractions, life changes, emotions, pain, and phenomena that can completely dismantle a mind. The wise accept the daylight as well as the darkest night, the Sun with the rain, laughter with sorrow, fulfillment with great longing. Our goal is to embrace these opposites on a daily basis, with no attachment, no aversion, no judgment, as the Will and Design of the Divine One, whether we understand it or not. The perspective of the witness or the observer is a healing meditation and precursor to profound change. But there is freedom in this change because it is not the result of the judgment of self or others. It is not for approval-seeking or a desire for acceptance.

You are the one person in this show, on this stage in this play called YOU. There is only one person in the audience. You! You are your only audience to the show of your most personal Self. You alone can choose to applaud yourself for your honest portrayal and acceptance of your own character, without judgment or concern for the judgments of others. Only you can give yourself a standing ovation as you witness your progressive spiritual growth in the study of your True Self. Only you can boo the performance as a witness or observer without judgment. It is not necessary to condemn yourself, just observe. The consciousness that seeks to evolve will modify and evolve all that is observed.

You are not demanding that your meditation produces vending machine answers in response to your Self-Inquiry and disclosure. There will be times you feel you have nothing to journal. When that happens, enter into your journal that you have nothing to journal, and continue to write, or not. There is often as deep an insight in that as if you had volumes to journal for that session.

Let us rise together out of our present perceived reality in this meditation and refuse to view this world as a hostile adversary. We can choose to make our every moment the conscious, visceral experience it was meant to be.

Journaling

If you choose to keep your journal in a digital file, it is advisable to journal your answers in a document secured by a password. If you choose to keep a hardcopy journal, obtain a three-ring binder and multiple copies of your questionnaire, then insert them into your workbook. Keep your workbook in a place that will ensure your privacy. Some of your answers may be too personal to share with even those closest to you. Enter your candid answers without censoring or imposing judgment upon yourself or anyone else. Some prefer to keep a video journal, which can offer an expanded experience of their journaling. Journal as your Higher Self, but make a note of any mindless or mischievous mental chatter.

Approximately once a month, on every full Moon, you should review your answers. Pay particularly close attention to your answers and insights regarding the last question. Record comments in the margins if you wish. Note any way your quality of life may have changed. Note any expanded insights you experience. Meditate upon the beauty of the many second chances you are given to do some of the things you may have otherwise neglected to do or may have taken for granted.

The creation and celebration of our bold spiritual adventures will take place within the journals of our minds. Continuing to keep this written journal will serve to document your travels between dream time and the temporal realm until you become spiritually unmoved by either, yet spiritually moved by both. We wish to view the dream time world and the world of form as the natural flip side of the same coin of reality while maintaining our spiritual focus. Our soul becomes the observer of this miraculous experience.

Keeping a written journal is important. Technology can track and record our "doings" reliably. But how do we track our "beings" in such a way that we would not worry that our very soul was being surveilled? We do not express ourselves the way we used to. We are equipped now with a spell check, auto-correct, and tight margins that weigh and measure our "published" material against the vision of a monitoring eye of judgment.

Pen and notebook in hand, we must journal outside of the framework of all of our *doings*. How often do we stop and quietly reflect on how and who we are *being?* How often do we have that conversation with ourselves? How often should we engage in Self-Inquiry, beginning with the meditation ... Who am I? We must inquire of ourselves ... *beyond* rank identifications, *beyond* personhood, parenthood, gender, religion, race, nationality, and career ... *Who* am I being? Who am I *really*? How am I *being* a force on a mission in this Self-created reality?"

Self-Inquiry meditation practice is vital to our holistic well-being. We must concern ourselves with our *being* at *least* as much as we concern ourselves with our *doing*. The Journal we keep of our contemplations and inquiries into the Source of our being will give us dots to connect when reviewing our Journal entries. Journaling gives us connecting bridges to build from a shape-shifting tapestry of our experiencing the illusory realms of Maya (the impermanent, illusory, material world) to our transcendence of it, and back.

The question, "Who am I?" is the beginning of a powerful conversation toward Self-Realization. Make a meditation of that consultation. Review it periodically to chart your progress towards accomplishing the spiritual goals you have set for yourself. If messages and information you receive in a meditation draw a complete blank and make no sense to you, by all means, record that in your journal. The meaning will unfold in its own time. Track related events using your journal. A journal is an excellent way of monitoring subtle nuances of multi-layered meanings that memory cannot be trusted to preserve. That will facilitate the decoding of cryptic communications from Spirit that tend to expand in clarity over time.

You will notice as you begin to establish a healthy relationship with the practice of Self-Inquiry that your dreams will begin to change dramatically. You will go into deeper REM states that can free you to astral travel farther than you ever imagined possible. You will receive communications and profound insights in your dreams. You may even be connecting with other intelligences, which is nothing to be afraid of, provided the communications are positive. Fear only attracts the object of our fears. There is nothing to fear if spiritual protection through prayer is practiced, respecting the sacred union between Creator and creation.

It is very important to record your dreams in your journal immediately upon awakening. If there was anything particularly disturbing about your dream, and you wish to determine its meaning, go into prayer, meditation, and even fasting. Always consult a medical professional before taking a fast. Do not take vain "demands" into prayer, meditation, or fasting. That is disrespectful of this sacred process. Be patient. No prayer goes unanswered. Answers will come, and guidance will be given. When you receive the understanding you seek, record this information in your journal. Pay close attention to the gradual unfolding of the meaning. Refer back to your notes to expand on your interpretations often.

Keep your journal under password, lock, and key. I trust that no one would be so invasive as to violate anyone in this manner. Still, I encourage you to *lock up your journal*. Your journal will contain very personal information that you may not want to share with *anyone*.

How to Practice the I TRANSCEND MY EGO SELF Meditation

The I Transcend My Ego Self meditation is an invitation to taste existence from the perspective of our pure Essence. This meditation ventures behind the veils and masks that blind us to who we really are. We experience our being in its original reality of formless consciousness, apart from all of the labels, identifications, and drama we have assigned to it. It is the part of us that the pain of our experiences of life on this Plane of existence could not destroy … or even touch. It carries a system of thought that alleviates suffering by keeping us grounded in the present, not focusing on the past or future. While this is a healing perspective in meditation, it is recommended that if you are in a depressed or troubled state of mind, seek help and follow the recommendations of a trusted medical, psychological, or spiritual professional before initiating a new meditation practice.

We seek to strip away the veneer of ego-based perceptions and expose internal and external counterfeit identities for their part in the grand deception we call life. We will meditatively go within and take a look at our lives from a transcendent perspective. We will return awareness to that Ultimate Reality from which we emerged, with a wealth of information. We will be grateful to discover that we are blessed to have the opportunity to change our lives by freeing our vision to see ourselves as we truly are. We will see our opportunity to shine as a beacon of guiding Light for ourselves and other people.

As with any spiritual practice, it is wise to resist a cursory approach. Study the phases of the Moon, planetary transits, and activities. Learn how they affect your meditation work. Study FEARLESS: PSYCHIC SELF-DEFENSE for a detailed overview of the protocol for mystical practice.

To properly perform this meditation:

Never engage in the meditation or play the recorded meditation while driving or doing anything that requires your full concentration.

Read the section called Basic Guidelines for Meditation *in this book before proceeding. Review the questions in your journal that you will be asked to answer at the end of the day.*

Designate a sacred place in your home that is energetically suitable for prayer and meditation. The room should be free of graven images, statues, pictures, mirrors, and symbols that may distract you from your singular focus on stillness and silence. Make sure you have turned off all electronic devices. The only electronic device you will leave connected and in use is the one that will play the digital file provided in your meditation study materials. You may prefer to use headphones to enhance your meditation experience. Refer to the Psychic Self-Defense manual, FEARLESS, at dreamuniversalmedia.com for detailed information on how to set up your sacred space. You will find instructions there regarding charging candles and other meditation tools.

Perform a ritual cleansing (hands to the elbows, face, mouth, ears, back of the neck, crown of head, and feet) before prayer and meditation, or according to your traditional manner of cleansing.

Before entering into this or any other meditation, you must offer the prayer of your choice in petition for the Light of Divine protection to surround you, cleanse you, protect you, and banish all that is not of The God.

Sit up to perform this meditation. Sit in lotus position or in a position that is comfortable for you. Energetic grounding is best accomplished by sitting on or as close to the floor as possible. If you have physical challenges, an executive office chair is the most comfortable seating I have found. Your feet should be on the floor or ground when seated in such a chair.

Close your eyes, and take deep cleansing breaths until you feel yourself relaxing. Observe the rhythms and sensations of your breath as a focal point to deepen concentration. Drop the "me" focus and move your attention away from the mind's preoccupation with self and others. Find the silent place within. In your mind's eye, envision a cord of light emanating from your navel to extend as far as you feel comfortable to travel on your meditative journey. That will serve to provide an anchor you may use to guide you back to your starting point and ground you again in alert consciousness.

After you have returned from your meditative journey and before resuming life as usual, make sure you have grounded yourself. Stretch, breathe, and have a snack, preferably fruit. Grounding can be achieved in many ways. You can wash your face, hands, mouth, and feet with cold water. Drink a cool glass of water. You can stand barefoot on the ground and visualize roots growing out through the bottom of your feet into the Earth. You can play rhythmic music. Do something to shake yourself out of a semi-trance, meditative state. Never forget that the silver cord of Light exists as a security device to assure a safe return, no matter how far out you venture.

This meditation is designed to get in touch with the driver of the physical body vehicle and keep you aware of the connection between the two. Enter your meditation without fear, knowing our temporal form is only a vehicle we have manifested to make this journey. The destination of this sacred journey is true Self-Realization.

You will continue this journey when you return from your meditation, with the advantage of knowing we have congregated here on this level of consciousness for many reasons. The first reason is to give praise and thanks for every breath we take along the way. We have been given our full experience of life as a gift. As we take our spiritual practice seriously, our lives will begin to reflect that knowledge and shine.

After the meditation and grounding, continue your day as usual. Pay attention to subtleties, knowing that there are signs, manifestations, and miracles occurring all around you. First, we will clothe our entire Self with *The Light Meditation.* Through the *I Transcend My Ego Self* meditation, our vision can be trained to perceive ourselves as the Higher Self in its realized state with no fear of death. We do not die. We have always existed in some form, and we always will in some form. Knowing that, we heal ourselves of our fear of death and life. We choose to live this earth-bound experience at the highest vibration possible. It is worth the energy of our commitment.

At the end of the day, review the questionnaire and journal your answers. Accept the opportunity of living a more peaceful life, spiritually seasoned, savoring the Essence of Eternal Light. Only then may we open up to the possibility of painting beautiful new dreams on the canvas of a profoundly spiritual experience of life. We become the artist and the art.

I TRANSCEND MY EGO SELF Meditation Transcript

From Timelessness my soul descends
I am earth and fire, water and wind
I am a spark of The Original Flame
now a being of form on the material plane

No one can know me
by what you think you see
this body is but a shell
wherein the real me dwells
the Ether, the essence
the spirit of me

I witness the many faces
I have chosen to be
Yet I am NOT them
and they are NOT me

I transcend my ego self

I transcend my ego self

I transcend my ego self

I unplug from all imagery

I have associated with my True Self.

I dissolve the costumes, labels, the identities

all of the many faces I have believed that I Am

only to discover the most Divine of mysteries

that the real I within the I, the formless I Am,

witnesses the many beautiful faces,

all of the shape-shifting forms,

peering back at me in the mirror.

I experience fear and suffering

in the face of a Sacred "letting go"
only because I have forgotten
who I really am.

I drop the identifications
that seek to define me
the many faces of time's conjured apparitions
as a mirror that does not cling
to the images before it.

I transcend my ego self
I witness the union … the harmony of opposites,
life and its many changes,
that which cloaks itself
in an illusion called death,
with its body of conditional realities,
I let go and invite liberation.

I see The Will of the Creator in all of the events of my life.
I affirm that this life of mine is mystical and sacred.
My Third Eye observes life spread out
over the multi-dimensional landscape of Timelessness,
free from the bondage of opinion and judgment.

I accept all that I see as a gift.
It is what it is. It is perfect.
I am as I am. I am perfect.
I see only in the present tense.
All exists in the Eternal Now.
Nothing behind me or before me
has relevance to this moment
and my present state of mind.
I am One with the Timeless Now.

I transcend my ego self.
I become a changeless state of consciousness
in the realm of no opposites
beyond all things dual in nature
I transcend my own dual thinking
spinning into freedom
away from labels of confinement
the bars that secure the cage of my immortal being.

I spin as the Dervish into the Eternal realms
into the embrace of the Divine One
My Divinity enshrouded in the tyranny of the flesh
cloaked in starlit thought-forms
expressed in this dream time world.

I remember the union of opposites

It remembers me and visits without invitation

I am the sacred symbol … the creative energy,

the order rising out of primordial chaos,

an awareness

a consciousness

a presence

traveling as Light manifested

of intention and desire

to rendezvous with destiny

I cleanse myself of counterfeit self-esteem

I transcend my ego self

I transcend my ego self

I transcend my ego self

I command the resurrection of my Light body

My Light body has emanated the illusion,

the mirage, the image, that I see in the mirror,

and I have called it me.

I release this clay body of opinion and vain preoccupation

with the ever-changing impressions I have of myself

I see myself as I truly am

peeking from behind the veil of all that I am not,

witnessing this existential dance

of shadows and Light.

I am a body of Light.

I am a body of Light.

I Am

I Am

I Am

I am One with the Ultimate

The Eternal I AM

The Light that I am breaks the container

and reveals the contained

I pierce the veil of form

and shift into the frequency of the Realized Self

I am pure Light energy

I am enduring beauty

I am undying

I am formless consciousness

I am enlightened awareness

Nameless, Faceless, Timeless

with no story that

precedes me or succeeds me

I am nothing. Therefore, I am everything.

I observe my physical form

from a comfortable, non-personal distance

through the Third Eye of my body of Light,
unattached, and objective.

I can shift from one reality
to another and back … at will.
I do not feel threatened
by my released attachment
to any particular reality,
only the Eternal reality of
my own beingness
engaged in perpetual becoming.

I command my inner child to grow up
I embrace the everlasting NOW

I accept and heal feelings of
loss of identity that the shift
between form and essence may bring.
I awaken from this dream and realize
there is no shift from one self to another Self.

There is only the Self,
transfixed in time as I have measured it
dissolving this figment of my imagination
into a sea of forgetfulness

of the lies I have called "myself"
Awakening from the hallucination
Ascribing permanent reality
to transitory states of being
I am free from that.

Nature abhors a vacuum.
As I empty myself of illusions of myself
I fill the void with Light,
Divine Light, Compassionate Light,
Loving Light … the brilliant Light of the Most High.
I become as nothing … melting into the warmth
of the Light that I Am
rising from the ashes of desperation
with its craving and clinging
attachments and aversions
breaking the spell
of this joyless hypnosis
rejecting my conditioning,
I rejoice in the continual becoming
One with all things.
I dissolve as light into Light.
I am not my own.
I surrender to the Unknowable Divinity
to Whom I am well Known and well Loved.

My body vehicle knows

its parking space

on the lot of humanity.

Grounded and anchored by a cord of silver Light,

my Light body frees itself of its container.

I am not distracted by the remains left behind,

regardless of their condition.

I disengage from the fear … the shock …

the drama associated with the container breaking,

regardless of the circumstances.

The Light of Ultimate Knowing

touches my Faceless being

and I relax and allow myself to be birthed into Ultimate Reality.

I escape time.

I feel the ambient surge of ecstatic energy

moving beyond the boundaries and limitations

of my own linear perceptions

I am no longer paralyzed by the innate fear and foreboding

of the inevitable transitions all souls are *born* to make.

I accept that there is no "transition"

The illusion of two selves is a dream.

I awaken from my slumber and arise in Love as I AM

I will no longer allow the tyranny of my attachment to worldly desires
and superficial, fleeting whims, to seduce me into forgetfulness of who
I am. I have unjustly wronged my Higher Self with my forgetfulness
that I am nothing … nothing … one drop
merging with an endless sea of consciousness.
I see my reality as a part of all there is … everything.
I accept that I am nothing …
nothing of form-filled definition,
judgment and conditioning.
I transcend these masks.
I see with clear vision.
I evolve from the realm of the perishable
into the splendor of the infinite.
I engage in a graceful dance in praise of my Divine Origin
The harmonious voices of the Universe have called me NAMELESS.
I am summoned to rise as a being of depth and beauty
I am a beacon of The Light from whence we all have emerged.
My spirit is quickened as I realize
the Ultimate Light is One with my own body of Light.
My Light body survives my ascent from the physical form,
just as naturally as it preceded it.
I release all fear of the loss of form.
I realize it is my original state.
All else is expressed from that.
I am That.

I am limitlessly able to recreate myself beyond common imagination.

I cherish my relationship

with The Most Sacred Ether …

the Comforter.

Protecting me, guiding me

through every stage of existence.

My Essence seeks luminous expression of our Sacred union.

Grace, Mercy, and Love fulfill my every dream

of being the dream born of the Oneness of Being.

Now that I have observed the beauty of my True Self, I feel free to

reach out in full embrace of both sides of my dual nature,

the perishable and the Infinite

I accept them both as one … I accept them both as one

One side, just as beautiful, just as perfect as the other.

I do not fear my Light.

I do not fear my shadows.

I do not fear for the container

that houses this beautiful Light that I am.

I am safe. I am comfortable in my own skin.

I am confident in my own being.

I place my complete trust in The Divine One

knowing that my life and death are the expression of That.

I release my fear of death as I release my fear of life.

Nothing can happen without Divine Permission.

Nothing threatens this formless being that I Am.

My formless Light body cannot be destroyed.

The container bears witness

that this infinite body of Light contained

is the evidence of my immortality.

The Eternal being that I Am cannot die.

I can only transcend my ego self.

I transcend my ego self.

I transcend my ego self.

I transcend my ego self.

We do not die.

Fear fades into the transformative Light

of Ultimate reality.

The opposite of fear is love.

I love myself regardless of my ever-changing form.

I love creation regardless of its ever-changing form.

I love the changeless and know that I am That.

The voice of my Higher Self advises me,

"You had better do what you came here to do."

The seed of this advice becomes firmly planted within my heart.

It is now my intimate companion and faithful friend.

This seed takes root in fertile soil.

This cherished moment and my physical life

become transformed into a beautiful, mystical, sacred adventure …

a grace and a blessing each moment of every day.

I am HERE NOW.

I am HERE NOW

and NOW I know

that NOW is FOREVER.

I transcend linear time.

I transcend linear time.

I witness my resurrection from my physical body vehicle.

My Light body emerges, whole, complete

and very much alive.

I am the observer of the fragile container

that is the Temple of my soul.

Death where is thy sting?

Flesh and bone is perishable by nature,

ultimately destined to fall into decay.

I am unmoved by that knowledge.

The physical form is my uniquely designed garment,

appearing as many faces, morphing in and out of many stages, the many mirrors of my life …

I thought each one of them was me.

Which one of them is me?

Which of them is the real me?

I see now that not one of them is me.

The One I am, the Light body that I am,

is the WITNESS who observes the snapshots

of all those selves I thought were me,

through each of the phases of my corporal life.

The physical container is a responsible host

and the Temple of the Most High,

the Light from which I was expressed

the Light into which I will be reabsorbed

in a glorious reunion with the Unfathomable.

I give praise and thanks to the Most High for this gift.

I rise into my new brilliance from the world of the perishable.

I accept who I am. I accept who I am.

I accept who I am. I accept who I am.

I transcend my ego self

I transcend my ego self

I transcend my ego self

I travel securely

in a sophisticated vehicle made of Light

on this Sacred Journey of my immortal Soul.

My Essence is transported in my Chariot of Light.

This medium becomes my room with a view,

my bridge between dreams,

my bridge between Ether and form.

I breach the time/space continuum.

I embrace Ultimate Reality.

I become One with All

and I breathe

(Breathe)

I inhale and radiate pure LIGHT

I exhale my fear of LOSS

I release my fear of DEATH

I release my fear of LIFE

I release my fear of CHANGE

I see life as fluid … not a fixed reality.

I feel so free.

I feel so free of senseless FEAR

My attention is drawn

to my Chariot of Light.

My transcendent journey
has led me to the Light
that I am within
the Light of the I Am,
within the I am, that I am
as I in I
I live.
I have always lived.
I will always live …
in whatever form
my Essence takes.
There is no veil
between worlds …
One World is our home.
The key to reentry
is the realization of Self,
a being of pure Light
rising to the occasion
of Union with Divine,
knowing our perception
of separateness
was pure illusion.

I return as the Chariot of Light
I have become,

grateful for my transcendent journey.
It is not a descent back into form.
It is a "shift" of perception into form,
a quickening of the spirit …
a fusion with mind, body, and spirit.
I reject the perception
that there is a veil between them,
without judgment.

I close my Third Eye and BREATHE
I am comfortably settled
back into my Light body container.
I am present to the resurrection
of my more evolved Higher Self.
I open my eyes prepared
to welcome this new day …
driven by deep gratitude
for the gift of my physical vehicle.
My worst fears subside.
The Light within me can never die.
The many roads I may travel
respectfully represent
the Will of That Which Created all.
I am both humbled and exalted.

I transcend my ego self, daily.

I rise from the ashes of my life

as a phoenix into the realm of enlightenment.

I transcend my ego self, daily. I welcome my daily resurrection.

I transcend my ego self, daily. I welcome my daily resurrection.

I transcend my ego self, daily. I welcome my daily resurrection.

I transcend my ego self. I stay in this moment of the Eternal Now.

I give thanks for my being in this moment.

I extend the manifestation of the Healing Light, that I AM,

outward to become a healing in the lives of others.

One of the gifts of the Divine One is the "power of naming things,"

and I name this day The Most Glorious Day of my Being.

I know who I am, with or without a garment of flesh and bone … with

or without the container. I am the contained. I am the scene.

I am not the scenery. I am the contained. I am not the container.

I AM.

I AM.

I AM.

I AM.

****

The I Transcend My Ego Self Meditation is available as an audio download at *Dreamuniversalmedia.com*. Please see the instructions in the chapter "Meditation Download Instructions" at the back of this book.

DREAMCATCHER JOURNAL

Go to dreamuniversalmedia.com to print out your cover page to your DREAMCATCHER JOURNAL and as many copies of the questionnaire as required.

How did I consciously die to my ego self?

What was it like?

What were the blessings I observed as I contemplated my physical life?

What were the blessings I observed as I contemplated my eternal life?

If given the opportunity, what would I do differently?

Who and what do I love about the physical world?

What do I love about the formless world?

What would this world love about me, if it had the opportunity to see me for who I really am?

What would the formless world love about me, as it sees me as who I really am?

What are my regrets, and how might I turn those regrets into healings?

What did I leave unfinished that I would complete, if given the opportunity?

What did I leave unsaid, that I would say if given the opportunity?

What do I love about myself?

What fences would I mend if I had the chance?

What and how would I contribute to humanity, if given the opportunity?

What did I learn?

What would I love to learn, if given the opportunity?

Who and what will miss me?

Who and what will I miss?

How have I contributed to a healing in my own life?

How have I contributed to a healing in the lives of others?

What do I see my purpose in life as being?

How am I fulfilling that purpose?

What changes would I make in my life to facilitate the fulfillment of my purpose, if given the opportunity?

What do I have to say for my Self?

How has realizing who I really am given me the gift of appreciating my life?

Am I happy to be back? If so … why? If not … why not?

How did my transcending my ego self on this day affect the way I lived it?

What did I do differently as a result of my meditation and contemplation?

What is my mission in the realization of my Light body, and how do I visualize achieving it?

What prayer of thanks connects me to my center … connects me to my Source … and heals my Being?

I PRAY.

In prayer, I transcend my ego self.

I transcend my ego self.

I transcend my ego self.

The Power of Affirmation

The following are suggested affirmations to help focus on your intention and get more specific results from your meditations. These suggestions may be used in a chant or be presented in the form of a petition written on parchment paper. Please refer to your spiritual protocol reference book FEARLESS, in the section regarding petitions, for more information. To anchor the energy of your intention to the physical Plane, it can be written or typed, photocopied, cut out, and placed in strategic places throughout your home, vehicle, and workplace as a reminder to allow you to maintain focus long after your meditation is complete.

These affirmations are ideas from my experience with Mystical Meditation, and in no way reflect an absolute formula to accomplish your spiritual objectives. The petition that you write for yourself may be the one that best accomplishes your spiritual goals. These are merely ideas that will hopefully assist you in the process of forming positive affirmations to improve the quality of your physical and spiritual life.

A mantra is a sacred utterance. Mantras are words of power or phrases of stated intentions and emotions. The use of a mantra dates back to the most ancient of times and is, in some form, used among most religious traditions and spiritual practices. Some use hymns and passages from sacred scriptures. Some use a mantra in the form of repetitive prayer or a personal mantra. One powerful mantra can be expressed in a single sacred symbol, the OM or AUM. The Sanskrit word "mantra" means "instrument of thought." A powerful mantra has a prescribed structure that transforms thought-forms into a manifestation of intention.

A mantra is often used in conjunction with prescribed mudra. A mudra is a symbolic gesture, posture, position, or movement used along with breath or prana, to activate and channel the energy evoked in meditation.

It is up to you whether you choose to approach the practice of meditation as a cursory study or pursue it to a depth that could last the rest of your life. It is important that you at least study it enough to find a system or tradition that complements who you really are. Meditation is a practice that can be tailor-made to conform to your own spiritual standards and goals. I do not promote one path over another here. I share traditions that I am familiar with and have benefited from in practice. A powerful meditation can be as simple as a heartfelt affirmation. A powerful meditation and mantra can be as simple as a heartfelt *Thank You*.

AFFIRMATION

In the image and likeness of The Creator, I affirm my innate Oneness with All that is, was, and ever will be. I am a spark of That Original Flame. I am an emanation of Its Essence. I am That.

AFFIRMATION

I affirm that the strength and fortitude of The Divine, of my ancestors, of human and spirit helpers, motivates the Essence of my being to realize the sacred nature of my immortal Soul.

AFFIRMATION

I am one with the Universe and all of Creation. I have access to the wisdom of all ages. I embrace the Light of Timeless Truth.

AFFIRMATION

I am thankful for the gift of Third Eye sight. I use my gift to help my Self and others. I choose to see only that which will contribute to the highest good of all concerned.

AFFIRMATION

My journey through the dream time world will be filled with the peace, protection, and the loving guidance of the Creator of all the worlds.

AFFIRMATION

Even though I walk through the valley of the shadow of death, I fear no evil. Nothing exists, but The God. My Eternal Self is safe in all worlds.

AFFIRMATION

I am released from fear. I take responsibility for my health and well-being. The Mercy of Divine Love and the Law of Cause and Effect heal my body and mind from the thought-forms that contribute to poor health.

AFFIRMATION

The Divine Protection of The Creator surrounds me. My footsteps are guided and blessed.

AFFIRMATION

I cannot know enough. I cannot love enough. I cannot be enough. I am in a continual state of becoming … from Essence … back to Essence … knowing that I never left. I Am That Essence. I am That.

AFFIRMATION

I affirm that every prayer I offer, every sacrifice I make, my living, and my dying are all for The One God. Nothing exists but The One God, and I humble myself in gratitude for the blessing and honor of carrying That Spirit within.

AFFIRMATION

I choose to see the wisdom of Divine, buried beneath the perception of any problem in my life. I choose to project the power of my Free Will, aligned with Divine Will, to influence a positive outcome in all matters.

AFFIRMATION

I respond to my innermost knowing with confidence and patience. I heed and trust that small voice within. My life is the sum total of the choices I make. Good decisions equal an opportunity for a good life.

AFFIRMATION

My breath takes me into my Truth. Stress is fear made manifest. I have nothing to fear as I let go of illusion, relax and attune my vibration with that of all of Creator and creation … I vibrate … Ommmmm. I observe my breath.

AFFIRMATION

I am the perfection of The God's Love for creation and now seek balance in my life to further manifest the strength and beauty of The Creator.

AFFIRMATION

Through reunion with The Divine, I am born again. Any displeasing perception of myself, encouraged by the standards of others, is a delusion of phenomenal proportions.

AFFIRMATION

No weapon formed against me shall prosper! I fear nothing. I fear no one. I rebuke any force or presence of evil in my life.

AFFIRMATION

I release (_____) to his/her highest good and happiness. I am cleansed of any shadows they may have cast over my life. Forgiveness is the gift I offer. Forgiveness is the gift I accept for having opened the door to this negative presence in my life.

AFFIRMATION

Any problem I perceive originates from within me. I attract into my life that which I am. I find peace within as I aspire to elevate the consciousness of my opinions and feelings toward others and toward myself.

AFFIRMATION

No matter how far I stray from Love … Love will bring me back. Love finds a home in my heart. The ambiance of Love radiantly lights my life with the brilliance of Divine Love. I radiate that same Light. I attract that same Light. I am That same Light.

AFFIRMATION

I don't have to look for love. I am that which I seek. I am love. I avoid conscious or subconscious thoughts of any particular person that I think I may be interested in. I understand that to intentionally project binding energy, within the context of spiritual work, towards any "particular" person, crosses the line into the dark side of manipulation. I understand that to ignore this truth could cause great harm and Karmic debt.

AFFIRMATION

I am as The God created me. I am perfect. I am secure in my inner beauty and radiate that same beauty, wearing it like a flowing robe of dreams waiting to come true.

AFFIRMATION

Our souls touch in the Eternal. Together we reflect the Divine Union of The Holy Mother/Father presence … blessed with Love that never dies.

AFFIRMATION

I turn within and center my energy, accepting into my home the peace that I am.

AFFIRMATION

I give thanks to the seen and unseen forces, which protect and guide me in Light.

AFFIRMATION

I release. I let go. I know that The God will heal my life. I step out of my own way, giving thanks with every breath. My heart is cleansed of the shadows cast by the illusions of this world. I forgive myself. I forgive others ... whether I think we deserve it or not.

AFFIRMATION

My immortal soul chose my mother/my father and my family of origin, to initiate the completion of my Earth Plane Karma. Even though the lessons may be painful, even if I find it difficult to embrace them, I embrace the lessons, loving, forgiving, and asking for forgiveness.

AFFIRMATION

I have created the sensation of loneliness I feel. I release the energy of neediness, judgment, and the illusion of separateness from any being.

AFFIRMATION

In times of struggle, I affirm that I am stronger than this. I am more than this. I find strength and comfort in the embrace of That Which Created me.

AFFIRMATION

Every end represents a new beginning. All of my relationships contribute something to my life as I contribute something to theirs. No meeting is a coincidence. No farewell is a coincidence.

AFFIRMATION

Nothing is static. I am constantly changing, evolving, and growing. I embrace change as a natural process of unfolding towards my higher good.

AFFIRMATION

I accept my freedom from the bondage of illusions as a gift from The Creator. I affirm my strength in Divine Love. I am a child of Divine Light. I rebuke the shadow principals of spiritual bondage and embrace freedom as my Divine Birthright. The seed of that freedom exists within me.

AFFIRMATION

I claim the healing of my heart in the face of the perception of loss. Nothing can be "lost" to me. All is changing. Objects and people come and go … but in no way are they lost. All is merely changing. I and all I know will come and go and change … I cling to the unchanging … I affirm that nothing and no one can be lost. I am healed from resisting change.

AFFIRMATION

I am healed from all deluded perceptions of prosperity. I pray for strength that I not be seduced from the Path by the illusions of material wealth without spiritual substance, material presence without spiritual substance.

AFFIRMATION

My soul was born in the success of Spirit. I stand in the knowledge of who I really am and what I have come to this Plane to master. The seed of my soul was planted in the fertile soil of the manifest Plane to experience the highest levels of the abundance of The Creator. I have come here to shine That Light. I am That Light.

AFFIRMATION

I affirm that I accept responsibility for knowing that I am the transformation of every environment I enter ... some by standing up and staying, some by standing up and leaving.

AFFIRMATION

My dreams of success frame my desire to make a positive difference in the big picture of the Timeless Now.

AFFIRMATION

I know my worth. I have a profound investment in raising the frequency of this entire planet.

AFFIRMATION

I can access assistance on this plane and beyond. I draw strength from within and from that which appears to be beyond me.

AFFIRMATION

The Universe supports me in the realization of my destiny. I now understand that I already am all that I need to be. I must never lose consciousness of who I really am. I am the remembrance of the indwelling ... the Ultimate I Am.

AFFIRMATION

Any appearance of lack is an illusion. The truth frees me to attract my needs as well as my desires. I see these "needs and desires" from the perspective of the I AM consciousness, never clinging, never craving ... with no attachment ... no aversion.

AFFIRMATION

I am a request for forgiveness. I am a request for the strength of Spirit to extend forgiveness as I wish to be forgiven. I release judgment, accusatory thoughts, and grudge-driven behaviors. I am a request for a healing in my life.

There is no closure.
There are no words.

I just want to pray with you.

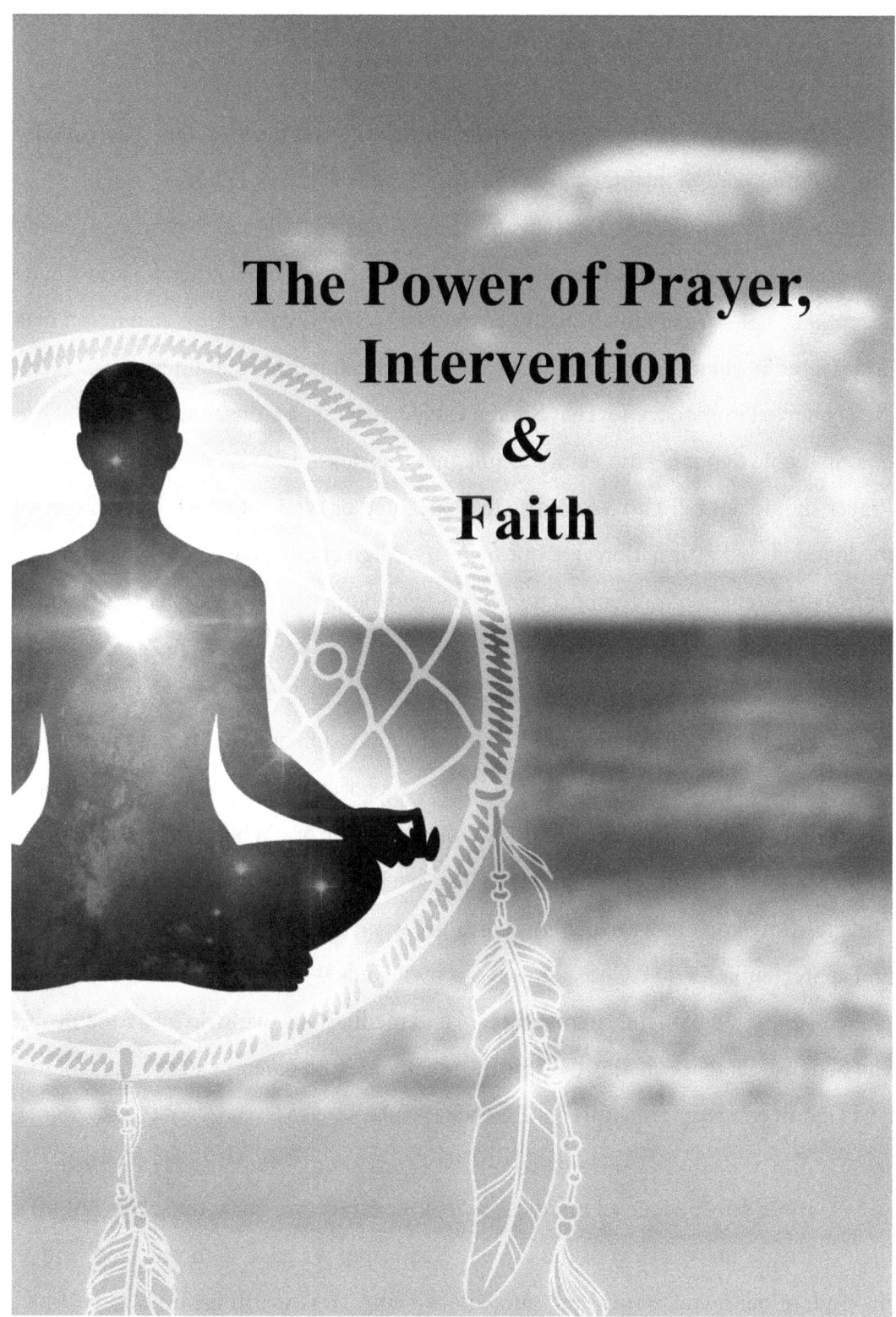

The Power of Prayer, Intervention & Faith

The Power of Prayer, Intervention, and Faith

It is tough navigating the unpredictable twists and turns on this road called life. It defies natural instinct and reason to adhere to limiting beliefs of fixed conclusions about just how fluid this mystical Universe really is. Nothing is fixed. Our greatest consolation is to know that we are not our own, whether we know and accept it or not. We are intrinsically connected to The Creator, God, in a union that is so sacred it cannot be named by our lower Plane languages and utterances. We are connected in Essence to That Source Consciousness, a Consciousness so unfathomable that it is pure vanity to imagine it is possible to speak Its Holy Name. Prayer should not fall into a category to be debated or argued to dust. The prayers, meditations, and affirmations are our own sovereign choice, based on what makes us feel the strength of our connection … understanding that our essence and That Essence are One.

Our regular affirmations of belief and submission are vital to our spiritual healing in times of fear, loss, and grief. If we waver in our belief of the miraculous nature of The God, all we need to do is look in the mirror. When we look into our own eyes for that spark of Light that we are, we know that we are looking at a miracle. Prayer is our way of communicating with The God. We validate our love and appreciation for The God and heal our own souls with every word of every prayer and sacred thought. In our prayers and meditations, we strip away the flesh and bone vessel that contains the spirit we really are and bare our immortal soul to The God in communion with That Essence.

If our prayers are but mindless verbal recitation, we cheat ourselves out of the experience and comfort of the sacred relationship we have with The God, and the truth of our own Divinity and miraculous being. It is worth the time and effort to respect the ritual process of preparing to experience that consecrated holy union.

It is worth the mindfulness of unplugging from the matrix of this confusion system to plug into a Higher Energy Source, that of the Most High.

It is healing to elevate the intensity of our longing by not just praying but remaining in repetitive prayer and chanting. It is well worth the time we allow in our busy lives for a departure from the vain drama of the perishable world to rest our weary souls in the loving embrace of Ultimate Reality. As we accept responsibility for our spiritual journey, we must be mindful of the fact that we are not alone. We are intrinsically connected at the core of our being to the Source of all healing. In the face of relentless pursuit by the spirit of despair, with its never-ending effort to capture and collect our souls for fun, we submit in prayer to the Will of the Most High in thought, action, and deed.

So why do we bother to pursue metaphysical studies and practices? I think we may do it for the same reasons we exercise the muscles of our physical body even though it is born perfect, even in spite of any of our perceived imperfections. Our perfection rests in the Loving Eyes of our Creator and has little to do with our or anyone's judgments, opinions, criticisms, or comparisons. Still, we naturally feel compelled to exercise, improve, and groom our already perfect vehicle because that inclination is a natural component of our perfection. However, we are not to bow down to the exercise. We bow down only to The Creator, not to the ritual around our practice.

Prayer is a spiritual exercise. Surrender is the spiritual muscle that results. There, in the spirit of that sacred surrender, is faith ... faith beyond evidence, beyond proof. The prayer must be a meditation of surrender. The meditation must be a prayer of surrender. From the killing fields of grief, all we can do is surrender what is left of us to the only Force capable of facilitating our healing. I do not represent any one religious or spiritual path over another. The prayers and meditations you choose to engage in are entirely up to you. If the energy of your prayer resonates with the energy of your Higher Self, you will feel it and know. Sometimes the best and most powerful prayer or meditation is simply, *"Thank You."*

I will share with you a few of the prayers from many traditions that I personally found comforting and healing. I encourage you to share prayers that speak to your soul at dreamuniversalmedia.com, to possibly be used in future publications.

Prayer of St. Francis

Lord, make me an instrument of Your peace;
Where there is hatred, let me sow love;
Where there is injury, pardon;
Where there is error, truth;
Where there is doubt, faith;
Where there is despair, hope;
Where there is darkness, light;
and where there is sadness, joy.
Oh Divine Master, Grant that I may not so much seek
to be consoled as to console;
to be understood as to understand;
to be loved as to love;
for it is in giving that we receive;
It is in pardoning that we are pardoned;
And it is in dying that we are born to Eternal life.

Every prayer is heard. Every prayer is answered. Sometimes the answer is no. Sometimes the silence is a test of faith. In the silence you may hear the answer spoken to your soul in your own inner voice.

Release Prayer

The Great and Holy Spirit,

Sacred Mother/Father God

the essence of I, Name ,

am your humble servant

and You are my Beloved

I seek refuge in your Guidance

and surrender my personal will to Thy Will

at this point where the river of my suffering

meets the shoreless ocean

of Your Love,

Compassion and Mercy

At this time, I stand before You

for guidance on this matter

My soul is burdened

My heart is heavy

and still, my faith

and my gratitude

are stronger than my suffering

I release and submit my willfulness

asking Your forgiveness

for every moment of

falling into forgetfulness

that only You are my sustenance, my providence

Our connection is Sacred

Our One and only reality is Our Oneness
I release my attachment to the outcome
I surrender my personal will to Divine Will

Here in the shadow realms of a desolate night
I release and let go as I seek only Your Light
Here in the brokenness of my heart
that beats only for You
that seeks healing only from You
I wait only for You

23rd Psalm, The Bible (KJV)

The Lord is my shepherd

I shall not want

He maketh me to lie down in green pastures

He leadeth me beside the still waters

He restoreth my soul

He leadeth me in the paths of righteousness

for his names sake

Yeah though I walk through the valley

of the shadow of death

I shall fear no evil for thou art with me

Thy rod and thy staff they comfort me

Thou preparest a table before me

in the presence of mine enemies

Thou anointest my head with oil

My cup runneth over

Surely goodness and mercy shall follow me

all the days of my life

and I will dwell in the house of the Lord

forever.

Amen

The Prayer of Life
The Rebuke of Self-Harm and/ or Harming Others

I was given the gift of this body to stay in it for as long as it takes
to hear it called back home in its perfect time
My own voice will never make that call

I realize this is not the home of my spirit
I recognize my soul's yearning for its return home
I evoke the awareness that I am already there, in or out of this body
no matter where else I may appear to be

I can die to this world and never leave my body
I can be here now
transcending the pain, the sadness, and the grief
transcending the loneliness and the suffering
transcending fear and rejection
I am not asking for my burdens to be taken away
I am asking for the fear to be taken away
and be replaced by the strength to bear it

Angels watch over me
I am never left alone
I cannot fail in this dance of destiny
I am here for that
for as long as it takes
to know that I do not need a body to exist

My body needs me to exist
Inside of it I am the transcendence of all materiality
Right here
Right now

I affirm that there is no such thing as death
I affirm that I cannot die
I affirm that it is not possible to end my life
I affirm that who I really am
will survive any attempt to erase myself
and be forced to witness the fallout
of the suffering my choice has caused

I am Eternal
There is no beginning of me
There is no end of me
Not by my hand, nor the hand of any other
Not by fire, air, water, or earth
I Am One with That from which my True Self emerged

I choose not to witness
the self-destruction caused by my misguided choices
by my tormented emotions,
by my troubled mind,
by my broken spirit,
by my own hand

I choose not to witness the pain such a departure would cause
on this side and the other

I choose to love and accept my True Self

My life matters

I have the power to reside in the domain of my Higher Self inside of this body

I have the power to transcend the stories, the faces, the masks, the theater

of the lower realms of my consciousness

I give up

I give up approval seeking, comparisons, and people pleasing

I give up imposing impossible, false, soul-selling standards upon myself

I give up force-fitting the vastness of my Self

into the tiny boxes of illusory realities

that have nothing to do with who I really am

I owe no offerings to the fake imagery of others

I am not this body

I was here before it happened

I will be here when it is gone

No thing, no person, no opinion, no circumstance

DARES to even try to invalidate the beauty

of this life, this breath, this Light, this Love, that I am

I am HERE NOW

I AM THAT which I seek

I am One with the Most High Creator Mother Father God

of my highest understanding

I am a spark of the Original Flame

There is no difference between us

I forgive myself for this thought of separation

I accept this perfect gift
this beautiful container
which is not me

It transports my True Self
through this experiencing
I own the power to OWN it.

The Power of Repetitive Prayer

The chanting of mantras and repetitive prayer dates back to the beginning of time. A mantra can be as simple as a single word of power, a vibrational utterance, a childhood prayer. This sacred practice balances and clears internal and external energies, bringing harmony to mind, body, and spirit. The sensation of this powerful energy results in our consciousness being shaken from the perishable realm into Ultimate Reality, the Timeless Now. All healing occurs there where the arrow becomes one with the mark ... the essence ... no beginning ... no ending ... no time ... where the prayerful one becomes the prayer.

Words of power in repetitive prayer and chanting can be used for very specific purposes, including the clearing of the dense emotional fog we call grief. The sound and vibration involved with the chanting of mantras can produce transformation and have a positive healing effect. Sacred sounds, repetitive utterances, mantras, chanting and prayer, date all the way back to the beginning of time. All we know began with the Sacred OM/AUM and is sustained by its vibration. It has no energetic beginning or end. It is well worth the effort to study how to engage the power of repetitive prayer, as practiced by so many traditions, on so many spiritual paths. It does not matter what language it is spoken in, as long as it is the language of the very soul of our being.

Repetitive prayer should not be a divisive issue. Among the core mystical groups of most spiritual traditions, the root language is ultimately Sacred Silence. What matters is the breath, and the heart's intention, as they are carried upon the magnificent wings of the most surrendered prayer, whispered into the ether. These are not the prayers and chanting of beggars with personal agendas and a list of demands. It is the sound of surrendered fusion with the Absolute Energy and finding the point of connection within. What matters is our ability to suspend our senses and drop all ego self-identification. What counts is how powerfully we are able to withdraw our attention from all distractions and focus it in such a way as to create change on a cellular level. What resonates with, and as Divine, is the purity of our hearts.

The information shared in this book is not meant to be purely remedial. There must be a wholesome, balanced lifestyle in place to support your practice. It makes no sense to have an elaborate altar, consecrated for healing and holistic well-being, if every door to the temple of the soul is swinging open to any, and every, random, sorrowful energy. Much drama would be averted by simply closing and locking the doors in our lives to the mental and emotional triggers that cause our suffering.

Most paths and traditions practice some form of chanting sacred sounds and words of power, each with its own unique method of repetition. Repetitive prayer is often practiced with a string of a prescribed number of prayer beads, or malas, for counting and focusing attention. There are specific "mudras" or hand and body positions associated with certain systems of chanting, meditation, and prayer. Some are practiced with instrumental accompaniment. Drums bring their own level of vibration and frequency. Some practices include spinning, dancing, or swaying rhythmically, while others require stillness of motion. Your best mantra is the mantra of your choice. The best mantra can be as simple as a childhood prayer, or even as simple as, "Thank You. Thank you for existence." You may feel drawn to a certain mantra or prayer system. Choose with discernment and in-depth knowledge of the meaning of what you are chanting or praying. Repetition of a mantra serves to quiet the over-thinking, reactive mind, inspiring transcendence beyond the origin of thought, into pure awareness. To enter the silence of Ultimate Reality is the goal of most meditation disciplines.

You would be ill-advised to engage in most traditional practices without mindfulness regarding the proper respect for its sacredness, and the strict protocol that must be observed, down to specific subtleties of perfect pronunciation, personal hygiene, and diet. It is worth the effort to study how to perform these very basic but profound healing rituals. This practice is prescribed in times of emotional suffering as a powerful tool for healing. Use that knowledge to empower your practice. The battle between forces of joy and sorrow is a choice and a perception. We are given the understanding that they are interdependent, and neither is "good" or "bad" … they just are. To see it in the context of a pendulum swinging rather than a balance being kept, we become an enemy to our own emotional stability. We may find the worst enemy of our happiness in the mirror. That is where the energetic cleansing begins. Removing the magnets that attract emotional drama will result in a more peaceful life.

One of the simplest of disciplines is the repetitive chanting of "OM/AUM." The energy from the vibration engages the Third Eye and has the power to induce a deep meditative and transcendental state of consciousness, which serves many healing purposes. The Sanskrit symbol for the sacred OM/AUM illustrates the four states of consciousness. Our spiritual practice strives for the fourth level, the transcendent state of the Higher Self. From that perspective, healing from emotional trauma is viewed differently. The first question would be, "Who is the 'self/Self' that is suffering?" If the personhood is suffering, the person must be dropped, and the matter must be taken to another realm to be resolved … or dissolved. From a transcendental perspective, there is no "self," consequently, no self to grieve. Once the trappings of the ego self, with its conditioned, subconscious, cultural narratives have been stripped away, the Self that remains knows that it cannot be harmed, damaged, or killed. It knows that it is Timeless, formless, identity-less, label-less, and without agenda or interest in carnal worries rooted in victimhood.

The Sacred Om

The Sacred Om is the diagram that represents the original vibration that resulted in the creation of the Universe and all we know. It awakens the light of the third eye chakra.

The Four States of Consciousness and the World of Illusion

1. Waking
2. Dreaming
3. Deep sleep
4. Transcendental state
5. Maya, the world of illusion

THE SACRED OM/OHM/AUM

This Ancient Mystical Sanskrit Symbol
represents the original
sound vibration
by which The Creator caused
the Universe to evolve
from chaos to order to creation
and all that sustains it.
It speaks of the dream world,
the waking state,
and the veil between them.
OM, when intoned,
vibrates the skull and the bones of the face
stimulating the Light of
the Third Eye, at the center of our brow line,
the sixth of our seven energy centers
known as the Chakra System.
The vibration and frequency of the OM
is the sacred connection between the Ultimate I AM
and The Divine manifesting in the I in I,
that Sacred link between Creator
and that which was created.
It is the voice of the Contained calling out
from within the container of our physical form
singing the song of its liberation.
The container can either be a prison
incarcerating our Essence

or it can be the sacred garment

which compliments and adorns It.

The vibration of the OM/AUM,

at the Fifth Chakra

in the area of the throat,

can be the medium

through which It is freed.

Sacred wisdom in wordless Holy language

through the representative visual art

of its evocative calligraphy

can cause the symbol of the OM/AUM

to become a catalytic connection

that seeds the mystical Essence.

This sacred symbol is consistent with the three Sanskrit sounds

A U M representing various fundamental triads believed to be a vibration

of the spoken essence of the Universe.

It is uttered as a mantra

in meditation, affirmations, and blessings.

Let us meditate every day.

We meditate upon The Divine Essence.

Do unto others as we would have them do unto us.

One God

One Love

One Breath

Born of the Eternal OM/AUM

of and into

The Light of the Creator our souls merge

as members of the same body of Eternal Light.

Let us join in this Universal dream.
We will once again
dream together.
Together we will awaken
our lives transformed
to emit our own frequency
and stop living in reference to
and under the influence of
discordant frequencies
that distort our perception of our own reality.

I am imperishable.
I choose a life that confirms this truth in every moment.
The Timeless tone of the Sacred OM/AUM is my meditation.
I must never forget who I am.
I remember I am that space
I share with no one.
I am
beyond time
beyond you and me
I am
That
Om

Service as Meditation and Healing

The best way to alleviate personal suffering is to cultivate a consciousness that reaches out to help and heal others. The beginning of healing unfathomable grief is to stand for the healing of others in the spirit of knowing we are of the same Spirit. In all of our spiritual endeavors, if we do not in some way seek to be of service to others, we have not earned our place on the grand stage of this phase of existence. Our first act of service is to embrace the Sacred Law of Impermanence as it sparks the awakening of our Essential being … our body of Light and awareness … patiently waiting in the realm of the Timeless Now.

After we accept the immortality of our True Being and the depth to which we are all connected, it is time to engage the healing process in a way that helps others. As we suffer from our own fears and loss, we must understand that becoming a healing in the lives of others is the answer to maintaining our own holistic well-being. We cannot effectively serve The God or humanity without the study of our own Light and resultant shadows. One is not good and the other evil, for That Which Created all created both.

Every day we engage in the same battle that began with our creation, the struggle to keep the balance between our physical and non-physical Self. We are given help on either side of the veil, between seen and unseen existence on this sacred journey. There are astral and earth-bound beings that are commissioned to serve humanity in keeping our delicate balance. Our willingness to serve humanity as an offering is our passport to a state of being that lives in love and service. To do this great work, we shift into the gears of our earthly vehicle, accepting that the mystical understanding of both our material and spiritual attributes is the balancing act that causes us to exist. There is no such thing as a coin with only one side. We can live our lives like a misspent, one-sided coin if we do not accept responsibility for bringing our natural contradictions into union. That union must then realize its union with the Unknowable. The committed search for the Source of the Light that we are is the beginning of our service to the Creator. To humble ourselves in service to creation is the Ultimate union with the Creator. Such a choice causes our rise into the empathic energies of a Light Worker.

A Lightworker is one who has chosen to become an instrument dedicated to the development of the expertise required to enable others to perceive and receive energy traveling at frequencies that are just out of reach to them. The Lightworker raises his or her vibration to the level or frequency required to become the medium through which healing energies and intentions are channeled. That type of energy cannot be channeled without resulting in a healing for the medium. We must embrace the task of becoming a healing force in the world we live in.

We are living in a world that is like a dream that the Creator is having of experiencing humanity through us … as us. Through us, a family was born of the purest Love. We were even given a choice to return that love or not, secure in knowing that within the Light of our creation, there would always be that Spark of Love within us as a bond. We do not serve a God of clay. We serve an Infinite Spirit so profound Its Name can only be expressed by silence. We are not merely beings of clay, but of Infinite Spirit. Clay is our temple of the Divine. Clay is also our prison. Spirit is our Ultimate Formless Reality, the Reality out of which we were born into this dream. The pain of our laborious journey on this Plane of dreams and illusions is the price we must pay, in service and in sacrifice, to deserve the blessings we receive. Even the pain is sacred. The suffering is sacred. The joy is sublime.

The Self-Realized being knows no conflict between spirit and clay, knows no pain, no suffering or grief, no death. We do not succumb to the lies these illusions tell, the most terrifying of which is, "This will last forever." We expand our Light through our experience of joy and suffering in the clay prison, in which our souls abide for a time. We live in the valley of the shadow of death. Yet, our consciousness may ascend into the realms of all Light, escaping time with a single thought. This is the process of expansion that justifies and qualifies our existence. We will ultimately return to our spiritual home with knowledge that no spirit unborn into this carnal Plane can even comprehend.

The God allowed the manifestation of Itself to be born onto this Plane of existence to experience the persecution, pain, and death that is our sacrificial offering. An archetypal crucifixion/resurrection scenario occurs every day with the rising and setting of the Sun. Because it sets and appears to disappear does not mean it does not exist anymore. These cyclical transitions are signs revealing the rising within us of the Eternal Light of our awakening and our plight of service and suffering through trials and tribulations. These Yin and Yang energies keep the balance without apology. It is a testament to the magnificence of our Creator. We have a Light within that seeks to comfort, enlighten, and attend to our needs, extending out to the needs of humanity. We are One with That nurturing Light.

The words of the sacred scriptures are now the headlines in the daily newspapers. I do not seek to be an alarmist. The world does not need another alarmist. I am suggesting that we strive to heal the energy in our own lives so that, in these trying times, when someone reaches out to us in a cry for help, we will have the spiritual tools and expertise to help them with an open and compassionate heart. No more is required of us than to know who we truly are. This knowledge is rewarded with the understanding that we are all the same in Essence, and that Essence is indestructible. To serve others is service to Self.

The most effective form of healing from fear and loss is understanding the importance of a spiritual discipline that nourishes our soul. We are required to cultivate the ability to suspend our senses, control our passions, conquer our addiction to immediate gratification of every fleeting desire and thought-form, and submit to becoming a less self-serving person. How can we help others if we are no better off than those we are attempting to help? We take on this honor of service not just for ourselves but for humanity in general and encourage others to do the same. We may be the next ones reaching out for help and be met with the cold indifference, arrogance, or ignorance that is so common in the cultures of this world today. Indifference is beyond hatred. Arrogance is a curse. Ignorance is inexcusable.

We must observe the spiritual mandates that give us wings to transcend everything; our own pettiness, race, religion, socio-economic status, gender, sexual orientation, ethnicity, politics, skin color, and nationality. We must be the keepers of our brothers and sisters, not their judge. We must see ourselves as the magnificent creation that we are and know that we possess the power to heal the wounds of spiritual disease.

Of course, we all have our own personal problems, more overwhelming in drama and character than ever before. If it were not for all of the confusing interference, we might all be able to raise our frequency to perceive the higher vibrations available to us to heal ourselves and others. The effect of such a shift of consciousness toward compassion and empathy would not only cause a personal healing but a healing for others through us. We are energy, surrounded by an endless sea of energy, like a wave that rises upon the ocean. It is crucial to keep our energy clean and refine our standards regarding the energies we allow ourselves to become exposed to.

There is much about the times and cultures we live in that can cause shifts in frequencies counter to our well-being, scrambling our senses, and controlling our consciousness in ways that are virtually imperceptible. The fact that it is invisible does not mean that it does not exist or is not affecting us. We may find ourselves living in reaction to things we do not think exist, just because we can't see it or prove it. If we are not paying attention, we have no idea how our limited, confused, and befuddled frequencies are creating physical and mental disease in ourselves and the people around us.

There is and always has been suffering in this world. Now more so than ever, it is a spiritual imperative to offer ourselves in sacrifice by committing our lives first to the service of our Creator and then to the service of creation. If our lofty goals and ambitions in life cause us to exalt ourselves over others, placing ourselves above serving others who have fallen into crisis and need, we will create for ourselves the Karma to become one of them. We will either be one of the ones administering healing or one of the ones begging for it. Those are our choices. It is our choice as to which side of that scenario we will be on.

There are people doing The Great Work of this spiritual journey who do not even know they are doing it. There are others who can be trained to enhance the powers and skills they have hidden deep within. These latent energies only need to be triggered by some spiritual force powerful enough to cause that spark necessary to jump the gap between streams of energy, causing change.

It is time that we drop the masks that divide and conquer us, threatening our very existence. If we do not remove the masks, we have no reason to fear death because that level of ignorance carries consequences that are worse than death. If we choose to live a life of such low vibration, seeking only the satisfaction of our own ego-based desires, death is redundant. We are already dead. That is the death we should fear the most.

We will not seek to transcend the fear-laced five stages of grief. We will go through them with impeccable courage. Denial, anger, bargaining, depression, and acceptance take on a different meaning, and the healing is easier if they are approached in reverse. We begin with acceptance … the acceptance of who we really are, and the infinite nature of our own mortality. We face depression, anger, and denial in meditation and prayer. We chant it down. We pray it off. We affirm our connection with Divinity. We embrace these stages and Love them into Oneness and Ultimate Light, affirming there is no such thing as death.

"You would know the secret of death. But how shall you find it unless you seek it in the heart of life? The owl whose night-bound eyes are blind unto the day cannot unveil the mystery of light. If you would indeed behold the spirit of death, open your heart wide unto the body of life. For life and death are one, even as the river and the sea are one. In the depth of your hopes and desires lies your silent knowledge of the beyond; And like seeds dreaming beneath the snow your heart dreams of spring. Trust the dreams, for in them is hidden the gate to eternity."

~ Khalil Gibran ~

"There is no death, only a change of worlds."

~ Chief Seattle ~

Epilogue

I write with the authority of my own experience. I represent no one particular religious or spiritual path over another. That having been said, I humbly submit this account of the many paths that led me here, from a place of courage enough to share my painful story, and peace enough to share the story of joy on the other side of that same coin.

I am reminded of the well-known story of Kisa ... a story about the wisdom and compassion of the Buddha. Kisa was a woman who could not accept the death of her baby. Kisa went throughout the town, desperately begging for medicine for her dead child. No one would help her. She presented the dead baby she had been carrying around to the Buddha and begged him for special medicine to heal her deceased child. The Buddha told her, "Kisa, if you want me to make some medicine, you must have some mustard seeds. Go into town and ask at each house, but you must only accept seeds from a house in which no one has ever died." She returned to him without the baby. She said she had no mustard seeds for the special medicine for her baby because she could not find anyone who had not tasted death. He sat with her and advised her of the nature of life and the seasons of its unfolding. She was finally at peace with her loss.

We, like Kisa, tend to desperately cling to the perishable. We will transcend our suffering, rise up out of the world of names and forms, and become the alchemy of healing if we choose to. We must choose enlightenment and know ourselves for who and what we really are. The pursuit of enlightenment should be undertaken with the same passion and desperation as someone whose hair is on fire pursues a bucket of cool water.

I was talking to my son recently about my mother, whom we affectionately called "Ma." The conversation took a familiar left-hand turn into my forlorn mantra called "I want my Mommy." Hardly a day has gone by that I haven't had that tantrum ... missing her from a place at the most profound level of my being. He told me something that would make me stop and check myself. His voice was laced with the joy of his boyhood innocence, and he marveled at how lucky ... how blessed ... how happy he was to have ever gotten the chance to know her ... to have spent time with her ... to have loved her and been loved by her. He mused, "I just thank her for her smiles, hugs, phone calls, and her melodic laughter. If we don't celebrate and remember life and what we gain from our fleeting moments together, we will one day find ourselves consumed by regret and misery ... then comes all of the physical ailments and diseases that we call into existence from the spiritual illness of ingratitude."

His words served to pull me out of that emotional whirlwind I was trying to spin around myself, and he made me remember in that weak moment that none of us actually exist in the manner we think we do. Death is the ultimate illusion in this Timeless flurry of our many forms, manifestations, and transitions. The formless being we really are cannot be destroyed and never ceases to exist. Remembering that will not stop me from missing my mother in the form she existed in my memories. I don't think that kind of "missing" ever goes away. Is it supposed to? Grief is not a disease to be cured. It is a sacred sacrifice we make upon the altar we call Love ... and we say *THANK YOU*. We honor the emptiness and the longing we know as grief by finding what is undying in ourselves. Every tear is a sacred offering. Every memory and every smile is an expression of gratitude.

There is no closure.

There are no words.

I just want to pray with you.

THE END

The moving finger writes
And once having writ moves on
Nor all of thy piety nor wit
Shall lure it back to cancel half a line

~ Omar Khayyam ~

Raushanah Hassain

Dedication

Raushanah Hassain

(Dorothy Louise Warren)

Sunrise – November 24, 1921

Sunset – January 5, 1954, and May 15, 2003

The artwork is a mosaic
of so many memories
of so many lives
she is still living through

In loving memory of my mother ...
The vehicle of her physical presence has transitioned
and her beautiful Spirit will never be forgotten.
The soul of such a vibrant, beautiful Light
gifted by The God will never die.

She was a soldier in the cause of raising consciousness
and healing suffering every place she found it ...
feeding the hungry, housing the homeless, clothing the needy, counseling,
supporting, and caring for the sick,
the disadvantaged, and disenfranchised.
She was committed to teaching those who had mistaken
themselves for ignorant, even hopeless ...
struggling against oppression and injustice,
from every source, with her every breath,
while remaining a pillar of strength, joy, and optimism.

Oh, my God … her smile was beautiful!
She braved many storms against relentless opposition for the strength of faith she cultivated in others. She was ahead of her time, a visionary, a sign of better days to come for many who could have given up hope.

Those fortunate enough to have shared in her world will testify to her loving contribution to the lives she touched.

She always had a smile to offer, a word of comfort and wisdom. She never met a stranger. She dedicated her life to being a gift of Light to everyone blessed to have crossed her path. She would give you the shirt off of her back, then take you into her heart and teach you how to make one. The door to her heart was always open to those in need and people from all walks of life.

Now her travels have taken her far from me, but closer to the love, beauty, and peace she so deserved. She walked with one foot in the Eternal and the other on solid ground. She found joy and freedom in her own heart. All she ever wanted was peace and sovereignty,
not just for herself, but for everyone.
The Eternal is the only peace
a spirit like hers could have hoped to find,
the only freedom to be found by anyone.

I dedicate this book, as well as my life,
to the loving memory of my mother, Raushanah Hassain.
Thank you for giving me the spiritual foundation upon which to build the solid structures that house and nurture my spirit now. Words are inadequate to express my appreciation for you.
Had it not been for you, I would never have written this book.

I certainly would never have been.
Rest in Eternity as the peace you have returned to again.
I will always love you.

Khalil Gibran is buried in Lebanon, in what is now known as the Gibran Museum.
Written next to his grave, as he wished, are the words,
"a word I want to see written on my grave:
I am alive like you,
and I am standing beside you.
Close your eyes and look around,
you will see me in front of you."

MY MOTHER, MY FRIEND

Strangers when we met
mother and child
nearly claimed
from the gate
by the angels of death
but the heavens
looked down
and cried for me
touched
your heart
changed your fate
and pushed
you back
into this
world
before it
was too late

I thank God
you were spared
from being taken
into the Light
leaving me all alone
that cold winter night

Your eyes reopened
with visions
of the future
of the present
and past
Upon my new life
your spell was cast

I offer my life as yours
Like you did for me
through victory and defeat
advances and retreat
the pain and trauma
of ecstatic ups
and my tumbling down

through loves I've lost
and loves I've found

You've always
been there
for me
with unclipped wings
flying free

A bond no mortal can break
My mother … my friend
born and reborn together
together from beginning to Zen

THE DREAMCATCHERS

Though many dreams
do not survive
the light of day
and distrustful eyes
of a world so damp
so cold and gray
in dreams that ran
from yesterday

Dreams are what life
is really made of
not hopes, nor trust,
not even love

Dreams are all
we've really got
that can't be stolen
sold or bought

Dreams dance in trance
through our minds in sleep
Dreams reveal the
secrets we keep

In dreams we glean
the mystical forever
but, best, are the dreams
we dream together

I WILL RISE AGAIN

Graffiti taggers
spray sin
upon the bones
of Lazarus

As time after time
I've closed my eyes
and with grace
I've embraced
existential demise

As many fragile
human forms
gave up the ghost
and left you to mourn

As surely as
I rest in peace
for just a little while
I'll be back in the sparkle
of some stranger's eyes
in a haunting familiar smile

Look out for me
I will return
I will rise again
I will find you all
my family … my loved ones
my enemies … my friends

Until I do
I will visit you
and walk all through
your dreams
Don't grieve for me
because I'm alright
I've seen the darkness
I've seen the Light
Now I know what it all means

As Maya beacons
I may choose
to descend
back into ash and clay
knowing the body
is a metaphor
just an elegant
robe I wore
for my part
in Time's
glorious play

Why must we bleed
from our hands and feet
before we can accept
our own immortality

Did you think
I haven't passed this way
many times before?
Did you think
there would ever
come a time
that I would be no more?

Did you think I was
my shadows and fears?
Did you think I was
the demons I had to fight?

Did you think
that I was anything less
than a being
of Eternal Light?

Did you think
I was my suffering?
Did you think
I was my grief?
Did you think
I was my
shortcomings
or the promises
I couldn't keep?

Did you think I was
the pain I've suffered
or the many
futile tears
I've cried?
Did you think
I would go quietly
Did you think
my soul could die?

As surely as time
has let me go
I will find a way
to let you know
I'm coming back …
A song of freedom
never dies!
Watch for me!
I will return!
Once again

I WILL RISE!

About the Author … JAI

With early beginnings as a published songwriter, JAI's passion has remained her poetry. She has been published in the Los Angeles Sentinel, SIC Magazine, Talisman Magazine, UCLA's NOMMO Magazine, Point of Light, The Drumming Between Us, and African Voices. Her Publications by Dream Universal Media are listed below. Dream Universal Media specializes in literature, audio, and video recordings, specifically designed to heal and elevate the consciousness of mind, body, and spirit through Mystical Meditation.

Jai is a student and teacher of metaphysical sciences and many mystical healing traditions, including Tibetan, Hawaiian, Native American, African, Caribbean, Middle Eastern, Chinese and Japanese, all of which inspired her work. Jai continues to teach, publish, and write.

FEARLESS: PSYCHIC SELF-DEFENSE – Transcend the Fear of Spiritual Warfare

SLEEPLESS: Transcend the Fear of Sleep Paralysis

SELFLESS: TURIYA – Beyond the Dark Night of the Soul

FACELESS: THE SACRED RELATIONSHIP

LIMITLESS: MADE OF LIGHT – Your Companion Reference Book for FACELESS

NAMELESS: A Poetic Journey to The Higher Self

I AM NOT A POET ANYMORE

SANDBOXES

DREAM UNIVERSAL JOURNAL

AUDIO and VIDEO MEDITATIONS INCLUDE:

The Light Meditation
I Transcend My Ego Self Meditation
Stone Meditation
Turiya Meditation

JAI (Jāy), literally means "Victory" in Sanskrit, representing the spirit of this sacred journey. Look for more at *dreamuniversalmedia.com* and the Facebook group: JAI The Timeless Now.

Works Cited

Gibran, Kahlil. *The Prophet*. New York: Knopf, 1952. Print.

Rumi, Jalal Al-Din, and Coleman Barks. *The Essential Rumi*. San Francisco, CA: Harper, 1995. Print.

Rumi, Jalal Al-Din, and William C. Chittick. *The Sufi Path of Love: The Spiritual Teachings of Rumi*. Albany: State U of New York, 1983. Print.

Thera, Buddharakkhita, trans. *The Dhammapada: The Buddha's Path of Wisdom*. Kandy, Sri Lanka: Buddhist Publication Society, 1985. Print.

Yogananda, Paramahansa. *Autobiography of a Yogi*. Los Angeles: Self-Realization Fellowship, 1971. Print.

HAFIZ. *The Gift*: Poems by Hafiz the Great Sufi Master

Meditation Download Instructions

To download the two audio meditations included in this book, go to Dreamuniversalmedia.com and select the OUR FREE BOOKS page, then select the Audio Meditations section and follow the instructions to download The Light Meditation and the I Transcend My Ego Self Meditation.

Recommended Reading

A Course in Miracles

Hazrat Inayat Rehmat Khan; The Soul's Journey

Idries Shah; The Sufis

Nisargadatta Maharaj; I Am That

Paramhansa Yogananda; Autobiography of a Yogi (Self-RealizationFellowship)

Sri Ramana Maharshi; Who Am I?

Thich Nhat Hanh: The Pocket Thich Nhat Hanh

Sayagyi U Ba Khin; What is Vipassana Meditation

Rupert Spira: Being Aware of Being Aware

Sun Tzu and John Minford; The Art of War

Recommended Meditation Music

Levi Chen of Yin Yang Records and Liquid Gardens at www.levichen.com

Joaquin Montoya (Joaqopelli) at soundcloud.com

Gabrielle Roth *(February 4, 1941 – October 22, 2012)* and The Mirrors